D0205915

JOHN CLARE

Selected Letters

A bust of John Clare by Henry Behnes, reproduced by permission of John Baguley and the John Clare Society.

JOHN CLARE
Selected Letters

Edited by
MARK STOREY

CLARENDON PRESS · OXFORD
1988

Oxford University Press, Walton Street, Oxford OX2 6DP
Oxford New York Toronto
Delhi Bombay Calcutta Madras Karachi
Petaling Jaya Singapore Hong Kong Tokyo
Nairobi Dar es Salaam Cape Town
Melbourne Auckland
and associated companies in
Berlin Ibadan

Oxford is a trade mark of Oxford University Press

Published in the United States
by Oxford University Press (USA)

British Library Cataloguing in Publication Data
Clare, John, 1793–1864
John Clare : selected letters.
1. Poetry in English. Clare, John,
1793–1864—Correspondence, diaries, etc.
I. Title II. Storey, Mark
821'.7
ISBN 0–19–818585–5

Library of Congress Cataloging in Publication Data
Clare, John, 1793–1864.
[Correspondence. Selections]
John Clare, selected letters / edited by Mark Storey.
p. cm. Bibliography: p. Includes index
1. Clare, John, 1793–1864—Correspondence. 2. Poets,
English—19th century—Correspondence.
I. Storey, Mark. II. Title.
PR4453.C6Z48 1988 88–4023
ISBN 0–19–818585–5

Typeset by The Alden Press
Printed in Great Britain
at the University Printing House, Oxford
by David Stanford
Printer to the University

CONTENTS

INTRODUCTION

As Auden says, 'A shilling life will give you all the facts'. John Clare was born the son of a thresher in 1793, in the small village of Helpstone in Northamptonshire. His formal schooling finished when he was 12; he began writing verse in his teens, and in 1818 had got local printers and booksellers sufficiently interested for some kind of publication by subscription to be a realistic possibility: Edward Drury, the Stamford bookseller, showed the poems to his London cousin John Taylor, and in 1820 *Poems Descriptive of Rural Life and Scenery* appeared. It was a considerable success; *The Village Minstrel* followed in 1821, but although it was a better book it sold less well. Clare made the acquaintance of local literary figures such as Octavius Gilchrist, and, through them, of the London literary circle, particularly those members associated with Taylor's *London Magazine*. There were few important writers of the day that Clare did not meet. But the instant fame did not, indeed could not, last; Clare's first really major work, *The Shepherd's Calendar*, did not appear until 1827, and by then many had lost interest in him as a phenomenon. Clare had begun the long struggle with ill health that drove him, in the mid-1820s, to the verge of suicide. The move in 1832 to Northborough, intended to set him up as a smallholder, was hardly a success; simultaneously, he saw his most spectacular manuscript, *The Midsummer Cushion*, reduced to what was thought would sell in 1835 as *The Rural Muse*. Within two years he had begun the dreadful institutionalization that constituted the second half of his life, first in Epping Forest, and then in the General Lunatic Asylum at Northampton, where he died in 1864; he was to spend only five more months at home, from the end of July to the end of December 1841.

As early as February 1822 Clare wrote to John Taylor, 'I live here among the ignorant like a lost man in fact like one whom the rest seems careless of having anything to do with'. His sense of himself as someone lost is a recurrent theme in his poetry and in his letters. Four months after that comment he returned home from one of his visits to London, and wrote to tell Taylor that he was so much the worse for drink that he thought people were joking when they told him they had reached Peterborough; this uncannily anticipates his tragic inability to recognize his wife Patty, when she meets him at the end of the long trek from Epping Forest to Northborough, after his escape in 1841 from Matthew Allen's asylum. So disorientated is he that he sits down to write to his first love, the dead Mary Joyce, a letter accompanying his description of his 'Journey out of Essex': in both he describes himself as 'homeless at home'. It is reminiscent of that other traumatic journey he makes, when, in 1832, he moves with his family the three miles from Helpstone to Northborough, and begins his poem 'The Flitting' with the lines, 'Ive left my own old home of homes | Green fields & every pleasant place. . .'. Not only does he feel a stranger in the new cottage, but the natural world itself has lost its bearings (just as he himself had done much earlier in his life, when as a child he went to see what lay beyond the horizon, and entered a strange world of which he knew nothing).

In the letters that he writes to his children, especially Charles, from the asylum at Northampton, a poignant refrain can be heard: 'There Is No Place Like Home'. Urging his son to write to him, he says, 'let it be about home & those who live there'. Some of the asylum letters consist of little more than a list of names of the people he used to know. By asking about them in such detail he goes some way towards reinstating himself as part of the community from which he is now excluded, except in his memory. The irony is that, even when he was an actual part of the village community at Helpstone or at Northborough, he was excluded by his very oddness, by the fact that he was a poet. One of his very earliest poems, 'Helpstone', had in fact turned on the ambivalent relationship between the place and the poet, and in an important way it sets the tone for the rest of his work. There is more than passing significance in the fact that he should write a prose piece on the subject of 'self-identity', and that so many of his poems—most famously 'I am—yet what I am, none cares or knows'—should confront the problem of who he is and where he belongs.

It could be argued that all the Romantic poets were obsessed with this problem of identity: at one extreme there is the 'egotistical sublime' of Wordsworth; at the other is Keats, watching with alarm as his sense of himself slips away, whether in a crowded room or in the Miltonic 'Hyperion'. Byron declares that his sole motive for writing has been to escape his 'cursed selfishness', and yet he has to give up the pretence that the hero of *Childe Harold* is other than a version of himself. Clare fits into this Romantic pattern, but there are pressing biographical reasons for him to be much more crucially obsessed on both the personal and the literary planes. There might have been a vogue for rustic poets, for 'uneducated' writers supported by generous subscription lists; but the vogue provided little reassurance beyond the moment. The eighteenth-century 'Thresher Poet' Stephen Duck had committed suicide; Robert Bloomfield was unable to repeat the phenomenal success of his first volume, *The Farmer's Boy*, of 1800; others, like Anna Yearsley, the Bristol milkmaid ('Lactilla') championed by Hannah More, were little more than names, warnings to those who, like Clare, were charged with too much 'ambition' for their own good. What is remarkable about Clare is that he confronts this problem of his proper place with such a persistence and determination that it becomes a central aspect of all his writing. And the privacy of the letter allows him to pursue it, and even to find some solutions to the problem.

Throughout his life Clare defined himself by his pen. He would often dismiss his writing—whether prose or poetry—as mere 'scribbling': such dismissal allowed him to disown any pretensions he might be accused of having. In his letters this determination to 'scribble without a thought' becomes a positive virtue, as it allows him to escape the constraints and expectations of art, to talk, as he puts it to Hessey, 'as to a Country friend'. One of the most engaging aspects of his correspondence is this ability to address directly the person to whom he is writing, to unburden himself of concerns both large and small. It is to Taylor and Hessey that he can be most free and unbuttoned. This is largely due to the fact that it is they who take him seriously as a writer, who in fact keep him going as a poet: 'the fact is', he writes in December 1820, 'if I cannot hear from John Taylor now & then I cannot ryhme'. He depends upon Taylor especially, for he is his publisher; but the dependence operates on a much deeper level, whereby he can use him as some kind of sounding-board. Whatever the rights and wrongs of the delays over the publication of *The Shepherd's*

Calendar, there is little doubt that the book owes a lot to Taylor's (and Hessey's) suggestions, to their ability to sort out from the great mass of material Clare sends them something that will make a satisfactory, saleable book. We can observe this relationship developing throughout the correspondence, and it provides one of the sheet-anchors for Clare's emotional life. When the angry eruptions occur, as they do, we can sense an underlying trust and respect which allows the anger its head. Taylor, Hessey, and Clare can write about details of poems with that same shared confidence that invites more personal truths.

The same is never the case with Edward Drury: from the beginning there is an uneasiness, a wariness, that taints the correspondence on both sides. It soon becomes apparent how Clare's fortunes are initially at other people's mercies: as early as December 1819 he is saying to his more reliable acquaintance the Revd Isaiah Knowles Holland, with reference to Drury, 'A Shabby Booksellers Word will be no advantage to me as self Interest is the Cause'. More than once he talks of Drury as a 'bear with a sore head'; how much happier he seems in the company of his other Stamford friend, Octavius Gilchrist, who sends him books that he treasures (Wordsworth, Byron), who asks him to dinner, or to the theatre. Clare experiences Gilchrist's death in 1823 as one of those many cruel losses that cannot be repaired. It is true that there are several times in the early years when he calls himself a 'clown' (even abasing himself before the attentions of Sir Walter Scott), but he is prepared to settle for the clown's dignity: he will not pretend to be what he is not. As he says, 'common sense gives me her spectacles to look upon everything', and it is the sturdy common sense of a countryman. Hence his fury with the dandified portrait of himself produced by William Hilton (pp. 21–2) (which, ironically, has served ever since for the common reader as the icon of John Clare, the Peasant Poet); hence his determination, in a wonderful letter to his artist friend Rippingille, to set off the pastoral myths against the hard realities of country life (pp. 105–6). This is all done with a lightness of touch which reminds us that Clare is the author of *The Parish* as well as *The Shepherd's Calendar*, *Don Juan* as well as *Child Harold*. The humour sorts well with his desire to capture the intimacy of conversation between friends.

Clare has a wide range of friends. From London he is receiving, every other week, regular as clockwork, a long letter from the redoubtable Eliza Louisa Emmerson; unfortunately, few of Clare's replies have survived, but those that have show him well able to stand up to her overbearing manner, and to supply her with the 'gossip' she requires. Also in London is the sculptor Henry Behnes, whom he gets to know in the late 1820s; they write to each other long letters of evident affection, covering the whole spectrum of activities from writing a poem to going to the fair, from presents for the children to the latest news of the 'Fancy' (one of Clare's perennial interests); a marvellous sense of warm domesticity permeates their correspondence, reminding us how much Clare needed to be the family man, the man firmly rooted in a house that was a home. Another correspondent who brings out the best in Clare is the writer H. F. Cary, who offers hospitality in his Chiswick house: in the early 1830s Clare can begin a letter with talk of family ills and ailments, and end with a general lament for the way the world seems to be going. As so often in those years, Clare demonstrates his astute awareness of what is happening in the country as a whole. Marianne Marsh, the wife of the bishop of Peterborough, corresponds sympathetically with Clare, and they exchange confidences with a refreshing openness. To George Darley, Allan Cunningham, Peter De Wint, William Hone, Thomas Pringle, Clare writes with a remarkable ease and freedom. To people closer to home, such as his friends at Milton Hall, Artis and Henderson, he writes briefly but often, and always sweetly.

Finally, and perhaps most importantly, there is his family, whether it be his wife Patty, his children, or Mary Joyce, the woman he comes to believe is his real wife. In all of these letters home there is a heart-breaking tenderness, an ability to love these people he has lost irrevocably. It is perhaps this more than anything else that stamps these letters with their particular poignancy and value. In *Child Harold* Clare writes, 'I sigh a poet & a lover still': for all the traumas, the contradictions of his life ('My life hath been one chain of contradictions'), Clare recognizes the importance and interconnectedness of love and poetry. These are what have kept him going, against all the odds. In his letters, even at the worst moments (and they are many), he finds a place, a refuge, where he can be at home and be himself, where he can sustain, within those private confines, the freedom of voice that is true to his sense of himself. His letters affirm that out of all those 'contrarietys' he had talked of to Behnes some kind of coherence can be achieved. And so these letters become part of a central narrative, a version—apart from the shilling one—of the writer's life.

The text follows that of my edition of *The Letters of John Clare* (Oxford, 1985), except that there are no textual notes, and no indication of deletions or corrections; for such details, as also for postmarks, for the case for a particular date where Clare gives none, and for the location of manuscripts, the reader is referred to the complete edition. I repeat my grateful acknowledgements, spelt out there in full, to all holders, public and private, of Clare's manuscripts. Something still needs to be said about the peculiarities of what remains. Clare's spelling is often extraordinary, his punctuation almost non-existent, and I have done all I can to be faithful to what he wrote. This certainly produces oddities, as any page will testify; I have avoided the disfigurement of Clare's text with ubiquitous [*sic*]s, in the belief that the context usually makes the sense apparent. If there is the likelihood of doubt I have supplied missing letters or syllables in square brackets. For much of his life Clare dispenses with the letter 'l' in 'coud', 'woud', and 'shoud', but by the end of the 1820s he seems to have taken a liking to the more conventional spelling; he is much more reluctant to resort to the apostrophe in 'hell', 'shell', 'well'. Clare is just as capricious in his use of capitals, and I have not attempted to regularize these, even if it means that a sentence often starts with a lower case. Superior letters have been lowered, and the inconsistencies in his use of inverted commas have been smoothed out. No points or commas have been added to his usually unpunctuated text (and where he has managed a comma, full stop, even a semi-colon, I have preserved such displays of adventurous conformity). But it seemed necessary to introduce one particular compromise, to spare the weary eye: I have provided a space where a sentence might be supposed to end. This form of editorial intrusion presents its own problems, as some sentences get lost in their own confusion, while others surge on through several lines, demanding no check. There is a similar compromise in the paragraphing: I have reproduced Clare's paragraphing, however whimsical it might seem, but where in a long letter Clare has made no attempt to break his prose into paragraphs, I have offered some kind of relief. Where he writes between the lines (as he often does in draft letters), or around the edges, or on the address panel, I have incorporated such additions into the body of the letter, or as a postscript, as appropriate. Clare's references to people by their initials (ED, OG, LR, ELE) are expanded on their first occurrence in any letter (E[dward] D[rury], O[ctavius] G[ilchrist], L[ord] R[adstock], E[liza] L[ouisa] E[mmerson]). Square brackets are used when the manuscript is torn: when, as very occasionally happens, Clare has left a gap, the fact is noted within square brackets. Any uncertain readings, whether because of a tear or because of illegibility, are placed within square brackets, with an initial question mark: [? dark]; a totally illegible word is indicated thus: [?   ]. Occasionally a word has been added in square brackets when it is clear that Clare has, in his haste, omitted it.

Abbreviations

PD	*Poems Descriptive of Rural Life and Scenery* (1820)
VM	*The Village Minstrel* (1821)
SC	*The Shepherd's Calendar* (1827)
RM	*The Rural Muse* (1835)
AW	*John Clare's Autobiographical Writings*, ed. Eric Robinson (Oxford, 1983)
LM	*London Magazine*
QR	*Quarterly Review*

LIST OF LETTERS

An asterisk (*) indicates a draft letter

CHRONOLOGY

1793	John Clare born at Helpstone, Northamptonshire, son of Parker Clare and of Ann, daughter of John and Elizabeth Stimson, 13 July.
1797	Mary Joyce born.
1798–*c.*1806	Attends schools at Helpstone and Glinton.
1799	Martha (Patty) Turner born.
*c.*1800	First meets Mary Joyce.
*c.*1806	Works as ploughboy for Mrs Bellairs at Woodcroft Castle. Buys Isaac Watts's *Hymns and Spiritual Songs*, Thomson's *Seasons*; begins to write verse.
*c.*1809	Works for Francis Gregory at Blue Bell Inn, Helpstone.
1809	Act of Parliament passed, 'for enclosing lands in the parishes of Maxey with Deepingate, Northborough, Glinton with Peakirk, Etton, and Helpstone'.
*c.*1810	Apprentice gardener for the Marquis of Exeter at Burghley House.
*c.*1812–13	Enlists in local militia.
1814	Buys his first 'blank book' from J. B. Henson, Market Deeping bookseller.
1814–17	Makes acquaintance of gypsies.
*c.*1815–16	Relationship with Mary Joyce ends.
1817	Works as limeburner for Wilders at Bridge Casterton. Meets Martha Turner.
1818	Henson prints 'Proposals for publishing by subscription a Collection of Original Trifles, on miscellaneous subjects, religious and moral, in Verse, by John Clare, of Helpstone'.
1818–19	Edward Drury, the Stamford bookseller, interests himself in Clare, regarding him as his protégé.
1819	Becomes friendly with Isaiah Knowles Holland and Octavius Gilchrist. Introduced to the London publisher John Taylor; arrangements made for publication of first volume.
1820	*Poems Descriptive of Rural Life and Scenery* published 16 January. Enclosure Award for Helpstone published.

	Visits Milton Park and Burghley House (February). Befriended by Lord Radstock, Mrs Emmerson, Dawson Turner, Markham Sherwill. First visit to London (with Gilchrist); meets 'Londoners'; has portrait painted by William Hilton (March). Marries Martha Turner at Casterton Magna, 16 March. Subscription list started on initiative of Lord Radstock and Taylor (April). Records one of his first 'fits'. Taylor and Hessey take over from Drury. Anna Maria Clare born 2 June.
1820–1	Lord Radstock and Taylor quarrel over Clare (December–January).
1821	Fourth edition of *Poems Descriptive of Rural Life and Scenery* (January). 'Sketches in the Life of John Clare Written by himself' completed (March). Taylor takes over *London Magazine* (May). Apparently sees Mary Joyce for the last time (August). *The Village Minstrel* published (September).
1822	Second visit to London (May). Eliza Louisa Clare born 13 June.
1823	Finishes *The Parish* (unpublished in his lifetime) (January). 'Second edition' of *The Village Minstrel* published (May). Octavius Gilchrist dies (June). Plans for *The Shepherd's Calendar* mooted by Taylor and Hessey (July–August).
1823–5	Spells of prolonged and severe illness.
1824	Frederick Clare born 5 January. Third visit to London; gets medical help from Dr Darling (May). Returns to Helpstone 8 August.
1824–5	Keeps regular Journal.
1825	Sends poems under pseudonyms to newspapers and journals. 'Essay on Popularity' published in *European Magazine*. Starts writing for Annuals.
1826	John Clare, son, born 16 June.
1827	*The Shepherd's Calendar* published (April).
1828	Fourth visit to London (February). William Parker Clare born 29 April. Visits Boston, Lincs. (September).
1829	Receives accounts from Taylor and Hessey (August). Takes issue over accounts with Taylor and Drury (November–December).

1830	Sophia Clare born 24 July.
1830–1	Severe illness.
1830–2	Contributes to Drakard's *Champion* and to the *Bee.*
1831	Plans next volume (*The Midsummer Cushion*). Plans essay on the 'Sublime and Beautiful in Poetry'.
1832	Moves to Northborough. Proposals printed for *Midsummer Cushion* (September).
1833	Charles Clare born 4 January.
1833–5	Increasing illness and despondency.
1835	*The Rural Muse* published (July). Clare's mother dies (December).
1837	Removed to Dr Matthew Allen's asylum at High Beech, Epping Forest (June).
1838	Mary Joyce dies.
1840	Reports in newspapers of Clare's death.
1841	Writes *Child Harold*, *Don Juan.* Escapes from High Beech; walks back to Northborough; writes account of the 'Journey out of Essex'; copies out *Child Harold* (July). Enters Northampton General Lunatic Asylum 29 December.
1842–50	William F. Knight transcribes Clare's poems.
1843	Frederick Clare dies.
1844	Anna Maria Clare dies.
1846	Clare's father dies.
1847–9	Some poems published in the *Bedford Times.*
1850	Knight leaves Northampton for Birmingham.
1852	Charles Clare dies.
1864	John Clare dies 20 May. Buried at Helpstone 25 May.

BIOGRAPHICAL REGISTER OF CORRESPONDENTS AND PERSONS FREQUENTLY CITED

ALLEN, MATTHEW (1783–1845). Apothecary to York Lunatic Asylum from 1819 until he opened his own asylum, in about 1825, at High Beech, Epping Forest (where Clare was taken in June 1837, and where he remained until his escape in July 1841).

ARTIS, EDMUND TYRELL (1789–1847). House-steward at Milton Hall, and one of Clare's closest friends; he was recognized as a distinguished archaeologist, famous in particular for *Antediluvian Phytology* (1825) and *The Durobrivae of Antoninus* . . . (1828, but published in parts from 1823 onwards).

BEHNES, HENRY (d. 1837). A less distinguished sculptor than his brother William; but his bust of Clare (now in Northampton Public Library) has become justly celebrated. His surviving letters to Clare are witty and affectionate. At the end of 1830 he started calling himself 'Burlowe', to avoid confusion with his brother.

BLOOMFIELD, ROBERT (1766–1823). The Suffolk cobbler-poet taken up by Capel Lofft, immensely popular for a brief period: *The Farmer's Boy* (1800) sold 26,000 copies within three years, and entered its 14th edn. in 1820. Clare admired him, and wanted to write his biography.

CARRINGTON, HENRY EDMUND. Editor of the *Bath Chronicle* in the early 1830s, son of the poet Noel Thomas Carrington (1777?–1830).

CARY, Revd HENRY FRANCIS (1772–1844). His version of the *Inferno* (1805) was not, initially, a success, but by 1819 a revised edn. of the complete translation of Dante had been called for: its powerful effect on Keats is a major fact of literary history. He wrote regularly for the *LM*, and in 1826 was appointed assistant keeper of printed books at the British Museum.

CLARE, PATTY (1799–1871). Clare's wife whom, as Martha Turner, he married in 1820.

COLLINGWOOD, MARY. One of several unidentified women to whom Clare wrote from the asylum at Northampton.

CUNNINGHAM, ALLAN (1784–1842). A successful poet, and collector of Scots tales and poems; he became assistant to the sculptor Francis Chantrey, and edited the 1829 *Anniversary*, to which Clare contributed.

DADFORD, ELIZA. One of several unidentified women to whom Clare wrote from the asylum at Northampton.

DARLEY, GEORGE (1795–1846). Poet, critic, and mathematician, remembered for a handful of lyrics rather than for *Nepenthe* (1835), and less fortunately known as the 'Irish Keats'.

DARLING, Dr GEORGE (1782–1862). He tended several distinguished members of the London literary circle, including Keats, Haydon, Wilkie, and Taylor. James F. Clarke (*Autobiographical Recollections* (1874)) described him as 'a man of very limited ability . . . He was of the old school of blue pill and black draught, and treated most cases as "bilious". He was a man about the middle height, and would ordinarily be taken for a Methodist parson . . .' Clare frequently resorted to his remedies.

DE WINT, PETER (1784–1849). A noted landscape painter, brother-in-law of William Hilton. He contributed the frontispiece to *The Shepherd's Calendar* (1827).

DRAKARD, JOHN (1775?–1849). Bookseller, newspaper proprietor, and publisher: he started the *Stamford News* in 1809 and the *Stamford Champion* in January 1830 (to which Clare was to contribute some political poems). He was renowned for his radicalism: on one famous occasion Lord Cardigan horsewhipped him in his own shop.

DRURY, EDWARD BELL (1797–1843). Moved from Lincoln to Stamford in 1818, to take over the New Public Library, and to set himself up in business as a bookseller. He persuaded his cousin John Taylor to publish Clare's poems, and then saw his own control over Clare's concerns slip gradually away. The distrust between Drury and practically everyone else is a common theme in this correspondence.

DUDLEY, DEAN (1823–1906). American genealogist and writer who visited Clare in March 1850.

EMMERSON, ELIZA LOUISA (1782–1847). Clare's most persistent correspondent, active in her self-appointed role as advocate and patron. It was she who persuaded Lord Radstock of Clare's poetic and moral virtues. Her husband Thomas Emmerson was an art-dealer who, in the 1830s, was to help Clare with his complicated finances.

EXETER, Marquis of (1795–1867). He was visited by Clare at his seat Burghley House, near Stamford, early in 1820, and undertook to pay Clare 15 guineas a year for the rest of his life; Clare dedicated *The Shepherd's Calendar* to him.

GARDINER, HELLEN MARIA. One of several unidentified women to whom Clare wrote from the asylum at Northampton; she is most probably related to Caroline Gardiner, a niece of Octavius Gilchrist.

GILCHRIST, OCTAVIUS (1779–1823). A Stamford grocer, critic, and journalist (editor of Drakard's *Stamford News*), he became a good friend of Clare's. He is best known now for his *Letter to the Rev. William Bowles* (1820), which indirectly drew Clare into a debate on the merits of Pope's poetry. He was responsible for 'presenting' Clare to the world in the *LM*, January 1820.

HALL, SAMUEL CARTER (1800–89). Founded the *Amulet, a Christian and Literary Remembrancer* (1826–33), in which some of Clare's poems appeared, and also the *Spirit and Manners of the Age*, where more of Clare's work appeared. His wife Anna Maria Hall (1800–81) was also an assiduous editor.

HENDERSON, JOSEPH. Head gardener at Milton Hall, a keen botanist, and a good friend to Clare.

HENSON, J. B. A Market Deeping bookseller who offered to print Clare's first volume by subscription, on the understanding that he would, first of all, print 300 prospectuses for £1. When Henson demanded £15 before he would print the poems, Clare decided to go elsewhere.

HESSEY, JAMES AUGUSTUS (1785–1870). Partner of John Taylor until 1825, when he tried to become a publisher of religious books; more successful, briefly, as a print auctioneer in 1830, before becoming a schoolmaster.

HILTON, WILLIAM (1786–1839). The historical painter who was responsible for the most famous portrait of Clare (now in the National Portrait Gallery), engraved by Edward Scriven for the frontispiece to *VM*.

HIPKINS, JAMES. A Londoner to whom Clare's last extant letter is addressed.

HOLLAND, Revd ISAIAH KNOWLES (d. 1873). Congregational minister at Market Deeping from 1815, removed to St Ives Free Church, Huntingdon, in 1820; an early supporter and encourager of Clare's work.

HONE, WILLIAM (1780–1842). A radical satirist and bookseller; tried three times in 1817 for blasphemous libel, and on each occasion defended himself successfully. Of numerous publications, *The Political House that Jack Built* (1819), with illustrations by George Cruikshank, was the most famous; noted also for his *Every-day Book*, *Table Book*, and *Year Book*.

HOWITT, MARY (1799–1888). A prolific writer, translator of Hans Andersen, and collaborator with her husband William on several books; the couple visited Clare in the asylum at Northampton in the mid-1840s.

JOYCE, MARY (1797–1838). The person who dominated Clare's

emotional and imaginative life, to such an extent that by 1841 he believed he was married to her (see *AW*, pp. 25, 72–3).

KENT, ELIZABETH. Sister-in-law of Leigh Hunt, author of two books, each published anonymously: *Flora domestica* (1823) and *Sylvan Sketches* (1825).

KNIGHT, WILLIAM F. Steward at Northampton General Lunatic Asylum, 1845–50, responsible for transcribing most of Clare's asylum verse during this period; moved to the Borough Asylum, Birmingham in 1850, where he stayed until 1892.

LUDGATE, MARY. Daughter of the family who ran the White Hart Inn in Northampton; a recipient of one of Clare's coded letters in 1850.

MARSH, Revd HERBERT (1757–1839). Bishop of Peterborough, 1819–39; his wife Marianne was a regular correspondent. Clare also knew their two sons George and Herbert.

MOSSOP, Revd CHARLES (1793–1883). Vicar of Helpstone, 1817–53, rector of Etton, 1853–83; his sister Jane was one of Clare's correspondents.

PHILLIPS, ELIZA. One of several unidentified women to whom Clare wrote in the 1840s; a song in *Don Juan* is addressed to her.

POWER, JAMES (1766–1836). Publisher of Thomas Moore's *Irish Melodies* (1808–34), set to music by John Stevenson; he published several of Clare's songs.

PRINGLE, THOMAS (1789–1834). Poet and editor of *Friendship's Offering*. After seven years in Africa, he returned to London to become, in 1827, secretary to the Anti-slavery Society. Author of *The Autumnal Excursion* (1819), *Ephemerides* (1828), and *African Sketches* (1834).

RADSTOCK, Lord (Admiral the Hon. WILLIAM WALDEGRAVE) (1753–1825). One of Clare's first patrons; he put intense evangelical pressure on Clare, and insisted on changes to several of Clare's early poems. He had known Nelson, and been Naval Governor of Newfoundland.

REID, GEORGE. An accountant who started a correspondence with Clare in 1834; he moved in 1837 from Glasgow to Alloa.

RIPPINGILLE, EDWARD VILLIERS (1798–1859). A painter who established himself as one of the 'Bristol School'; he exhibited regularly, and edited, in 1843, the short-lived *Artist's and Amateur's Magazine*.

ROBERTSON, WILLIAM (1799–1872). A member of a well-known theatrical family in Grantham, and father of Thomas Robertson, who was noted for his 'realistic' comedies.

RYDE, HENRY. The estate agent at Burghley, for whom Clare had scant respect: an 'impertinent fellow . . . who occupys a situation which proves the old Farmers assertion that the vilest weeds are always found in the richest soil' (*AW*, p. 121).

SHARP, WILLIAM. A friend who worked in the Dead Letter Office and helped Clare with his finances in the late 1820s, while also exchanging botanical information and cuttings.

SHERWILL, Capt. MARKHAM E. Author of *Ascent . . . to the Summit of Mont Blanc* (1826) and a *Brief Historical Sketch of the Valley of Chamouni* (1832); he edited *Modern Antiquity: And Other Poems*, by his friend Charles Caleb Colton, in 1835, after Colton's suicide.

SIMPSON, FRANCIS (FRANK) (1796–1861). Nephew of Octavius Gilchrist, and one of a large artistic family. His *Ancient Baptismal Fonts* appeared in 1828; his brother Octavius was a landscape painter.

SIMPSON, SAMUEL. An unidentified correspondent from Lancaster, who asked in 1832 for some sonnets in Clare's own hand; no relation to the Stamford Simpsons.

STEWARD, Revd JOHN. A Market Deeping clergyman who invited Clare to visit him in 1828.

STRONG, Revd WILLIAM (1756–1842). Archdeacon of Northampton, 1797–1842; an early benefactor.

TAYLOR, JOHN (1781–1864). After working for James Lackington, and then Vernor and Hood, he set up in business with James Hessey in 1806. They were to publish many of the most important writers of the day. Taylor took over the *LM* in 1820, but sold it in 1825: for its first two years it was one of the most sparkling literary journals of its time. Apart from Mrs Emmerson, Taylor was Clare's most regular correspondent.

TOWNSEND, Revd CHAUNCEY HARE (1798–1868). A writer and poet, author of *The Weaver's Boy: A Tale* (2nd edn. 1825), a book on mesmerism (1840), and *Sermons in Sonnets* (1851); dedicatee of *Great Expectations*.

TROLLOPE, Sir JOHN (1800–74). Elected MP for Lincolnshire South in 1841.

WATTS, ALARIC ALEXANDER (1797–1864). Poet and editor of various journals, including the *Literary Magnet* (1824–8) and the *Literary Souvenir* (1825–36).

WESTON, JOSEPH. Editor of Robert Bloomfield's *Remains* (1824).

WILSON, ELIZABETH. Daughter of the Stamford bookseller Samuel Wilson, who was a partner of John Drakard.

To J. B. Henson

[1818]

Sir

I send you some of the principal Subscribers which I have procured lately: the first of which is a Baronet!!! who speaks very highly of my 'Sonnet' in the prospectus°—Good God, how great are my Expectations! what hopes do I cherish! As great as the unfortunate Chattertons were, on his first entrance into London, which is now pictured in my Mind—& undoubtedly like him I may be building 'Castles in the Air' but Time will prove it—Please to do all in your power to procure Subscribers (as your address will be look'd on better than that of a Clown) when 100 is got you may print it if you please so do your best—& if ever it lies in my power to give friendship its due you shall not go unrewarded

yours

John Clare

To Isaiah Knowles Holland

[mid-1819]

Sir

I Return one of the Books—Shenstone is a Good Poet but his pastorals (as I think) are improperly call'd so the rural Names of Damons Delia Phillis &c & rural Objects Sheep Sheepfolds &c &c are the only things that give one the slight glimps of the Species of Poetry which the Title claims

—Putting the Correct Language of the Gentleman into the mouth of a Simple Shepherd or Vulgar Ploughman is far from Natural—Pope for the Harmony of Numbers surpasses all I have ever seen—Your Criticisms of the 'Trifles' sent wou'd oblige—'The Jewel of all' 'To an April Daisy' & 'The Winds' are the Productions of a Moment & as such are always the best in my Opinion—Seemingly happy Suggestions & easily attain'd

Yours

John Clare

To Isaiah Knowles Holland

[October? 1819]

Sir

I Return your Book with my thanks I have many New Pieces but no time to Copy them—My First Atempts at Poetry are nearly Publishd They have this Title 'Pastoral Sketches in Poems Songs Ballads & Sonnets By John Clare A Northamptonshire Pheasant' Printed for Taylor & Hessey London.°—I could have wishd to began a Corespondence with you from Casterton° But dare not venture for fear of Offending I am now writing 'The Woodman' in the manner of Burns Saturday night you Recollect giveing me the hint the last verse concludes in a Dedication to you I hope youll alow its Insertion° I send it in Letter—You was my first & best Friend—& as such I shall always Esteem You—Drury wishd me to mention that when you next came to Stamford he should be happy to have the pleasure of your company°

Yours Ever

P.S. Return to Casterton on Wednesday & could wish an Answer by Return—I would have sent the Last Verse of the Woodman but cannot Recollect it at present but you may expect the whole Piece the first Opertunity—

The Following Pieces are either Written or now Writing

—Pause before the Battle
Woodman
To Solitude
Many Songs & Ballads
Thunder Storm
Winter
Autumnal Day
Autumn
Ways of a Village
To a sprig of Barley
Letter to a friend
Ryce Wood
& Dissapointment

Sir I hope you will Excuse my Scraps of Paper but you know it is a Scarsity with me

J.C.

To John Taylor

[24 November 1819]

To the Right Honourable Charles William Lord Viscount Milton° These artless Rural Delineations are most humbly & unostentascously inscribed with the Gratitude of the Northamptonshire Peasant who feeling the blessings of his Lordships benevolence to an helpless & afflicted Parent thus dares to declare his admiration & thankfulness.

Dear Sir

I was very pleased with the dedication which Mr Gilchrist wrote for me on Sunday but after a little Consideration percieved it was too Refined & Elegant to flow from the pen of a Clown & as such Unsuitable for the Book Altogether. Therefore I have done one in my own way above which your Taste will model in shape most Suitable°

I am yours with Respectful Regard
John Clare

P.S. Mr. Drury has not yet recieved the Book you promised & I am very anxious to see it particular[l]y the 'Memoir'°

To Isaiah Knowles Holland

[December 1819]

Sir

Lord Milton is come home would you do me the favour to acquaint him with the Publication of 'Trifles' you are a Gentlman of Learning your Word will go a great Way in such matters & as I can find no one in the circle of my acquaintance & Friendship that appears better quallified for the Undertaking I eagerly solicit your Condesencion & rest assured of you[r] agreement thereto—Please to hint the Dedication if he will not agree to it I am undone but I am in no fear as to that When you come to Inform him that I am the Son of the *Lame Man* at helpstone° Please to hint Like wise the Intention of Sending me to the National School°—to Enable me to act in the

Capacity of a Schoolmaster which has dropped for the Want of Friends

—P.S. The sooner done the better as I am affraid Drury will Interest himself in the matter   A Shabby Booksellers Word will be no advantage to me as self Interest is the Cause—What Copies you take to Lord Milton please to Write over again as they are the only Copies & he may loose them—'The Suprise' & 'Epistle to a Friend' will be sufficient—Return the 'April Daisy' 'Jewel of all' 'To the Winds' 'Sonnet' 'To hope' &c what you have done with—send your remarks for correcting   I am going to Casterton & it will be an amusment

A Gentleman in Stamford has kindly offerd to put any of my Pieces to Music which I may oblige him with—'The Jewel of all' I think will suit him you & Opinion

Sir   Yours
John Clare

To William Strong

Stamford Feb 9 1820

Revd Sir

I had this day the pleasure of reading a Letter you sent to Mr Drury of Stamford & I must tender my gratful acknowledgments for the present it enclosed.°

I beg you respected Sir to accept the simple thanks of a Clown who little dreamt of acquiring the honor you have done him by thinking his ryhmes worth your notice and I am Respected Sir

Your Gratful Servant
John Clare

To Markham E. Sherwill

[Captain Markham E. Sherwill, of Mortlake, Surrey, had written to Clare on 7 Feb. 1820 ('I am a perfect stranger to you . . .'), enclosing some money for Clare's parents. He was writing to Sir Walter Scott the same day, and would mention Clare. Lord Radstock encouraged Sherwill to foster the correspondence with Clare, partly for the sake of Clare's moral improvement.]

Stamford Feb 9. 1820

Sir

I thank you for your kind notice of me & the present your letter containd I percieve by your mention of the Celebrated Walter Scott you are a Gentleman of Literary pursuits & one who can do me a great deal of good which you have so kindly under taken the trouble to do

Your mention of another Vol. has made me impertinent enough to inform you I have been preparing one for the press this Winter shoud this succeed—It contains Ballads & Gossip Stories & two or three long poems viz 'Peasant Boy' 'Solitude' 'Reccolections after a Ramble' &c° the Gossip Tales are taken from the mouths of my unletterd Parents & nearly related as they told them The chief is 'The Lodge House' & 'Robs Terrors of Night'°

I was this Morning shown for the first time one of Walter Scotts Works viz 'The Lady of the Lake' the mention of him in your letter (as I was just reading him when it arived) seemd to me so very singular that I coud not help to remark the circumstance—you will excuse my uncooth & unconected manner of letter writing when I own I am a very bad hand in it & have scarcly had occasion to write a Letter

Your kindness of proffering me a book has emboldend me to mention my wish of seeing 'Kirk White'° which I have heard great talk of being one I understand as humble in circumstances as my self

I reamain with gratfull acknowledgments your Humble Servant

John Clare

To Markham E. Sherwill

Helpstone Feb 24 1820

Hond Sir

With a clowns gratfull way of blunt return I can but thank you—& shoud have answerd your kind Letter sooner but had thoughts of coming up to London & then getting Mr Taylor to inform you of my next intended publication—I fear your expectations are too warm respecting the pieces I informd you of they little satisfy me but it will make some excuse in their behalf when I tell you Solitude was written by scraps last summer in all the bustle of hard labour—as to the rest they are all of them the Gingles of this winter the Lodge House I must confess this bit of pride is I think the best as it is the most original subject it is in the measure of 'Crazy Nell'°—last monday I went to the Marquis of Exeters to say that he has behavd kindly is saying too little he has proposd to alow me a yearly present to assist my leisure to write my success at Milton Hall° you have no doubt heard of who put it in the morning chronicle I dont know but I fear it has done me harm good men dont like their kind actions to be made so public° I must get some friend to hint to Lord Milton that I was strange to the matter & have been sorely hurt since I heard of it—the day clears up & I am again preparing to start for London° but as I have got so far with my scribbling at all adventures you shall have it I have a great deal to say & little art to express it therefore with telling you some country News about your humble poet being (what we call) ask in church on Sunday to 'Patty of the Vale'°

I conclude your Humble Servant
John Clare

Dont direct to Drurys no more but to
John Clare Helpstone | Near M[arket] Deeping | Northamptonshire
I must hint the Second Edit of my Poems Will be embelishd with my old Hut drawn by a friendly Gent° & then I shall beg leave to present you with a Vol as soon as pub. they went to press on monday

J.C.

To John Taylor

Helpstone Wednesday [8 March] 1820

Dear Taylor

Excuse the warm expression—according to promise I send you a note to tell you of my safe arival home & glad enough I am for I was weary of noise & bustle I send you 'Solitude' The 'Lodge house' next time Lord M[ilton] flatters me I doubt in saying many parts of it please him much as I found a note to that purpot when I got home my book is to be sent me in a weeks time give Mr Hessey a hint of the fiddle & if you please you may send me the Head of Lord Radstock as you proposd° give my sincere Respects to Keats & tell him I had a great desire to see him & that I like his first vol of Poems much I coud point many beauties in my thinking if I had time but as soon as I got home I found the tables in the Hut coverd with Letters 18 in No 10 of which I found it nessesary to answer so you will excuse the hasty scrawl—I must not however forget to tell you to give my respects to Messrs Reynolds Woodhouse° Percival° Hilton Dewent Mrs D[ewent] & little Girl & all whom I may forget

in great haste | your humbl Servt

John Clare

(With Speed) Send 2 or 3 Copies of 2nd Edit as Lady F[itzwilliam] wants 2 directly

To John Taylor

Sunday | Helpstone | March 19 1820

Dear Taylor

I recieved the parcel by coach this day but the other is miscarried & I fear lost will you take the trouble to question the waggoner about it the next time hes in London—as to drury° I think we are under no obligations to him for any thing I shoud always wisht him to have been a partner in the things I publish but as he cannot speak well of me when he has no longer hopes of Interest in my conscerns I think I can have done with him alltogether in my next which I shall not [h]esitate to do I was mentioned by sombody in Stamford Town Hall this week (it is from good authority) & Drury I suppose answerd him stuntly° 'no more Clare for me' you know thats enough I think he is paid very well for his journey to helpston & I think to pay myself with resentment is to wipe out his name at the bottom of the next book—If you & I was to part tomorrow I dont think you woud find reasons to say any thing against me as he does shoud you I never set no price on my writings to him I always humoured him with new pieces as soon as wrote & went to

Stamford Weeks & weeks only on his account when I had more need been at work still I dont wish nor mean to speak ill of him to no one I shall always respect him as long as I live but when he got his agreement upon foot I quickly grew jealous of his fidelity & resolved to keep my pieces more to my self you will no doubt say this thought was timley put in practice after the hints I gave you at london I doubt you will think I trouble you with letters but the 'lodge house' was just posted off when I got your letter speaking of the parcells—You talk of cutting me about in 'Solitude' I can only say have mercy I have provd your judgment & patiently submit—my lodge house I think will be above your thumbs & Keats too° it is undergone the Critiscism of my father & mother & several rustic Neighbours of the town & all aprove it you will agree they beat your polite Critics in that low nature which you never prove but by reading & which them & I have daily witnessd in its most subtle branches so much for this—you will laugh at my conesceit but dont humour it by looking over what you may think faults I always heartily wish for you[r] plain judgment about everything you know that—now for somthing else there is a rumour in Stamford about putting in force a Subscription° for me of 100 Guineas I told O[ctavius] G[ilchrist] at the fair but he knew nothing of it tho the person that told me had it from the Mayor himself tell O.G. your self if he woud have the goodness to put a paragraph in Drakards 'News' it woud soon be put forward you might hint it as your own opinion—If Lord R[adstock] woud do this in the London papers instead of his puffs perhaps it woud produce me a benefit—this hint is for your opinion—now I will give you my opinion—if by subscription I coud get £1000!!!! dont be struck I should be satisfied & shoud want not a farthing more £50 a year woud keep me capital & I shoud have no dread to look forward this is not the case now I even shudder to peep at whats to come I cannot write a line in this suspence & never shall while I percieve my doom to turn out good or bad Excuse my freedom it is always my way to unbosom my thoughts to friends which I believe as such tho I know I have paid dearly for it by times to you at a venture I dont hesitate to say any thing just as I think I speak to you & always shall

Farwell

P.S. Respects to Messrs Hessey Hiltons Mr & Mrs D[e]went & little girl Reynolds Keats Woodhouse & all whom I may forget Pattys best Respects to you & wishes very much to send a piece of Bride Cake tho she thinks it will [cost] you too much Cariage but I shall venture ont I coud say much more if paper & time woud hold out | Yours

John Clare

To James Augustus Hessey

Helpstone April 2 1820

Dear Hessey

I am happy in having for the first time an oppertunity of addressing a letter to you in ansr to yours accompanying the fiddle parcel which I recieved last night (1st of April) I had not time to put it in tune but I can agree with your opinion readily that I think it is not got worse with age I shall not fill my letter with thanks neither to you nor Mr Taylor for his present as I am obliged to do to others tis fulsome flattery downright I shall only tell you I esteem both gifts gratfully & believe that your fiddle will remain with me as a standard for life tho I shall not despise my old one I may lay it on the shelf but cannot sell it as it is like an old Friend when I behold it, it reminds me of what is past many pains & pleasures mingld together in banishd days—I have found out the No 35 Fleet Street it is Mr Hoar a Banker° as I have been so pesterd with fussing puffs from booksellers chiefly country I thought this was one & some time shall send M[r] T[aylor] a Copy of his Letter with my Ansr which for the first time I purposly copied

Lord Radstock has promised me 'Curries Burns'° did you know of it it is a good book I think & will be as valuable a present as his Lordships first 'Blair'° dont forget to hint that I am highly pleased at the mention he made of such a present in his last letters for I do assure you Expectation is on the look out for it every day here I must stick Mr Hilton tell him I dont know what hes about with my pictures I am a blunt fellow & if he is likwise short questions will please him best which I think he is & the most unlike a Londener I saw all the while I coud not help feeling a sort of friendly gratification at my first Interview with him he appeard to me like a neighbour of the Country & when I was told it was Hilton the Painter I was more supprised then ever as I had heard of him much at Stamford my foolish opinion of these Celebrated London Writers & Painters was that they was somthing different to other men & if Mr H[ilton] & D[ewint] took notice of my staring at them so strictly I dont wonder at it as I did it as matter of curosity to find where the distinction was which the fact is I coud not see you will readily excuse my silly remarks it is only for your own eye I shall never get that polish which some recomends to me I cant abide it I write to you & T[aylor] as I shoud do to a Country friend I tell you my most simple opinions of things that strike me in my own rude way as I shoud have done 3 or 4 years back—dont mention to Hilton what Ive said only give my respects to him & Mr Dewint his wife & little girl some folks tell me my letters will creep into print & that it is a serious benefit for me to try to polish I only tell them I must then make an apollagy to creep after them as a preface & all will go right—what a polishd letter this woud be if it was printed!!!—& my last wild thing to Taylor there[s] two specimens for ye.—but as I am in one of my half fits of good humour I must consider before my papers filld what I have got to say of information as you will have a long roundabout of silly blunders & nothing else—I must tell you (tho Taylor has took all the pride away that I had in the poetical line of judging) that I have this last fortnight wrote a good many Sonnets 2 of which to 'Taste' & 'Poetry' I like best I have begun a Long Poem on Spring but cannot finish it I send Taylor the only prospectus left he very much desired it so make him pay for the letter

yours &c
John Clare

I have lookd in all Drurys letters but not a word T. mentions is in them I had a good mind to send them but thought they woud not pay for carriage O[ctavius] G[ilchrist] wants a prospectus you must not (if he mentions it) say you had one from me so latly as I said I had none which I then thought

NB if Lord R[adstock] says any thing of Burns tell him you have it as I shoud like it from your shop then you can send it & it will be a good Copy

To Markham E. Sherwill

Saturday night | 9 o'clock | 8. April 1820

Dear Sir

Your notice of the kindness of the Hon Baronet Sir Walter Scott° towards a Clown so unworthy of his notice has affected my feelings in such a dergree that I can scarcly write an Answer give him my gratitude you can prove it sincere give him a thousand thanks had I been told last year that I shoud have been noticed by that Celebrated Poet—I dont know but I think it woud have overwelmd me & turnd my senses I am scarcly able to bear up with my success I have felt very poorly a kind of slight Fever with frequent Faintings but I have kept it secret besure dont tell Lord Radstock—2 days ago I was greatly alarmd by a kind of fit but I hope it is wearing off I have nothing now only a cold—I hope you will keep me more in the dark respecting the kindness of these great men till I recover my Strength—God bless you you are the Second Gent in London that noticed me the first was one who signd himself 'AB'° 32 Red Lion Square you woud oblige me some time when it is in your way to call of him I have not heard of him latly—

Lord R[adstock] is under a mistake respecting a Gent who wote to me I said his name was 'Hoar' & that he livd at '35 Fleet St' I shall send a Copy of his Letter to you which I beg you woud answer if you please

you told me to unbosom myself I have done it what I hinted at was the elated stretch of my feelings which affected me the last time I wrote to you that I even dreaded my dissolution was nigh & that I shoud not see my harvest got in—I was rather disapointed when you mentiond the 'Lady of the Lake' as not accompanying the letter—if you purchase Curries Burns which I shoud like with the Honble Baronets Bounty besure to tell Lord Radstock as he proposd to send me them & then it will hinder him as he may send somthing in lieu of them at some futer time for I think his Lordship has been at expence enough in buying books for me at present—you wish me to state what I shoud like else I am fearful of overrunning the Sum but you need not send them if I shoud—I often wish to see poor

Chattertons Works & shoud like Whites Life & Funeral of Lord Nelson° I feel a great Regard for that Saviour of his Country & shoud be happy to posses an account of him I once saw 'whites' & likd it much I have seen none that I like better—besure dont say nothing to none of my friends respe[c]ting my alarm of the fit or rather swooning I tell you & you only my parents knows nothing of it if they did they woud be very uneasy it was in the fields & wether I lay down or fell down I cant tell but when I came to my self my hat was lying at a distance frome me & my coat was rather dirtied my throat was rather sore & I felt as if suddenly attacted with a cold—this 3 weeks or more I have had many shiverings on me somthing if I may or can describe it so like a momentary Ague—I have now easd my mind I hope you can give me some comfort in your next by telling me what the appoplexy is I did not bleed anywhere which I think they say accompanys it I have made the best of it by fancying it was only a strong drowsiness that came upon me—I said I woud send you a Copy of Mr Hores Letter but [I c]annot find it—never mind—he wish[e]s to know my Cirscumstances you know them & you can tell them better then my self I shall not trouble his Lordship about it any more—I forgot to ask you if Sir Walters Portrait accompanys the 'Lady of the Lake' as I shoud like it much Taylor promised me Lord Rs Picture but I have not got it as yet—if I have misd anything in answering your letter you can forgive me

God bless you with every one that befriends me | Good night

John Clare

To John Taylor

Helpstone [19 April] 1820

Dear Taylor

You will not write to me so I must take the trouble to force you if I can how is the 2nd Edit° going on when do you intend to publish a new vol. the matireials are all ready the M.S.S. are came safe from Milton & O[ctavius] G[ilchrist] has got them now as soon as he has done with them he sends them to you I suppose with the Chauser &c of yours I have recieved a ¼s Pension from burghley & am writing an Ode to the Marquis as I think I must certainly be his Laureat now by profession have you got a Copy of the unpublished M.S.S. which you have if not can you spare the M.S.S. as I think a great many of the pieces with a little alteration might do well at least they may be too good to be lost I have happend of good luck since I heard of you having in this last day or two got about £11 I have had a gentleman from Cambridge° purposly to see me he says I am admired at Coledge much & thats not bad News you know is Mr Hilton dead & gone you know what lies in that question reccolect as I am renounced all work for this month or 6 weeks if you coud wish to have any of the old MSS alterd nows the time as I am not in Q° to write origionally get the old MSS copyd out if you like D[rury] dare not trust 'em again with me I am getting a deep shifty designing scoundrel so be upon your guard & have your eyes open—I sent to D. for the book I told you but he woud not let me have it there he is more out of my favour then ever—you must do what you can with him he has got too many pieces to be lost in fact I know not what he has got—you say nothing more about the 'Lodge house' I coud say a coud [*for* good] deal about here but my paper wears away—I have been teribly plagued with the muses since I saw you I think I have wrote 50 Sonnets—wether they are inspired by those ladys I cant [say] I am almost afraid that some evil spirit is fond of personyfying them to torment me—Expect the 'Review' in next Quarterly°

Goodbye
John Clare

To Markham E. Sherwill

Helpstone 3 May 1820

Dear Sir

I am happy to inform you I recieved your Parcel safe but am sorry you shoud be at more expence then proposd as I did not wish it I knew not the price of the books & therefore you shoud not notice my claims any further then the sum amounted to but it is done & I thank you once more for all favours you have so kindly bestowd—there is mistery in not sending 'Lady of the

Lake' perhaps Sir Walter Scott is returning by Stamford & if he does you shoud tell me he has gone that way before now often as I understand by O. Gilchrist Esqr—I am not so carless as you think in loosing my corespondence I dont think there is any lost they are laid aside & I have now got a box made on purpose & shall look up the whole to put in it after a bit—Hoars letter where ever it is is very short & very misterious a few questions about the Publishers & myself thats all—I have had a letter from my old friend 'A.B.' I thought he was lost but was happy to prove my notions wrong whoever he is his advice is to me of great value & I shall always esteem him greatly I am very glad to hear your opinion of my complaint° & have made my self very easy about it ever since

I am very sorry for his Lordships misfortune°—I understand from Mrs E[mmerson] he has written twice to Lord M[ilton] & recieved no answer I did not feel easy for such neglect he coud but have been as carless with me he had a right to have answerd it—I therefore took up my pen independantly & wrote to him my self stating the kindnesses Lord R[adstock] had done towards me & that all done was without any proposal what ever & that if such things troubld his Lordship I was independant & did not wish it therefore when you see Lord R. again tell his Lordship not to write any more about requesting the cottage° as it seems not agreeable to Lord M[ilton]s intentions I have no doubt he will do somthing but I believe he is one that must have time to consider he is not so open hearted as Lord R. you make me laugh when you tell me to try to spell better indeed it is a hard task had you saw my first writings you might have hinted it then but I thought I was a fel hand at it now however I will do my best with your advice & you know I readily excuse you in finding fault with my learning—I have had a Revd J. Plumptre° wrote to me latly he is an Author & has sent me some of his publications which I cannot commend 'Dramas' after the way of Mrs Moore is one—I have had a visitor from cambridge 'Chauncey Hare Townsend Esqr' he has flatterd me with a fine Sonnet & as I promised Taylor it in his letter & then forgot it please to let me trouble you to copy it out for him next time you write to him or are in town this is the

Sonnet

There is a vivid lightning of the breast
Flashd from a kindred spark of poesy
Which poets only know when rapt they see
Some hidden thought some feeling unexprest
Upon the pages of the bard imprest
In all the warmth of natures energy
O Clare such answering electricity
Darts from thy numbers to my soul addrest
Thou hast read nature with a poets eye
Thou hast felt nature with a poets heart
Not the broad page which all expansd descry
But the fine secrets which poetic art
Alone unravels—can alone impart
And to which none but poets souls reply

C.H.T. | Cambridge 18 April 1820

This is a Copy you can judge of its merits people tells me he gaind the prize for poetry° this year I know no more of him his journey to me was purposly made—& as soon as I get more good News to tell you off you may depend you shall not fail to be troubld with its hearing tho I fear my scrawling sensless corespondence is almost wearied you

your Humble St
John Clare

To John Taylor

[4 May 1820]

My dear Taylor

I cannot help answering your letter nearly verbatim & directly tho you need not return one I have got Sir Walter Scotts Books with the addition of Ramsay from you safe I am glad you have made straight with E[dward] D[rury] tho ED is not my favourite now I went to see him on friday & shoud have gone before then only I woud not have it said I stood in the way of either while the job was settl'd you are right in saying you think we need no other bond then friendship in keeping you

& me together for I took such a liking to you from the first appearance at Stamford that ED knows I often said if you did not give me 6d for my new pieces no one else shoud have them but you all the vexsation that set me agen D. was him wishing to be first as to the publication when he stood as much indebted to your as my self (between you & me) as a Secret he talkd very slightly of you as he says I did of Lord R[adstock]—it shows his wisdom by depending on such gossiping tales as facts I never did do any such thing if it was so you know very well where it came from—his speaking lightly of yourself was I suppose only a tradsmans folly it was I expect wishing to make you less magnified in my eyes then himself but his Elocution coud not efect it I knew when I had found a friend that coud bring me before the public in the best manner & when that was done it was nothing but gratitude to esteem his as such;—& as such I will esteem you in spite of all that may be said [to] the contrary—if D. has the merit of first procuring you as my friend I will let him to see I have merit enough as bad as I am to value you accordingly—thats how the fray began & I vowd no agreement shoud rest upon any bodys proposal but your own & that Ill stick to wether Im wrong or right he has no doubt by my orders sent you origionals & copies by this but the first book I told you off is kept back for my purpose as there is in the margin fragments of pieces which I want at this time—but you shall have it as soon as you want it tho he says he has copyd all the best out of it which is not much I know it was only for your jud[g]ment that I hazarded it into his hands but you never had it—you need not be in any doubts as to materials for another vol: as I know theres plenty—I have a great many short pieces written since I left London these are only known to you & me nor I dont intend they shoud be known to—you know you do—therefore when they are again written off you shall have them under my seal thro O[ctavius] G[ilchrist]s or E.D.s care with the book O G has got I wish he woud get forward with it I shall give him the hint—I reccolect the sonnet to Autumn & have a fair idea of one to a violet but what Mrs E[mmerson] mentions about the 148 Psl. I know no more then the dead have I been paraphrasing one to her I cant recolect I sent her any such thing°

I am sorry for Lord Rs misfortune but hope he is getting better as I heard of it a day or two ago   you need not be very sorry about my complaint as I wrote to Cap Sherwill the particulars of the whole just after my fear had workd up apprehensions of death in me & I am happy to hear he thinks but little of it some effect of mind from my success &c &c   I intended 2 or 3 times to have been blooded & as you advise I shall have it done imediatly   the Shiverings I was so fearful off dont attend me so much as at first   I get more into the company of the rustics in the village harmless cottagers reccolect & there I am at home again & hear things which I formerly was accostomd to   this puts all thoughts of other things out of my head & I think will be the only means of getting well till I am accustomd to the ways of the world her overpowering flattering reception or overwhelming disgust which like an unrestraind torrent bursts out in applause or censure & till her victim is exalted or debased no restraint Can force her into bounds   keep me as blind as you can in these matters & all will be well   you are right in saying £30 a year is as much as I got at hard work & gratitude wispers to tell me I am right in thanking you as the cause which I do from my very soul   the Gent from Cambridge you wish to know of is 'Chauncy Hare Townsend'   I understand (only by hearsay mind) that he won the prize this year for poetry   he made a purpose journey to see me & has flatterd me with a complimentary Sonnet which you shall have in the course of the letter—I had a kind enquiring letter after my cirscumstances from Mr 'A. Hoare 35 Fleet street'   I sent him a answer but recieved none in return   it is a long while since   has he been to you   I understand latly he is a great Banker & very rich

I am glad your taste & mine agrees in Friend Keats° & I am glad you are making a selection of his Poems for publication   I heartily wish you woud accompany it with a preface as you did mine   I know it woud do him good   every body is anxious to know somthing about an author & woud even buy the book to satisfy that curosity   if you do it as simple as mine it will never fail to please or be of service to the author whom I sincerely wish success only keep it close from O.G. if you say any thing about the Quarterly—but you know that you do—I shoud like to see somthing of 'living poets' handld simpley & easy which you know has never been done yet—but your Essay° may be a good subject as far as I know   you percieve I am no judge in such matters—

'Nutting' I have begun nor am I so carless as you imagine if you think I have lost sight of the 'Ways of a Village'° you will have it before next christmass if I guess right your hint of loosing the 5th lines of 'Midnight'° I cannot do I doubt without working it all over again but Ill try when I get it from drury I am glad to hear the success of the 2nd Edit—& now shant fail to remind you of the Cottage it is a copper plate wood cut or nothing at all—aye—I think I hear you say as well as not—but mind ye I look for it—& if you leave it out I am dissapointed—but to speak plain if the Hut is engravd for the third Edit send—A.B. a copy as I promisd his daughter one with such embelishment if not you may save your-self the trouble—I have heard of my old friend A.B. this last week he tells me this time to direct to Mr Turners 32 Red Lion Square as usual—as usual he never said so before but I imagine he thinks we have smelt him out & thinks very right if so he does think—I cannot but say you behave very handsome to ED considering his behaviour too I think he has got off well—I knew long enough you had no disguise but I must tell you you may save the trouble of informing me about any such matters I am not inquisitive & can but say you have acted uprightly on all sides

J. Clare

I have had a letter from an Author latly with a collection of his works the Revd James Plumptre & I have answerd him he dont like my notions of *fate* & *fortune* & in rules for song writing: an Introduction to one of his Books he tells me to model mine I read it & found to my suprise he is a modern puritanical reformer or at least woud be for I hope he will get but few followers he sets his face against all mention of fairies muses passions in love & forbids all belief of gohsts hobgobblings witches &c &c I soon found his rules woud not do for me & bluntly told him my superstitious Grandmother had instilld those notions into my nature so very early that it woud be hard matter now to make me disbelieve em if I deny their existance in the day I soon recant my opinions at night when I am wandering alone by haunted spots & if he preached rules & Reasons of their nonexistance as long & as often as he preaches his sermons his reasons woud not fortyfy me with courage at them times enough to keep me from looking back & trembling with terror over my old supperstitious stories

I have nothing more to add only my best respects to Mr Hessy & all my other London friends which as soon as you see I hope you will not fail to rem[em]ber me to & that I remain your

faithfull St

John Clare

P.S. I coud not help smiling when O.G. told me Mr Hessy had heard fearfull news of my having had a appolectic fit—tis wonderful how such things get out I never told my apprehensions to any one but C. Sherwill as I know of only dropping a few hints to O.G. but I often hear things that are reported to have belongd to me that I am till then entirely unaquainted with both to their origin & subject

J.C.

To Chauncey Hare Townsend

Helpstone [after 6] May 1820

Dear Sir

I must trouble you with an Answer to say I have recieved the parcel safe & to give you my gratful thanks for it my fathers sees the benefit of the plasters° imediatly & I hope that they may succeed the 'Minstrel' is a sweet Poem & far as I have read a many thoughts occur which are in my 'Peasant Boy' I doubt the world will think them plagarisms therefore I must alter them or cut them out altogether but nature is the same here at helpstone as it is elswhere—I am now employd in writing songs° for a musicseller in Town If I succeed it may perhaps be to my advancment If I dont there is not much risk to run—so I am carless as to them matters I shall be glad of your advice when ever you give it I shall be happy to see you again at helpstone likwise your first visit found me in a glowering desponding condition that often gets the sway but when I have been inspired with a pint of 'John Barleycorn' & in one of my sun shining moments you woud not know me I am a new man & have too many tongues tho your visit did not find it still I can be cheery but In my sullen fits I am defiled with the old silence of rusticity that always characterized me among my neighbours before I was known to the world—I was reckond a 'glumpy half sort of fool' amongst 'em you will excuse all this it is only to make apology for the ill behaviour that might seem predominant at our first interview—excuse likewise my writing so soon had I neglected perhaps It might have been too long before I had pluckt up my spirits to address you—I am obligd to answer every friend imediatly while gratitude is warm other wise indolent neglect woud defer it too long to be thought as such—you will look over my faulty corespondence Letter writing is a thing that I dont give any brush of correction or study too tis just set down as things come to my 'tongues end' I am affraid I shall weary you with my stupid scribbling therefore I must conclude with acknowledging myself to be your | gratfull St

John Clare

To John Taylor

Helpstone May 20 1820

Dear Taylor

You seem supprisd at my scribblings of late but you have none to be supprisd at what D[rury] sent you are the silly stuff of my young days generally speaking some songs sonnets & ballads included—what will you be when you come in for the tail piece now at O[ctavius] G[ilchrist]s you may be supprisd then & more so when I tell you all of them or nearly are the productions of this winter—'my good old chuckey'° you are blind in my manners & plans of writing when I am in the fit I write as much in one week as woud knock ye up a fair size Vol—& when I lay down the pen I lay it down for good a long while—reccolect the subjects are roughly sketchd in the fields at all seasons with a pencil I catch nature in every dress she puts on so when I begin to ryhme & polish up I have little to do in studying description I am like the boy that gets his horn book alphebet by heart & then can say his lesson with his eyes as well shut as open—dont be under aprehensions of an offence to Lord M[ilton] I know my friends too well to offend em so cheaply I know very well the Milton family is my best patrons & I am in no fear but of them continuing to be so—Lord Radstocks letter° was all I did—I only professd my ignorance in the matter—

what a fool the Editor of the morning post must be he has left a line out of Townends Sonnet & spoilt the whole get it reprinted in some other paper°—I will give you a specimen of poetic madness—

Address to the clouds

O painted clouds sweet beauties of the sky
How have I viewd your motion & your rest
When like fleet hunters ye have left mine eye
In your thin gause of wooly fleecing drest
Or in your threatnd thunders grim black vest
Like black deep waters slowly moving bye
Awfully striking the spectators breast
With your creators dread sublimity
As admiration mutely views your storms
& I do love to see you idly lye
Painted by heaven varied as your forms
Pausing upon the eastern mountain high
As morn awakes in springs wood harmony
& sweeter still when in your slumbers sooth
You hang the western arch oer days proud eye
Still as the even pool uncurvd & smooth
My gazing soul has lookd most placidly
& higher still devoutly wisht to strain
To wipe your shrouds & skyes blue blinders bye
With all the warmness of a moonstruck brain
To catch a glimpse of him who bids you reign
& view the dwelling of all majesty

This is just a bit of eye salve for my cursed prose—I shall frequently sprinkle such in my letters in future

Dear Taylor

I this morning got Hiltons sket[c]h° of your humble St his hardship John Clare dont let him find frame & glass in the bargain pay him at my account—& as to the picture I will well thresh him for it in ryhme so caution him wi my threatnings—the fact is I mean to write him a jingling letter ere long to 'W. Hilton R.A.' ask him wether he woud as leave stand pillory an hour as stand in my ryhmes I think myself the disgrace is only equal & if he is in my opinion I will surely search in my new vol of poems to torment him so tell him bluntly he has forcd poor J.C. from his flail & spade to strut on canvass in the town of lunon & I will take him from his 'water nymphs' to lye on the hobs of our dirty cottages to be read by every greazy thumbd wench & chubby clown in spite of his 'RAs' &c &c so tell the gentleman his doom—nor are you out of the mess for I have already dressd you out in a letter to Captain Sherwill I expect you know it ere now you know you do I think it the best ryhming humour I have yet wrote in that way I was pleasd wi the verse on your worthy self° let you find it as you will I expect to see you & Hilton down next week, so look to't if any more delays postpone it O.G. expects too remember—good bye & kind respect to all friends

J. Clare

Sonnet. C.H.T.
'Thou hast felt &c' the next is left out
'*Not the broad page, which all expanced descry*'
The line out is the 10 mind that.

C.

To John Taylor

[10 June 1820]

My Dear Taylor

I am sorry to hear you have been unwell but hope you will weather the storm & make your appearence soon my visit was not far but good company entices me to make long stays you know me well & woud know me better if I was nigher London I have seen the critique in the Quarterly & a deal softer it is then I expected as for what he says of 'book sellers'° care not I dont—I am glad you was pleasd with the verse on Sherwill as it pleasd me I think your taste & mine had I education woud be as like 'as pin to pin' your selection of my poems gave me plenty of consciet of your abilities I asure ye—& if I have any fault it bears to the flattering side [?mum] for that—I 'smell the rat' in the fancy° & shoud have wishd his autograph much—Poor Keats as a brother wanderer in the rough road of life & as one whose eye picks now & then a wild flower to cheer his solitary way who looks with his wild vain & crackd braind friend to the rude break neck hill where sits the illustrious inspirer—fame—who looks with me—as carless of her anointed few—but who as he turns away cannot help with me but heave a sigh I judge colors by complexion & for his feelings his love of nature & his genius I heartily love him I like the extracts from his poems & wait their publication anxiously—you will think me diligent when I tell you to expect my poems soon they will come directly from me I think next week but the presise day you shall know of before hand wait till then to answer me either you or Hessey will be expected to give an imediate notice of their arival as you know the feelings of mad braind ryhmers for the safty of his childern—but if you come down next week I think they will be ready for taking up with you if you will take the trouble

I dont think D[rury] right yet therefore the best is the best & you shall have them direct from me the only copies so take care of em I often see D. but we are not so familiar as usal poor fellow he had too much consiet of me he vallued me more as a poet then I deserved & when his expectations fell he met like all others dissapointment he is now in your hands use him well he is like me a stranger to the world & therefore like mine his congectures for the most pa[rt] are wrong founded the Song 'Here we me[et] too soon to part' is published & dedicat[ed] to Marquis Exeter by Hayden Corri° the opinion of the town is a mean performance—the next book forgive my pride I shoud like in 8vo well printed with a head & vignette cottage it is only vanitys conjecture & left to your judgment as usual

God bless you

The 'Fancy' is R——ds I think remember me to him & Hessy to Hilton Dewent Mrs D[ewint] & little girl

To James Augustus Hessey

Helpstone July 4. 1820

My Dear Hessey

On thursday the M.S.S. starts to London I have some new ones but shall trouble you wi' them in letters as I finish them I heard from Lord R[adstock] last week & answerd his Lordship this morning—weres my old friend Sherwill—I began on our friend Keats new Vol:—find the same fine flowers spread if I can express myself in the wilderness of poetry—for he la[u]nches on the sea without compass—& mounts pegassus without saddle or bridle as usual & if those cursd critics could be shovd out of the fashion wi their rule & compass & cease from making readers believe a Sonnet cannot be a Sonnet unless it be precisly 14 lines & a long poem as such unless one first sits down to wiredraw out regular argument & then plod after it in a regular manner the same as a Taylor cuts out a coat for the carcass—I say then he may push off first rate—but he is a child of nature warm & wild Campbell & Rogers° must be fine very fine Because they are the critics own childern nursd in the critics garden & prund by the fine polishing knifes of the critics—they must be good no soul dare say otherwise—it woud be out of the fashion—dont ye think a critic like a gardener uses his pruning knife very often to keep it in action & find as he calls it a job—an old proverb is among us 'a gardener woud cut his fathers head off were he a tree' so woud the other if his father was a book—to keep his hand in—I have skimd over Keats & noticd the following as striking

——'Often times
'She askd her brothers with an eye all pale
'*Striving to be itself*'

Isabel

'*Season of mists & mellow fruitfullness*'
'Then in a wailful choir *the small knats mourn*'

Autumn

'& joy *whose hand is ever at his lips*
'*Bidding adieu*'

Mel:

'No stir of air was there
'Not so much life as on a summers day
'Robs not *one light seed from the featherd grass*
'But *where the dead leaf fell* there *did it rest*'

Hyp:

'A stream went *voiceless by*'
Hyp:

——'let the maid
'Blush keenly as with some *warm kiss surprisd*'
Hyp:

'& poplars & lawn shading palms & beach
'In which *the zepher breaths its loudest song*'
Hyp:

I think this Vol not so warm as 'Endymion' why did you not print some of his Sonnets I like them much—I shoud like Endymion bound with his autograph inserted if he pleases & shall send my copy up purposly the first opertunity—'Chauser' I shall send by Drurys care quickly—D[rury] has sent me 3 vols calld 'Percys Relics' there is some sweet Poetry in them & I think it the most pleasing book I ever happend on the tales are familiar from childhood all the stories of my grandmother & her gossiping neighbours I find versified in these vols—I shall now make a beginning with 'Ways in a village' I think a series of little poems connected by a string as it were in point of narative woud do better then a canto poem to please critics I mind no fashions

Farwell
John Clare

Give my remembrances to Taylor Hilton Dewint Reynolds Woodhouse Keats &c. &c. &c. &c. J.C.

I had forgot to say 'Patty' has got to helpstone & I think will prove a better bargain then I expected—

To James Augustus Hessey

[10? July 1820]

My Dear Hessey

I have seen the third Edition & am cursed mad about it the judgment of T[aylor] is a button hole lower in my opinion—it is good—but too subject to be tainted by medlars *false delicasy*° damn it I hate it beyond every thing those primpt up° misses brought up in those seminaries of mysterious wicknedness (Boarding Schools) what will please em? why we well know—but while their heart & soul loves to extravagance (what we dare not mention) false delicasy's seriousness muscles° up the mouth & condemns it—what in the name of delicasy doth poor Dolly say to incur such malice as to have her artless lamentations shut out—they blush to read what they go nightly to balls for & love to practice alas false delicasy—I fear thou art worse then dolly say nothing to T.—he is left to do as he likes you know—& if we controul him he will give us up—but I think I shall soon be qualified to be my own editor—pride once rooted grows very fast you percieve—I expect Drury is in London—he will tell you my eagerness of having a new vol I hope you will be as eager & then 'tween us all three we shall get Taylor to work—I hope he will come home from bath a new man & be so far recoverd as to master his puzzling job with pleasure I have a great many more old & new things which I shall muster up for a third Vol if its ever calld for—the people round here are very anxious of a New Vols appearance—send me a letter by Drury tell me your opinions & intentions how you will proceed with the new vol wether the '*head*' (vanity agen you percieve) will be engraven—I have made out '*Scriven*'° he is historical Engraver to his present majesty—as to the cottage for the sake of my young friend I must insist on thats being inserted so T. must let me have my wish there—but in these matters false delicasy I think will not interupt him—I have felt long enough for poor T. I asure you I know his taste & I know his embaresments I often picture him in the midst of a circle of 'blue stockings' offering this & that opinion for emprovement or omision I think to please all & offend all we shoud put out 215 pages of blank leaves & call it 'Clare in fashion'—the hut he may have done just as he likes on wood or copper as a frontpiece or vignette but tell him I expect & hope & after all bluntly insist it must be done—T. woud not be offended to find me vext I think at the omissions he k[now]s him self in so doing the gold is lickd off the gingerbread—'Dollys mistake' & 'my Mary' is by the multitude reckoned the two best in the book—I have lost my tail—by it, but never mind what think you by the new poems brought by D[rury] just glance over them & tell me I like Keats last poem the best Hyp:°—R[eynolds]'s lines on Shrewsbury are passing sweet I read em over & over if that man (noticing nature instead of the foibles of the day) is not a future poet I am mistaken give my best respects to all—dont print nothing under the hut when engravd let it pass silently & leave people to guess—you know by now I have been writing for 'Powers'° he wanted 100 Songs but am wore out—I think I shall take another sheet

To John Taylor

Help: [31] A[ugust] 1820

My Dear Taylor

I have been out on a Visit to Revd Mr Hopkinsons° Morton so did not answer your last till now—I had just got seasoned into Harvest Work when the express arrived they sent a horse for me so busy excuses was usless I have been to Grimsthorp castle° & saw many curosities & several other places & have returnd as idle & listless as ever its no use making resolutions to work you see now—they will not let me keep quiet as I usd to be—they send for me twice & 3 times a day out of the fields & I am still the strangers poppet Show what can their fancys create to be so anxious & so obstinate of being satisfied I am but a man (& a little one too) like others still as they will come I will still sit in my corner in readiness for them & ryhme & jingle in the teeth of trouble & scrat away on my 'Cremona' striving to make the best use of the world while I am in it—I fancy my W—— 'you know you do' will turn out a termagant she is one of the most ignorant & I fear will turn out the most obstinate of woman creation—I am cobbling up some pastorals but dont know how I shall succeed I have done 4 or 5 & thought little of them—but a second reading has given me a higher opinion & encouragd me to proceed tis your long wishd proceeding 'Ways in a Village' you need not write often—do it when you please only in your next tell me how you mean to print the next I must insist on the *Cottage* for the sake of my *friend*° do it in Wood or Copper as a frontpiece or Vignette only 'you know you do' it must be done—he is taking many local spots about the village which may somtime be usful to you & me perhaps & you know friends have vanity & must be a little humourd &

encouraged—he is not a Dewint—that I know well—nor is he half an artist—but his drawing, tho somthing deficient in perspective is far from being unfaithful in a general way & must claim a good share of merit by coming from a self taught pencil—give my respects to Hessey, Hilton, Keats & '*Tothill fields*'° Woodhouse & all others are you coming in the country if you intend calling on me I will wait for you I have a barrel of 'Barley corn' ready so if you are going downwards say so in your next but if you are not for tramping I am & mean to be in London° the middle of next month I have 11 Cards of adress in town & want to make use of em but reccolect yours is this time 'head quarters'

farwell

J. Clare

To John Taylor

Helpstone Octr 3 1820

My Dear Taylor

I write you imediatly & as you seem to wish a long letter I have taken a leaf out of my ryhming ledger to pleasure you & a long letter you shall have I am determind if I end with the same spirit I begin with tho its not often the case for I am very short winded & if ever I mount my old rawbone hack of a pegasus determind for a long journey we are sure to be both of us d—— d——ly cut up ere we end it & often cursedly sick ere the half way is accomplished—the fact is if we begin long things we always make bad finishes as the prancing hunter scarce kept in his reins at the beginning sickens by toil & scarcly hastens from the spur in the close—first I shall answer your kind letter where I see any answers are nessesary I think with you about the 2 lines° & cannot see any thing justly condemning them to oblivion I mean 'Ease & plenty' &c the 'dawning of genius' pleases me but I am so conceded in your taste that I seldom fancy anything displeases of your alteration in fact it makes me a bad judge of any body beside as I never can yield in the least to any of them—what I can remember of the Quarterly (as I cant find it just now to refer to) it is a long way off of an error insomuch that I believe it correct & which I have more then once told D[rury], who fights very shy with the cirscumstance°—he never saw a M.S. of the setting sun then I'll be answerable for as this proof is convincing to sense & reason—hark ye—I was a few shillings indebted to Thompson D's predesessor & thinking he woud do me some service for his own interest in hopes of the possibility of discharging the bill which then had been hopless I sent him three prospectuses as specimens for his customers & a short note wishing him to do me a kindness by giving me time to discharge the bill & using his interest in my new adventurious station of an Author all which as I learned by the bearer he treated with contempt but now to the proof if I had sent 3 printed copies of the setting sun what was the nessesity of sending a M.S. I never was fond of copying nor Ill be answerable when there was such good reasons to shun it woud I take the trouble I had but 2 copies in writing at that time Hensons & my own the first of which you have—do you want any other proof or is this sufficient I can say the M.S. story is a lie tho a friend has said it which I woud not wish to injure any further any thing of information you want in matters I am in power to dechyher° be free with—my word is my bond mind & they shall rest in my bosom & go no further then satisfaction desires—I saw it just to place you on a level with D. & I was determind to accomplish it—I did not like the slight mention of the London Publishers in the Review & have hinted it home more then once I have many things on that head which I shall tell you of in london or at helpstone I am very happy for Hiltons news° as he is a man I value not only for his genius but his plain blunt & honest manners which suits me to a tittle—I hope poor Keats will return to England as he coud wish—& shall feel honoured with his corespondence I assure you nor shall his advice° be thrown away if I can help it tho you are well aware of my stubborness I am glad you like my Pastoral & as I think I have better you have clapt a spur to old Peggy° which starts her off agen at full trott you shall have all as soon as I can set too to copy them—The 'Vignette' suits & the 'nob' of 'sir John'° tickles him I assure you 12 months is a long time but the materials is not yet ready or it woud seem longer nor do I know if they are ready by then—I shall never dream of John Taylor acting roguishly as Nature never woud belye her self by putting such an honest looking face on a rogues shoulders tho the 'great & good' are so charitable to give their advice for a twelvmonth longer 'as such things are' I doubt not, but not among Hesseys & Taylors mind; my opinion is stubborn & so it aught to be thank you for the mile stone before its put down as then you are aware I shall not have the oppertunity you shall see some of my friends poems° when I get them I shall write him to day & bluntly ask him for them he has not got the knack of song writing as the attempts he [has] shown me are very weak & dry—you never mention the proof sheet poet° so shall not trouble you with it as my opinion tells me its not worth it—dont hint a word to J[ames] D[rury]° as I told you of the matter. I shall expect you in november but mind ye the barrel will not hold in till then I feel no inclination to see London when you are from it so 'good speed & guerdon to ye Johnney' till we meet agen as you likd my last Sonnet you shall have another & a specimen of rural courtship from a new pastoral 'Close of Eve'° & then if my memorys wore out its good bye & god bless you

To the Ivy°

Dark creeping Ivy with thy berries brown
That fondly twists on ruins all thine own
Old spire points studding with a leafy crown
Which every minute threatens to dethrone
With fearful eye I view thy height sublime
& oft with quicker step retreat from thence
Where thou in weak defiance strives with time
& holds his weapons in a dread suspense
But bloom of ruins thou art sweet to me
When far from dangers way thy gloomy pride
Wreaths picturesque around some ancient tree
That bows his branches by some fountain side
Then sweet it is from summer suns to be
With thy green darkness overshadowing me

Now from the pasture milking maidens come
With each a swain to bear the burthen home
Who often coax them on their pleasant way
To soodle longer out in loves delay
While on a molhill or a resting stile

The fondling shepherds try their arts the while
With glegging smiles; & hopes & fears between
A snatching kiss to open what they mean
& all the utmost that their tongues can do
The hony'd words which nature learns to woo
The sweets of language 'darling love & dear'
With warmest utterings meet each maidens ear
Who as by magic smit she knows not why
From the keen look that waits a wisht reply
Droops blushing down in loves delightful swoon
As slinks the blossom from the suns of noon
While sighs half smotherd from her throbbing breast
& broken words sweet trembling oer the rest
& cheeks in crimson burning turnd aside
Betray the plainer what they strive to hide
The amourous swain now breaks the thin disguise
& sees the fondness she at first denies
& with all passions love & truth can move
Urges more strong the simpering maid to love
More freely using toying ways to win
Tokens that echo from the soul within
Her soft hand nipping that with ardour burns
& timid gentler pressing its returns
& stealing pins with innoscent deciet
To loose the 'kerchief from its envyd seat
& unawares her bonnet to untye
& auburn ringlets wiping gently bye
To steal a kiss by seemly feignd disguise
As love yield kinder taken by suprise
While she near conquerd less resentment moves
& owns at last in tears & sighs she loves
With sweetest feelings that this world bestows
Now each to each their bosom thoughts disclose
Vow to be true; & to be truly taen
Repeat their loves & vow it oer again
& pause at loss of language to exclaim
Those purest pleasures yet without a name
& while in highest extacy of bliss
The shepherd holds her yielding hand in his
He turns to heaven to witness what he feels

& silent shows what loss of words conceals
& ere the parting moments hustle nigh
& night in deeper dye his curtain dips
Till next days evening glads the anxious eye
He swears his truth—& seals it on her lips—

You see thoughts taken from poems of mine not fit to see the light I deemd them too good to loose & think I have not made bad use of em here—your opinion in your next will oblige—the poem is 'Evenings close' & when finished will contain many rural scenes—how do you lik my uniform measures of tens I have got usd to it & cannot break myself of it.

J.C.

P.S. I made a cursed blunder last week at Drurys shop which had nearly slipd the letter—the Marquis of Exeter came in & very condensendingly askd me how I did—I not knowing him said very bluntly 'middling thank ye Sir' he next askd me when my poems woud come out as that he said causd him to call 'sometime ere the spring sir I dare say' was my answer he lookd hard in my face & went out—& when I was informd who it was I was most confoundedly vex'd & all the way home at every stile I got too sat & repeated it over to my self how I acted which every repetition made more rediculous but I have now nearly overset it—D tells me there is nothing the matter so I rest upon it—& now I think of it you must not forget to speak very kindly of The Marquis Earl Fitzwilliam Lord Milton & earl Spencer & as you can say a little about each in the narrative way as I was noticd by them the classification will not be conspicuous—& the annecdotes will I think be entertaining—as to an Introduction one there must be so never try to shuffle off the task & if you begin it in as happy a vein as the other the longer you make it the better—I'll furnish you with trifles if you think additions to the former narrative nessesary—put in G[ilchrist]'s verses° from the london Mag: in introduction & name him: as better 'make a friend then miss one' you smell it—the 3rd Vol I think will do with out 'old chuckeys' assistance but I cant feel myself safe in the second—so fare well for the present—

J. Clare

To James Augustus Hessey

Helpstone Dec 1. 1820

My Dear Hessey

I got your kind letter this day & am cursed mad at myself for my last blunder° but you then see I woud not believe any thing wrong in Taylor & I hope you will burn the stuff & say nothing about it to him & before I answer your enquireys I shall say somthing conserning myself Sunday last I fancy I had good news the *Bishop of Bristol*° wrote Mr Mossop wishing to know somthing about 'Clare the Helpston poet' as he calld me in his letter as the Society of Christs Colledge Cambridge (to which our living belongs) intends to do somthing in the way of acknowledging the merits of your humble Servant! I told him Taylor & Lord R[adstock] was at the head of my affairs & that the Bishop had better write any of them if he pleasd & in particular I gave him Taylors adress & he said he woud refer him to write there so I expect ere long you will have a Letter from the Bishop if you have forward it to T[aylor] immediatly now supposing as they cannot make a parson of me they shoud grant which woud be far better an equal income with our Vicars salary £50 there'll be for ye!! I have nothing of T. yet but expect & expect every hour till I am weary with expecting if he comes he will find helpstone a rum shop & have a very rum tale to tell you I dare say—I am glad you like the wild flowers° the last verse is such a favourite of mine that it is the only one I can repeat of any of my poems & my selfish consiet is constantly repeating it twas first pointed out by a stranger reading the M.S. who begd to transcribe it—no Londons this year for me your 'cold drizzly half-wintry weather' has got me so low livd & mopish that your noisey town woud instantly craze me

are you 'St Caroline' or 'George 4th'° I am as far as my politics reaches 'King & Country' no Inovations on Religion & government say I—this night is the grand illumination for our City in honour of St Caroline the woman that is to personate her majesty is a deformd object who is to be dressd in white & all the rest are to have 'white favours' the windows are to be illuminated but as the grand characteristic of an Englishman is liberty of consience I will for once sustain it—I am persuaded to light up in consequence of keeping the peace & my windows unbroken—but they have their whims & jack will have his & I am now soon as your letter is done making preparations of defence a large oaken bludgeon & if the devil heads the mob let him head it so as he passes my door peacably & if his develship throws one stone at my window mind ye hostilitys begin & if his hide is not cudgel proof Ill feel for it & for once let him know I am as rebellious against his opinions as he was in old times against a superior adversary

Lord R. ask'd my opinion of the present matters & I bluntly told him that 'if the King of England was a madman I shoud love him as a brother of the soil' in preference to a foreigner who be as she be shows little interest or feeling for England when she lavishes such honours on the menials of another which Nelson has long characterizd as a set of 'whores scoundrels poets & fiddlers'° still poor St Caroline she has seen much trouble & perplexity god forgive her—I am glad the head is going on with & hope Scriven will do hilton justice as he was my choice you know—when they are done perhaps you coud spare me one or two for a friend—& now I must hint you to tell Taylor soon as the book is out he shoud send Lord Fitzwilliams & Milton Earl Spencer & the Marquis a book each with a letter as he can do such things far better then I so dont forget it—Lord R is at Brighton he sends me 5 or 6 newspapers every week & I have had 2 letters from him this 8 week & 1 from Mrs E[mmerson]—my Wife is well & the child gets on bravly I myself am in as low ebbs as melancholly can reduce me & as idle as need be sulking in the corner from day to day & scribbling by fits—I am about 'martinmass Eve'° but am stalld with it—I have written 'the Cress gatherer'° & am pleasd with it—I send you additions to 'Reccolections' &c°

& left free to every whim
Resting oft ones weary feet
Seeking joys that suited him
While I shard the shepherds seat
Counting colours in their wings
As each butterfly did pass
Marking miles of namless things

How they jumpt along the grass

As he eat his lunch of bread
Wondering much when beatles stopt
By what knowledge they were led
To the crumbles which he dropt
Loading off in order free
Trackless oer the fuzzy dust
When he calld em 'wise as we'
Sure enough I thought they must

Sonnet to Autumn°

Come pensive autumn with thy clouds & storms
& falling leaves & pastures lost to flowers
A luscious charm hangs on thy faded forms
More sweet then summer in its lovliest hours
Who in her blooming uniform of green
Delights with samely & continued joy
But give me autumn were thy hand hath been
For there is wildness that can never cloy
The russet hue of fields left bare & all
The tints of leaves & blossoms ere they fall
In thy dull days of clouds a pleasure comes
Wild music softens in thy hollow winds
& in thy fading woods a beauty blooms
Thats more then dear to melancholly minds

I had some time back an invitation to write for the 'Ladies Museum' & promisd the Editor I woud but alterd my mind & gave it up as it dont suit my taste to please boarding school Misses & such like paper Van[i]ties—give my best respects to all & believe me dear Hessey | your faithfull friend & gratful St

J Clare

To John Taylor

[Lord Radstock had written to Taylor, suggesting a written agreement, along the lines of one made between Southey and his publishers, whereby all expenses were paid for by the publishers, and the profits from sales would be divided equally. Taylor had responded with a note of cool anger; he none the less asked Clare to consent to 'the Execution of an Agreement between us on the Terms of assigning to you half the profits, and dividing the other half between Drury and us'.]

Help: D[ecember]. 18. 1820

My dear Taylor

With some supprise I opend your last in mourning thinking by the seal you had taken a tour to the other world & written me from thence—but respecting your request wearied vanity dare not say what she woud willingly say if no reason was attach'd to the matter what that reason is you well know & I hope you will never loose sight of John Clare when such correspondents become burthensome Lord R[adstock] I own as a friend & as one in the first order but what induced him to write you in such a manner I know not as my last to him was a plain proof of my satisfaction after Hesseys Letter whose simplisity of manner woud not fail to convince any one that I harbour the highest opinions of T[aylor] & H[essey] Lord R. well knows I now come to certain points in your letter which I dont fail to reeve° clear off—as to his saying 'you aught not to be in possesion of my M.S.S. without first signing an agreement' that opinion must be his Lordships own & a very new one too as I understood him the very same thing was long ago proposd by yourself & him without me & to that I returnd an answer of the utmost satisfaction that is giving me half & half yourselves (the publishers) which if I mistake not his Lordship hinted as being Southeys way such manuvering has been practisd that I know not what I might say but I dont remember giving the least hint of an agreement proposd—but your note to Lord R tho perfectly appropriate on your part will not pass in its progress without (I fear) taring a hole in my next subscription list which Lord R. long ago told me he shoud resume with his wonted ardour & moreover that he had influencd Lord Liverpool° to take my part in the next Vol: whose words I cannot turn too but somthing in this manner 'Your Lordship will inform me when Clares next poems makes their appearence as I shall be willing to do him what service I can' Liverpool—these things you will look too I hope as for myself interest urges me I must & therefore I must keep the peace with his Lord ship—you know long ago my opinions & I must own the matters you complain of are very troublesome—as to your opinion in thinking he wishes you to throw it up I cant fancy so but as to 'doing justice' the highest vanity cannot concieve the extent of that bubble there I readily see with the same spectacles as T. & H. & all who has ever had a specimen of the person woud as readily give the like reply as to his Lordships opinion that 'had no Lord R stepped forth in support of the work—a second Edition woud not yet have appeard—' this urges me to give it readily the lie which (when my merits is put aside for puffing to come strutting in & say I am the mountebank that got Clare a name with the public) I woud contradict in the face of any man let his titles be what they may—as to your yielding to any ones controul is & has been all along at your own option you know it—& you are as free to use it at this present moment as you ever was in respect to the poems—your request of an agreement I will agree too let my friend Woodhouse° draw it up as he thinks proper in the way you proposd half & half & he had better put both in some regular way as Drury somtimes complains of your not complying as you proposd with so doing will stop all mouths & save me a deal of answering the bother of calumny & gossiping enquirey if agreeable to you it is to me to put all together published & unpublished in the same agreement on the same princaple—'that J.C. is to recieve one half of the profits arising from the sale of the poems alr[eady] published & from any that he may publish after & that no other persons then T.H. [   ] has any right to the publishing or copy right what ever &c &c' you see by this I am ready to do by consent what D. put on me by force which does not argue that I doubt the sincerity of T. & H. I doubt not your acting towards me well afterwards as I shall reckon nothing of the Bond myself but appear as free as ever I have had temptations enough already from booksellers if I had wishd to go astray—as I wishd to say more I must take another sheet—& as I may not forget it I wish you to send me a little paper of letter & other size as soon as you can for I am out & has been along time & giving a penny a sheet for it here is more then I can expence with

P.S. Dont misguide your judgment by fancying good pieces in the old M.S.S. from the praises of their late [?printer]

To John Taylor

Helpstone De: 21. 1820

My dear Taylor

On Saturday the 'Ways of a Village' comes to London all the pieces that are corrected none else for the remainder are so far from it they are of little use to you as they will give me a puzzling to make them out if they lie long—my last scrawl was written in such haste that it was wrong dated & the letter I quoted from being such a bad scrawl even worse then mine that I made a blunder in the quotation tho it is as rediculous as ever: & twas rediculous in me to quote it as a proof of my ignorance in the consern but I was so damd mad with such encroaching meddlings that I scarcly knew what I wrote or read 'Dear Emma has been making much or such exertions for you in going to fleet St that deserves from you more then you will probably ever have it in your power to repay—Do not let this dishearten you' I punctually write from the letter & this is it Lord have mercey on me & free me from such sallies of vanity as soon as possible or convenient is the prayer of John Clare—& I hope he will hear me when I come to London I shall bring a specimen of the precious honey drops of vanity for an hours amusment—for my part last winter I hardly dreamd such beings had existance in your wonderfull Exebition of absurditys in London I have been mustering up the songs one copybook is lost but that copy has been selected for your Quarto & when I consider: there is few but what you have got that is worth any notice if you turn to the letters to Mr Hessey & yourself you will find what I mean however I will make all out I have bye me good bad & indeferent & then you do as you please have a good care over the Sonnets & I think you will find first & last a Selection far superiour to the first book I shoud not be crampt for room if I was you but heedless of the price (as the sales nearly safe) put all in thats good of poems tales ballads sonnets & Songs—here I am upon unlawful ground prating were I have no business but you know me my advice is harmless after all my pratings you are left to do as you please—often write me at least when you find amusment in so doing for I can asure you I myself feel a great itching always to trouble you with my scrawl very often—this moment I am interupted with a parcel of Newspapers from my old friend his Lordship but no letter—tis impossible to feel otherwise than gratful for the many trifling troubles he takes in my behalf weak as some actions may appear such trifles as these (whatever the simple design may be) warms & binds him closer in my esteam & affections & I realy think I shall dye with his praises in my mouth do as he may do afterwards—I always told you to act as an Editor you may get above such insinuating bother I must knock under for my own advantage I find it far easier to have [an] hours work of flattery then I usd to do an hours threshing in a barn & tho I have not yet been swore at Highgate° I have judgment enough to chuse the most easy method in such things—If E[liza] L[ouisa] E[mmerson] & L[ord] R[adstock] had found me out first & Edited my poems what monsters woud they have made can it be possible to judge I think praises of self & selfs noble friend & selfs incomparable poems undoubtedly shovd into the bargain woud have left little room for me & mine to grow up in the esteem of the public but shoulderd into a dark corner they woud have servd as a foundation for their own buildings & dwindled away like a tree surrounded with Ivy while the names & praises of patron & poetess flourishd in every page—when you get the 'Ways &c' tell me as soon as possible how you like them or I woud not send them had it not been to get on with the rest or leave them altogether—my dear Taylor with the warmest affection I remain | your humble St

John Clare

To John Taylor

Helpstone Jan 9 1821

My dear Taylor

I just got your letter ere I started for Stamford this Morning to recieve my quarters anuity from the Marquis but I shall never loose the pleasure of answering a letter of those whose correspondence is always enliv[en]ing & welcome   I wish I coud say so by every one—Drurys conscieted ways often provoked me   dont notice his pencil dashes no were   if you had been mistaken & led astray by them my vexation woud have certainly fell home upon him as it did last winter on other matters—respecting the mistake you had better wait till Im gone & say nothing of it   poor fellow he is humble enough now & I have many pleasant Evenings with him at Stamford & what is past is past   I dont like to hurt him so let it pass   Ill leave plenty behind me to correct the mistake which in any mans reason I think is already corrected at least in yours   shoud we three ever come together you bring it up & his arguments will be like childern playing with burning paper 'there goes the parson & there goes the clerk'—but I can assure you if no John Taylor & Hessey had been in the mess poor Drury woud have quite lost me after his agreement   I have no confidence in him   I now always look up to you as the head & I only wish to keep up my friendship with him for the early good he did me for had it not been for him I shoud never have met with John Taylor & this he often cracks of for it is all thats left him after his foolish proceedings but I still think twas ignorance in trusting to others selfish opinions that led him astray   I am glad you like the 'Peasant Boy' for I have read the rough sketch a second time & think some of the things the best I have written   I sent off all I had bye me yesterday & you will have them tonight I expect   send me your letter I shoud have had°   besure ye I shall entirly hate D. at last if he plays that with me   I have often thought he stopt letters directed to me & have greater cause to strengthen that jealousy—put in *despotic*° & in the 5th Edit: alter it agen to 'cursed'   never mind Lord R[adstock]'s pencelings in the 'Peasant Boy'   what he dont like he must lump as the dog did his dumpling   I woud not have 'There once were lanes' &c left out for all the Lord Rs in

Europe d—n it do as you like I tell you if you like to print 'cursed' too print it—'& a fig for the sultan & sophy'—I wait anxiously for Tothills poems if he has got any more like 'Shrewsbury' & 'Tothill Fields' he'll do for the Byron of Byrons never produced their superiors—I wish him success heartily my returns to Mr Hessey warm as the winter alows me

I am in haste for my journey | so farwell & god bless you

John Clare

To John Taylor

Jan 23. [18]21.

My dear Taylor

Having betook me seriously to think about my latter end I send you the fruits of my repentance—in reading 'Gastrels Institutes'° I found some most beautiful images which I had never noticed in the Scriptures before & which I never coud have believed existed in them had I not seen it they are chiefly from Job on mans Mortallity—Lord R[adstock] is meneuvering uncommonly now he has written to D[rury] & to Lord Milton about me being ill he fancies such flummerey pleases me but hes mistaken for I wish all such bother far enough & am glad Lord M[ilton] has learnd to disregard paper kites & pass over trifles without notice—for I have not heard from him—I wrote Mrs E[mmerson] & have given her a thought or two from the bottom of my mind as naked as possible but I fear shell dream over it & make two meanings of it & chuse the best for herself—Lord R. has sent for his first Letter back—whats this mean—Ill readily send all if he wants me—O Vanity thou vapouring idol of weak minds whats thy value? the 'lumination of the rainbow & the painted clouds of sunset is more lasting then thee thou wordy war of nothingness & sounding symbol of empty delusion whoever listens to thee goeth 'into the wilderness to see a reed shaken by the wind' thou breath of an emphemeron I have lived to experience thee & am left to sigh with an elder witness of thy folly 'Vanity of Vanitys all is vanity'° When you write me again I want some instructions respecting making a will as life is unscertain I intend to leave my parents 5s a week of the funded money & patty the rest with an eaqual share of what comes from the publications till she remains a widow & then it drops to the child if I dont make a will she gets all & I shall be d——d mad at that I assure you so gi's your opinion sometime

farewell & god bless you
John Clare

To John Taylor

[*circa* 17 February 1821]

My dear Taylor

You will see agen that I agree in almost every particular of your alterations—I am pleased to see you drive on so fast tis just my hobby when once begun to go forward—the word '*pounced*' is what it is in the origional—The 'Milton Hunt' on a second thought I am loth to leave out but I always disliked the 4 last lines what say you to this proposal—suppose we repeat the 4 last lines of the first verse agen 'The bugle sounds away away' &c &c after '& scampers from his plough' & cut 'The muse &c &c' out I think it woud make a good hunting Song then & free me of being fond of the barberous sport what think you—the alusion to Milton is what I wish to preserve but do as you please—as my ink runs very much it may lead the printers into errors by seeing letters blotchd that was not intended—please to look over them & rectify it—be careful in perusing the Songs & Sonnet as they are my favourites—those Songs repaid long corespondence with Hessey in your abscence are many of them not in the book nor are several of the Sonnets &c sent on your return—I only do this to remind you as you might think the Book contained them their rough sketches are most in the last MSS but the corrected ones in the letters are much better you may print the *hunting song*° I say it reads well here it is—

The Milton hunt again begun
  Break autumns dappld skys
While yon red east its blushing sun
  Awakens in supprise
The bugle sounds away away
  The chevy chace begins

The praise the honours of the day
The hardiest hunter wins

For blood bred steeds no reigns can check
& true scent nosed hound
For sportsmen fearless of a neck
No chace is more renownd
The echoing woods are all alive
The hounds are on the run
Oer hedge & gate see how they drive
The daring routs begun

The cracking whip & scarlet coat
Draws all eyes round em now
Een startld giles puts in his note
& scampers from his plough
The bugles sounds away away
The chevy chase begins
The praise the honours of the day
The hardiest hunter wins

It reads capital dont it—if you think so besure & print it I send them back imediatly—I dont intend letting any one of Stamford see them—Drury may be content to have his share in the publication thats plenty for him I wish I coud get such a job in being paid for doing nothing—But my good nature I dare say has made me my own fool agen in writing the Songs in summer for him which I fancyd nothing more then a recompence for the suppos'd injury done him in forcing the agreement out of his hands which if he coud he woud have made me believe was an unjust piece of justice—he is now getting some of them set to music—& sent me with his last flaming threat of hostilitys (for he sadly wants me to believe he is sole proprietor of my poems still—but stop Mr Conjuror your own word is only great in your own mouth thinks I—Napoleon may say to the winds I am emperor of france while the rocks of St Helena daily tells him to his eye he's a liar)—a Mutilated Skeleton of one of the Songs° which made me so d——d mad that I am half sorry I wrote my answer at the moment—still if I see my merit at stake I am aright to cry stop thief—I stopt him however Ill [be] bound fort yet sooner then eat my first conscent I said if his music man lik'd to take the words as he found em they was there—if not let them alone for my Name shoud never accompany such affectation & consiet—If I did wrong in writing these Songs° dont be offended at me 'chuckey' for I knew little what I was about but fancyd it a fine thing to have ones name on a music sheet—I have not had one single farthing for doing them nor dont know if I ever shall—still if Drury had not proposd it they had never been written so if I get any merit by them he has the credit of being the origin of it—& if not I have the credit of being a fool—I think hell not write to you now after I ript him up at such a rate—he was always complaining of injurys & I thought this request woud satisfy him but I am mistaken it seems so he must (like a bear with a soar head) keep growling on—he said he shoud stay while the selection was made in the Vols—but I have found him long ago to be dealer in falsities—thats why I feel a desire of having the best Songs in as their after mutilations of the M.S.S. may not pass as genuine—I cannot write further as the parcel is ready but shall answer your promised letter if I see its requird which is now at Deeping I expect

yours &c &c
John Clare

To John Taylor

[7 March 1821]

My dear Taylor

I have got the proofs safe but have such a severe indisposition upon me that I cannot look the corrections over this day so you will excuse me—they shall be ready for going off on thursday—I heard of Poor Scotts death° by the Stamford Mercurey—Lifes not much to be regretted when we loose her she is such a lump of trouble & deception that I my self care not how soon I am done with her & if there was not such a fence of pains & heart aches between this world & death I shoud at this moment certainly be trying to break the bounds for a break neck leap into that unriddled blank of fancys terrors & confusions—my two favourite Elm trees° at the back of the hut are condemned to dye it shocks me to relate it but tis true the savage who owns them thinks they have done their best & now he wants to make use of the benefits he can get from selling them—O was this country Egypt & was I but a caliph the owner shoud loose his ears for his arragant presumption & the first wretch that buried his axe in their roots shoud hang on their branches as a terror to the rest—I have been several mornings to bid them farewell—had I £100 to spare I woud buy their reprieves—but they must dye—yet this mourning over trees is all foolishness they feel no pains they are but wood cut up or not—a second thought tells me I am a fool was People all to feel & think as I do the world coud not be carried on—a green woud not be ploughd a tree or bush woud not be cut for firing or furniture & every thing they found when boys would remain in that state till they dyd—this is my indisposition & you will laugh at it—answer Drury as you please but I think any thing of reasoning or argument or quarreling will be no more then wasting pens ink & paper—his foolish pettishness is too trifling for notice I only wish he woud keep quiet if he dont I shall burn his open Evening which I dont wish to do but my good naturd silliness has often made me act the fool for him I thought the writing the Songs would stop his mouth—he let me know the alterd Song was stopt—I shall have the 'Sketches of my Life'° ready for sending you in a fortnight at most I shall be very minute in Hensons & Drurys affairs that your judgment may decide—& what I shall say you may take for the truth for I shall not withold praise unworthily or spare censure where its nessesary—I am in that muddy mellancholy again my ideas keep swimming & shifting in sleepy drowsiness from one thing to another—this letter will denote the crazy crackd braind fellow it has left behind—I do think from my soul that this comical complaint will carry me off ere long—but god knows best—perhaps before thursday I may be another thing fancying myself as far from death as doomsday—theres no notice to be taken of me in these matters so for the present farewell & god bless you

J. Clare

P.S. I forgot to say I got the last proofs 2 days before the letter that was to warn me of them coming I thought you might think it odd in me sending the proofs first & answering the letter afterwards this was the cause J.C.

To John Taylor

March 24. 1821

My dear Taylor

Having had either a visit or a hoax from the muses I lost no time in sending it to you which if you like it t'will urge me to dip deep & frequently in their bath of inspiration from which I have long been an indolent idle wanderer—wether it be poetry or fustian, inspiration or bombast common sense or nonsense your judgment will soon decide & as the paying the post is the only serious consequence belonging to it be what it will—I shall rest very quietly for your opinion—having the free ope[r]tunity of exempting myself from that expence & the impudence to make use of it—the poem is 'To Time' a Sonnet

To Time°

In fancys eye what an extended span
Time, hoary herrald has been stretchd by thee
Vain to conscieve were thy dark burst began
Thou birthless *endless* vast stupendity or boundless
To mortal wisdom thourt already ran
A circled travel of Eternity
Vain all consceptions of weak minded man
Thee to unravel from thy mystery
Still but a moment of thy mighty plan
Seems yet unwound from what thou art to be*
Consuming tyrant of all mortal kind
& what thou art & what thy age shalt see†
Is known to none but that immortal mind
Who reigns alone superior to thee

I had a letter from Drury last night enquiring wether I had any thing to send up to London as his brother James is down but as I dont intend to go Stamford in haste I declined sending this by him as I at first intended—Patt is a great deal betterd since I told you of her being ill—I find its only the natural progress of things—you understand me—by G—I may rant & ryhme if its

* This word was first *see* & this line† thus '& what thou art & what thou art to be' I did not know which was best so you decide it if worth deciding—

to be thus but 'such things are' & such things will be in spite of—Economy or what you will—yours to this worlds end with the hopes of begining the other as warmly & friendly together is the wish & ever shall be of

John Clare

I forgot to say I thought Keats Epitaph° very superior to any I had seen in that line & shoud certainly think like you if seen in the place describd that no common dust slept there

To John Taylor

April 3:d 1821

My dear Taylor

I waited to send off the sketches of my life° by your parcel but as its not yet come I have put you to an additional expence by sending it off alone—as it is written expressly for your eye I have been perhaps punning particular in some places especially about my first meeting with your cousin Drury were by so doing I thought your opinion might more justly decide on things as they ought to be—when I am no more—what is written is the truth in which when I speak thus much you will doubtless have no hesitation to believe—I am prompted neither by favour or affection to utter a falsity & I hope you know enough of me not to be jealous of my guiltiness in such matters—its only to furnish you with particulars—remember that—& not to stand as I have hobbled it over—you are the person if you survive me that must do me justice—to you I give these sketches & to no one else shall I copy a repetition of them tho I have often been urged to it—what comforts you have procured for me I shall never or at least never ought to forget—for what I posses at this moment boasts its origional in you—I readily agree with Lord R[adstock] that without your Introduction the right hand of my success woud have been wanting but as to his Lordships goodness good as it is it remains at a great distance behind—& to sum up every thing—those silly beggerly flatterys in the morning post &c &c &c—I think Ive gaind as much harm as good by it—& am nothing in debt on that quarter—I went last Sunday to 'Lolham Brigs'° in our Lordship no doubt you have heard of 'em—they are very ancient & are said to be built by one Lollius Ubicus tis the King street road or old roman bank on the end of which stands 'Langley bush' the produce of this walk is a poem 'The last of march' which if you have any curosity to see shall accompany the next parcel till then I am | yours &c &c &c

John Clare

P.S. Remember I am just got from the blue bell & am damnation drunk & consequently as happy as possibility can make me—god bless you & if my errors make him my enemy I hope you have conduct enough to keep him your friend

To John Taylor

[between 3 and 14 April 1821]

My dear Taylor

I send you my sorrows for poor Keats while his memory is warmly felt—they are just a few beats of the heart—the head has nothing to do with them—therefore they will stand no critisism—

To the Memory of Keats°

Thy worldly hopes & fears have pass'd away
No more its trifling thou shalt feel or see
Thy hopes are ripening in a brighter day
While these left buds thy monument shall be
When rancours wounds are past in nought away
Enlarging failings known to more then thee
& beautys feign diminish few display
When these are past thou child of poesey
Thou shalt survive—ah while a being dwells
In natures joys with soul to warm as thine
With eye to view her fancinating spells
& dream entranced oer each form divine
Worth wild enthusiast shall be cherish'd here
& thine with him shall linger & be dear

If you dont like it dont utterly condemn it I did it as I felt it at the moment your mellancholy news woud give me pause for reflection—I wishd I had made an Elegy afterwards of it as my ideas was crampt they flowd freely & I coud have gone a great length—but words are of little value—be as it will I can do nothing more now—the moment is gone I cannot call it back I wish I coud—the apathy of mellancholly has again laid her cold hand upon my heart pointing with a carless finger to my own fate that awaits me & alowing but a common feeling for the fate of others to go before me—viewing such in a course of natural occurences—but dear Taylor with the affection that one brother feels at the loss of another do I lament the end of poor Keats

I am glad I have got your opinion turned to the Cottage agen—each vol with a front piece will be uniform & quite bewitching at least to your humbl[e] St. but the head only in the first & nothing in the next woud be unfair to my twin childern leaving one a favourite & the other neglected—a cheap rough etching will I think be quite sufficient & have perhaps better effect then a fine engraving the time I expect in doing it as I mean will be nothing—but you know best: what a fool must I be to preach so profoundly knowing about things that I know nothing more of then their existance—I take all for granted & like a child when promised a ginger bread house feel pleased with the expectation of seeing it—so remember if its not in your child will meet a trying dissapointment—if not in this I shall not live to see it in another so while I am here I want to see all I can—your critsisms on 'Time' are just the thing & your alteration capital—but certainly you paid me no compliment when you asked me wether I understood you—I must either have been drunk or blind had I not—you never desert common sense & therefore common sense never mistakes you—your alterations & omissions in the proofs are by what I see good but as I send this off without em I shall say nothing more about them till they come

I cannot correct the proofs yet but they shall start tomorrow or next day—you must forgive me I am in such a tottering trembling state of nerves & have such sickly sensibilitys about me that I cannot correct yet—things that Ive once done are quite loathing at these times to repetition—

Song°

Fill the foaming cups again
Lets be merry while we may
Man is foolish to complain
When such joys are in his way
Cares may breed in peevish minds
Life at best is short & vain
Wisdom takes the joy she finds—
Fill the foaming cups again

Fortune she may slight us boys
Boast her thousands to our crowns
Give to knaves her smiles & joys
We can feast upon her frowns
What care we how rich she be
Present needs but meet supply
Kings may govern so will we—
Foaming cups before we're dry

Fill them foaming oer again
Fill wi' cordial to the brim
Let the peevish soul complain
Care is worthy none but him
Hearts of oak were born to dye
Toast for comforts while we reign
'Present needs to meet supply—
'Foaming cups be filld again'

To John Taylor

Ap: 24. 1821

My dear Taylor

Just to pass time I am sat down to write somthing—but what—yourself nearly knows as much as I do—however somthing Ill scribble—I have been idle agen—but I have to make up for it proffited by your lecture & have kept sober ever since & I am still determined on the plan in thus proceeding—visitors comes on me every other day or nearly & I had a sensible Gent: yesterday   no doubt you know him 'Dr Noehden°

British Museum' he talked civily & unasuming & I felt the loss of his company after he left me—he has given me an Invitation when in London to visit him & see the Museum which he thinks will please me—he odd enough said 'he had seen my *pretty poems* & that curosity had urged him to seize the first oppertunity of seeing the author' he was accompined with 2 other gents who did not leave their names I didnt much like pretty but well alter these things when out a second time twas natural enough—childern say so about playthings—& this first book is our plaything I consider it nothing more now—the muse is there in the bud in the next she will be in the blossom If I mistake not—& these will alter the note a little—a smile shant dimple to say them pretty—but admiration shall redden the cheek with pronouncing they are good—& if not in the next—if we are left as I hope we shall to wind up the story: in the last admiration shall let fall her muscles into reverence—like one reading a monument & with sacred enthuseasm between a smile & a tear—in pity & supprise pronounc em best of all—the blossoms shall give way to their crimson berries which shall shine in every leaf as bright & as lasting as the vanity of a crackd-braind aspiring hopfull & harmless son of the muses coud ever wish for—I coud have gone on dreeming thus to the end but have stopt to read it over found it very foolish stuff & desisted—but knowing innocent foolishness will meet with all possible indulgence at its journeys end I leave it as it is—what is written is written—I am going to write to Bloomfield very soon shall I say that you will send him the new poems as soon as published I know he will like to see them—& I think you will like to write him as I always feel entertaind with writing to those I esteem I think so by others—& as to John Taylors liking Bloomfield there is not a doubt—nature has so orderd it that he cannot help but love such people—who are made of somthing more then the shreds & patches of this world—so wether I am to tell him you will send him one—or wether I am to say nothing about it—tell me when you write me agen—remember you neednt hurry nor be put out of your time one second only when you do write tell me—I shall write to Montgommery after a bit for he spoke warmly of me—aye as affectionatly as one poet can speak of a brother—you know what that is without being told—I felt it & shall for ever—I forgot to thank you for your invitation but youll excuse me: when you mention it agen I shall tell you wether I mean to come or not—its a very long journey—& theres an equal hazard wether I ever see it agen or not—tho nevertheless I shoud like to see very much indeed J. Taylor & his circle of friends once more & if I knew I had seen my last of them I am sure I shoud be hipt° with new mellancholy—its a good method of providence in giving no distance in her pictures painting the present & stopping the eye with darkness from seeing further—it saves 100s of heartaches—it gives 100s of pleasant sensations as we always hope for the best before she draws up her curtain—we may meet agen yet—god bless you—

John Clare

To John Taylor

[5 May 1821]

I have just got the proofs (Saturday) & shall start them agen on monday—I always like to tell you as I get them—you have not got 'last of march' in yet—you will do may be—I will write for the 'London' if you like & shall feel spurd to do it by having your approbation°—the 'New Monthly' in my eye has sunk into insignificance—it perhaps may be sufficient to say that all your alterations suit me well & with your proposd ommisions do as you please I feel very satisfyd with them myself—do as you like with the lines on Lord R[adstock]°—but I think the dedication now to any one woud be almost presumptious—there is a debt owing to Earl Fitzwilliam Earl Spencer & the Marquis tho the last is certainly my greatest patron at least in my own bosom & you can do him justice with the rest in the Preface—thats the best way as I think: time will tell us more & then we can dedicate you know were we think best so we'll do without dedications this time unless your further reflections on the subject convinces you that your first notions are right—if so Ill readily agree to any thing you propose—I am anxious of getting my book out & not only that let me tell you but am as anxious of seeing you do justice to Keats by bringing him out agen which I hope you will loose no time to do—excuse my conscieted meddling advice—else I think the sooner you publish a vol of his remains with an account of his Life &c the better while the ashes of genius is warm the public look with a tender anxiety for what it leaves behind—to let this get cold woud in my opinion do him an injury—the ill treatment he has met will now be productive of more advantages—tho the warm heart that once felt it—is cold & carless to praise or to censure now—still he left those hopes behind him—which his friends cherish in remembrance that justice woud be done him—is the cold hearted butchers of annonymous Critics to cut up everything that escapes their bribery or thinks contrary to them is polotics to rule genius—if it is—honesty & worth may turn swindlers & liberty be thrown to the dogs & worried out of existance—& that she has been long ago—I have been reading his 'Eve of St Agnes' agen—were madeline is describd undressing herself it is beautifull & luscious to describe how much so—

'—her vespers done
'Of all its weatherd pearls her hair she frees
'Unclasps her *warmed jewels* one by one
'Loosens her *fragrant boddice*: by degrees
'Her rich attire creeps *rustling to her knees*
'*Half hidden like a mermaid in sea weed*
'Pensive awhile she *dreams awake*, & sees
'In fancy fair st Agnes in her bed
'But dares not look behind or all the charm is fled'°

Look for such a description throughout Barry Cornwalls Endless amusments°—& were will you find it—you may as well look for the graces of simplicity at night throughout the painted ranks & files of Drury Lane or Covent Garden & you will meet with equal success—I shoud have taken a large sheet—but my child is very bad—& I was not in mood for scribbling

god bless you
John Clare

P.S. I look for your promise of a letter remember soon—I had nearly forgot to thank you for your kindness in sending me the 'London' & the promise of continuing it—but youll excuse all omissions for my d——d thick head makes a many that are not intentional the man you direct the parcels to is become tricky & shifty— as there is few more to come when you send the rest direct to the 'Bull Inn' as usual & send a letter to inform me of their arival & I will fetch them myself—

I have a d——d bad opinion of the Sonnets in these vols & think most of em poor stuff—lets hope my judgments good for nought—what think you—you never sed

To John Taylor

[Clare gives away the joke of this spoof letter in his concluding note. Hessey acknowledged it on 23 June 1821: 'but we do not think it one of your happiest efforts—The best thing you can do is to write in your own natural Style, in which no one can excel you.' Neither the letter nor the poem was published; but Clare continued to write and send off poems under pseudonyms (especially that of 'Percey Green').]

To the Editor of the London Magazine

June 14. 1821 past 10 o'clock

Mr Editor

I am a countryman in a very humble way & my friends will have it I may rise by trying my tallents at poetry which they consider as very exellent indeed

To try this experiment Uncle Zebedee & my poor Grandmother Ailsey Timms urgd me to send a Specimen to your Magazine; Uncle Zebedee had it lent him by a friend & thinks it a very good one that is he fanceys theres no Envy about it to shove merit out of sight or stick ones hopes in a corner to scoff at. Uncle Zebedee was greatly delighted in reading Humphrey Nixons letter° he was so mortgagously° pleasd with it that he laughd till the tears stood in his eyes at his funny sayings about Mrs Gale & other things Uncle thinks him a promising genius. His opinion upon most of the rest is not quite so favourable he says that writers have imitated each other so long that one may as well look for any thing new among the first chapters of Genesis as [amo]ng the books now adays—Granny (as you might expect) is all for 'Walter Selbey'° she wishes me to do somthing in that way after a bit, h[er] expectations are raisd uncommon high since I read this letter to her & she says if she dont live to see her hopes come true she shant rest in he[r] grave so pray do what you can [for] her comfort [& I shall] do my best to serve you

I [rem]ain &c &c
Stephen Timms

Some account of my Kin, my Tallents
& myself. a Poem

Ryhme is a gift as our folks here suppose
Nor wealth nor learning ever makes a poet
Tis natures blessing so the story goes
& my condition goes the way to show it
Tho up to Bible classes I was taught
My school account is hardly worth the telling
I staid no time to master as I ought
A hardish chapter in it without spelling

A timber merchant father was—that is
A maker & a seller out of matches
This honest truth somes very apt to quiz
That can do nothing but such meddling catches
These I woud ask is the prime strops of Packwood
A pin the worse cause he has humbler been
Then why—but hold—I quake at Mr B——
Hell rap my knuckles in his magazine

Things may (as gran observes of Turners Blacking)
Be very good & very worthy praise
But theres such puffing & such swindling quacking
That merits next to nothing now adays
Some praise themselves some by their friends are stuck
As highs our weathercock upon the steeple
While all beside are trampld in the muck
I humbly hop[e] youre no such kind of people

Truth waits times touchstone as the just attacker
To burst the bubble & to put to rout
Each pompous sounding literary cracker—
Mine lives as long as many Ive no doubt
[I wi]ll but print them as I hinted at
[Suc]cess may be decievd its no grate [m]atter

[ ]ps frog I a [ ] bir[ ]t with that
[ ]e [? sights] me up [b]ut she is [a]p[t] to flatter

Still tho my genius cant be reckond rich
Thats its origional youll all agree
& tho my pen is often on the itch
Ive kept as yet from thieving pretty free
To tell the truth Ive hardly stole from any
Save some few things from worthey mother Bunch
A joke from Miller (praisd as mine by many)
For an old pedlar once who acted punch

If you like this Ill tell you tales by dozens
Which youll find pretty or I miss my aim
To strengthen this I might bring in my cousins
Who swear Im hastning up the hill to fame
But of friends praise I cant say Im a lover
For they like all are very prone to puff
Oft magazines laud books upon the cover
That prove when read most disagreeable stuff

So here Ill leave this sample to its fate
Send me the 'London' if you take the hint
Twill get you halfacrown at any rate
For Ill give that to see my name in print
& be [wha]t will Ill wait & hope the better
Gran poor old creature will be all delight—
& as Aunt Prissey often ends a letter
When getting late—I wish you all good night

If this pleases [ ] more [to] Morrow for Ill be as regular in [ ] correspondence as your Nos [ ] in the Callender—

[? thank] T[aylor] for the Engraving's & hope the last proofs will [reach] helpstone so[on]

J. Clare

To John Taylor

Helpston [18] Aug: 1821

My dear Taylor

This letter is written to tell you that after thursday next you need send no proofs of your progress (which by the bye seems a foot founderd & bad traveller) as I shall be gone so if it be not got ready before you may publish it without my seeing it as I dont fear in the least but it will suit me—I have put on the black waiscoat you gave me for this last week & shoud have done so with the coat but it is too dandyish for this country—but its not to mourn for the injurd quean°—I hated her while living & I have no inclination to regret her death—I hated her not as a woman or as a queen but as the vilest hypocrite that ever existed—common sense gives me her spectacles to look upon every thing Im of no party but I never saw such farcical humbug carried on in my life before & I never wish to see it agen for its lanched me head over ears in politics for this last twelvemonth & made me very violent when John Barleycorn inspird me—every one has his share of humbug & I have mine the black waistcoat is for the last twin childern° which I fancy as still born & gone hom agen so I am driving away at knocking up stuff for another as hard as I can & I send you with these a specimen of my new beginning you do as you like with it—we have got Mathews° coming here next friday (to Stamford Theatre) I dont know wether I can resist stopping to see him but wether I do or do not you shall hear from me directly after I get to Whittlebury the person Im going too is a Mr Bunney° an Artist & Poet!! a pupil of the late Wests° he has a poem by him of 10 Cantos which Ill tell you of soon as Ive seen it

Sonnet°

England with pride I name thee—& with pride
I boast thee as my birth place—where is one
That thou has given life too breathes beside
Nor feels the honour to be calld thy son—
Who reads the pages of thy glorys won
Victorious stripling on this jiant earth

Who keeps in memory what thy valours done
Nor feels the value of such noble birth—
Hast thou one heart that dwells amidst thy fame
Thy heroes living & thy heroes gone
That from thy soil a brothers right can claim
Nor warms in triumph to be counted one—
If such there is tho nourishd with the free
Tis bastard breed—& not a stain to thee

yours sincerly
John Clare

To John Taylor

[28 August 1821]

My dear Taylor

Mathews got the better of my travelling intentions & I accordingly went to see him on Friday night harangue over his dialogue on 'Air Earth & Water'° & was rather dissapointed in the beginning were nothing struck me except the old Fisherman but the 'Polly packet' paid for all 'Daniel O'Rouke' 'Moses the Jew' 'the Frenchman' 'Old lady' 'Major Longbow' & a spindled shankd silly fellow who kept bawling out 'mamma' & 'papa' were acted admirably well. Has Gill: been to see you hes up in town I understand & Mrs G[ilchrist] likewise—I shall not start on my journey till thursday week now as the weathers unsettld so you may send the Mag: when published & pray lets hear then when the books are to be out for my patience is crackd & I can settle to nothing—your cousin D[rury] fancys I believe that you & I are confederate in dark misterys about the publication for he grumbld like a bear with a sore head last friday when I calld on him & seemd discomforted I told him I was going to write for the London a short time before & I dare say thats what gravels him—at all events it will be as beneficial as writing his Songs for Ive got nought yet either by dedications or music—save a small sum which I borrowd at times with the intention of never paying agen

I will begin a series of 'Village Sketches'° for the Mag: as

Hessey hinted a while back & you may insert those you have got when you please upon that head

Your delay makes me swear cursedly by times that is grumbling to ones self for I say little elswere still I am yours sincerely & affectionatly & ever shall be

John Clare

To John Taylor

Helpston Sep: 3. 1821

My dear Taylor

I did not get sight of your parcel° till sunday night so the delay of mine is unavoidable I am again on the stool of repentance but how long I shall keep so I dont know—I am like Job broke out in b[o]ils from head to foot & have been for advice to Dr Michael who tells me its the nettle fever—

Respecting whats laid at your door as its laid there by a literary porter its not to be wonderd at if some serious make weight has been added to the luggage—I may have said as I did by the first book I am anxious to have it out to hear whats said of me & shall not settle till it is—But I never laid any thing to your charge further in all my life & I always concluded it by saying that I thought what ever was done was done for the best & that you knew better about such matters then my interference coud advance or suggest—so thats settled°

As for getting any one else to edit them to forward their publication I woud sooner have had them delayd till christmass twelvemonth remember that—I am not started to Whittlebury yet & if Im no better shall not go at all—

Now for correcting the mistakes in the proofs° first the milton affair was thus Lord M[ilton] gave me £10 Earl F[itzwilliam] £5 & Lady M. & Lady F. £1 each the childern gave me nothing

The Marquis's Anuity is *15 Guineas* & not pounds

Patty is no kin to Turnills her maiden name was *Turner* & not Turnill I married her from Walkerd Lodge in the neighbourhood of bridge casterton (she is the Rosebud in humble life where mention of that spot is made)

Richard Turnill & not William was the brother of John the

Exciseman he was one of the earliest friends I ever had being intimate from childern & the first whose loss accostomd me to the lorn sorrows & feelings expierencd in departed friendship that comes with increasing substance of pleasures till it passes away in a lingering shadow of lonliness & misery

Poor Keats I mention his name with reverence & regret as to letting his name stand do as you please but it strikes me that 'except one' woud be more appropriate not so personal & less fear of being misjudgd partialluty as some woud assuredly call it—you know from what quarter I mean—it may pass in the first Edition & in the next advance the name at once—but do as you please—°

My opinion of this Introduction is that it is as much to the purpose as the first & as well written which coud not be betterd by you or any one it pleases me very much indeed

Your mention of the patrons are capital & at the same time as modest & unasuming as heart can wish the end with its accompaning couplet is very good indeed

> 'The kindly dew drops from the higher tree
> & wets the little plants that lowly dwell'°

is a beautiful allusion & the finest compliment that coud be paid to patrons.

I shall like to see the book before the world as soon as you can get it out which wont be long now—I woud agree with you that october is best but restlessness will not let me so I must have my humour & vanity gratifiyd for once—I am heartily gratified with the vols of the London & my thanks is the smallest return that can be made for them—

I must tell you if you dont give somthing up you will dye without joking—why the devil cant you sit in your chamber with as much indolent pomposity as the Albermarle Bookseller° does—why need you trouble your self about Mags &c &c while Editors are employd for that purpose—take my advice get a wife & be happy & let the world wag as fate wills it—youll remember Bloomfield when the books struck off—Ive a deal more to say but am so unwell that it wearys me so for the present good bye | & god bless you

John Clare

To John Taylor

[6 September 1821]

My dear Taylor

I merely send this letter to hitch of[f] the sonnet as I am began to scribble agen vehemently Ive a long piece in hand 'Wanderings in June'° were I indulge reflection perhaps too much but you shall see after a bit when its finishd here is the sonnet

A Reflection in Summer°

One well may wonder oer the change of scene
Now Summers contrast thro' the land is spread
& turn us back were winters tempest fled
& left nought living but the Ivys green
The then bare woods that trembld over head
Like spectres mid the storm of what had been
& wrecks of beauty neer to bloom again
Are now all glory—nature smiles as free
As the last summer had commencd its reign
& she were blooming in eternity.
So in this life when future thoughts beguile
& from past cares our spirits get relievd
Hope eggs us onward with as sweet a smile
As if before she ne'er had been decievd

I am agen recruiting from my complaints & shall wait till the book is publishd ere I start so when it is you may let me know & send me what copies you think fit—you will then hear no more of me for a time unless I do any thing to my mind & send it for your opinion

Do you fancy that Dewint will call at Helpstone if he did I shoud be sorry to be out of the way but I dont believe either him or yourself ever once meant it when you said so & I shall always reckon on that head when you talk of it hereafter—I am sought after very much agen now 3 days scarcly pass off but sombody calls—some rather entertaining people & some d——d knowing fools—surely the vanity woud have kill'd me 4 years ago if I had known then how I shoud have been hunted up—& extolld by personal flattery—but let me wait another year or two & t[he] peep show will be over—& my vani[ty] if I have any will end in its proper mortification to know that obscurity is happiness & that John Clare the thresher in the onset & neglected ryhmer in the end are the only two comfortable periods of his life—I sent you 'The Vicar' long ago did you get it

god bless you & farewell
John Clare

To John Taylor

[6 November 1821]

My dear Taylor

I got your noveltys° on sunday & had a rare days work & a pleasant one too to peruse them   sir R[ichard] P[hillips]° is a meek milk & water knight or at least he affects to be so—but I believe he has took the pains to sift out all the chaff for his sample & cast the wheat behind him with a modest wish it seems to aid its obscurity as the thief did the caskett while he is persuading his readers that he is doing justice & adding his mite in my success god help his readers brains if such doggerel moves them either one way or the other—but an author that lives by his own puffs & has to keep up his placard as the rival of Newton cannot be expected to have much time & many wishes for the praise & success of any body else be they poets or philosophers—thus much for the worstedstocking might of the Monthly Magazine.—

Mr Carys opinion° has done me great service indeed & started my muse agen full gallop   while such mens praise comes due—puffers & bluestockings may rant as they please for I care but little for them   Incognita° was sent me in the Morn: Post & I suspected

I shall come to London but I cant say when for the expence is tickling to a Poets Purse so I shoud be very happy to hear of your voyage in the [?dark] tho some of the companions° you mention I posses as visitors already   Mr C[unningham] & that rouge of a Peter with yourself I shall feel great pleasure in seeing & if youll tell me the precise time when you meant to be at wansford Ill walk there ready to meet you & youll find the scenery more pleasant then you expected that way to Helpstone & then the Author of the visit° may have a second subject—is the other Peter as droll & as wicked as the origional.—Dewints not been he never will now—you was mistaken in the book account Scott gave me the Burns & Southeys Nelson in addition to what you mention & I have no Wordsworth tho I cant say but it woud be pleasant if another Milton woud step forward to correct the mistake with its addition

I am happy to see the Mermaid of Galloway° reclaimed by her farther at last after being so ungratfull a fugutive your Mag is livlier this month then ever tho I feel the loss of Opium° & a Cooks oracle°—the article of the New Monthly° is very tame but calm weathers & meek motions are suitable things to its Editors constitution & its what I expected for I have no doubt of his good manners & meanings—I have finishd 'Jockey & Jinney' 'Wanderings in June' & a ne[w poem] the 'Workhouse Orphan' & am now about a po[em] on 'Burghely Park' but shall not finish it till next summer as I mean to take another review when in its beauty—'The Fate of Genius' will soon be started I mean for the Parish Clerk to be the relation & my vanity fancys I shall make a good thing of it—what think you by the insertion of the 'Lodge house' in one of the 'Londons' some time or other—My consciets not dampt about it yet & I fancy it one of the best I have still written you might do it without the name & it woud pass calmly to its destiny I have never seen drury nor heard of him since since you & I parted silence speaks for its self & keep an eye on the 'Patchwork skreen for the Ladies'° in future—for that Sonnet was inserted there by him & no one else Im convincd of it & have felt cursd mad about it ever since I care not when nor were Im fixed with good company but such trash as those periodicals disgusts me for Id as lieve stick in the pillory an hour as any ofspring of mine shoud stick in the worsted stocking knights puffs of dignity—I must cease but cannot help noticing 'Summer'° in your last London as a beautiful poem in my opinion —I shall not be without additional pride at seeing more room occupyd by me next month—

yours &c
J. Clare

To John Taylor

[24 January 1822]

My dear Taylor

I have just nothing to do & to pass time away I scribble this with not a single thought to begin with nor one perhaps worth reading ere I get [to the] end—I wait impatient for the end of the month to see the dream° in print—you must not decieve me as you have often done by saying so & so is to be in the Mag: & then nothing of it when it comes—I think of writing a love tale in the measure of Spencer but have not exactly pitchd on a subject unless I call it 'the Deserter'°—I have been to Milton & spent 3 days with Mr Artis the Antiquary very pleasantly

he has discoverd a multitude of fresh things & a fine roman bath is one of the latest discovereys the painted plaster on the walls was very fresh & fine when I saw it & the flues of the furnaceses was a proof without the least suposition of its being a bath he has also found the roman road that led to the river & the pavement is as firm as when first laid down—next summer when the water is low he intends to try for the iron bridge which is said to be sunk in the river—his plan of the Roman City is nearly compleated—he has a great many drawings of curious things & I think his book when published will be very entertaining—he is going to take a plaster bust of my head somtime for myself—his own he has taken himself & I think very like he seems to me quite a clever man & every thing but a poet—lets have the Mag: this time as soon as its possible as I am all anxiety to see how the thing will read in print & shall not settle to ryhme a couplet till I see it—I dont know how to account for it but the good & bad parts of a poem are very rarely distinguis[hed] by me while° its in print—the M.S.S. book is been out a fortnight or ne[arly] so if its missd you its lost—but I harbour no other opinion then that of your having it safe & that you have said 'this will do' & 'this wont do' long ere now—I think very much of 'Jockey & Jenney'° now its gone & fancy it one of the best Ive written reflection dwells long upon things that are favourites & when thats the case with me I always remark it that I am seldom mistaken—excuse this scribling—

yours &c &c &c

John Clare

I have broke my brass seal coud you get me one engravd with 'J.C.' on a bone heft   mine was a wooden one & its come off & left me at a loss—I gave 2s for it to drury & its turnd out very dear get me one done if you please as it will be a little better engravd then I get them here & no doubt the expence will be less

To John Taylor

[31 January 1822]

My dear Taylor

I have had some reflection on the following subjects before I put them to you & tho rather preposterous I think not impossible—what the D——l this mean youll say or think & well you may—this it is that 'Bachelors Hall'° is on the wreck or nearly so   when the inclosure was they mortgagd the property for £200 to a Jew a second Iago who employs a lawer at deeping to lend money of the name of Baker as big a rogue as himself & they both go hand in hand like a brace of bloodhounds bent on destruction & as sure of their game as death when once in the scent & thus it is that the Billings being my oldest & now only friends in the village I cannot see these rogues pursue their prey uninterupted—nothing is a greater hell to me then to see an old friend wrongd by intentional villany by meditated fraud—hell overtake them but I make one desperate struggle in behalf of an harmless man—this is my design—Ill publish a vol: of poems under a feignd name were I will try my uttermost to excell—they shall be all out of my way   here are some of them: 'a Vision of Hell' 'Shadows of Fate' or 'Life death & Eternity'° but this is all idea for not one word is yet begun & the blood hounds is on the heels of their victim—a long paper has been sent them from this Baker about 'Kings bench' & 'John Doe & Richard Roe' & a damd set of mystic bother as obscure as the workings of hell to which they belong—the Cottage is a beautifull spot of 6 or 7 Acres   there are crowds for it if it be sold but if I coud get hold of the mortgage it woud be mine & still doing a kindness to a friend I shoud like to make sure of it as 'Poets Hall' instead of its old name of 'Bachelors' which must soon be extinct if I dont succeed—Ill do this way if you like Ill sell you my writings for five years for that sum which cant be dear—however be as it will give me your free opinion for I know its a bargain—since I wrote thus far he has been to Lord Milton who has got the before mentiond paper to do somthing—still I shoud like it as in handhold & if you seem to think it worth while Ill write to Lord M[ilton] to say Ill pay off the Mortgage —but do as you list I myself hate to be troubld or to be troublesome—but my feelings are rousd to madness at such acts of violence & my imagination cannot withold an attempting struggle to save a sinking fellow creature & more especially a friend—tho it be like the shadow by ones side mocking our motions in idle deception & empty nothingness—I have a[t las]t pitchd upon a subject for a 'nov[el]'° it is 'Cares & Comforts' or 'Notes from the Memoirs of Uncle Barnaby & family as written by himself' I shall write it in Chapters & confine myself to no mechanical plot but go on just as things jump at the moment—'The Misterey'° a dramatic Pastoral I shall quickly proceed with—I am all madness for writing but how long its to last I dont know—I want £3 to get straight this year & hope you will send it soon as you can find time—

yours &c &c &c &c
John Clare

To John Taylor

[5 February 1822]

My dear Taylor

I write this to tell you that the bother of Lawers & Jews is all setteld Lord Milton has lent the 'Old Bachelor' £20 to pay off the interest & thats all thats needed at present so you need say nor send nothing about it but pass it over in silence as nothing had been the matter.

I think 'Bradgate Park'° in the present No a good article I can see in a moment the Dream will do tis the best Ive done yet 'uphoped sight' is hard mouthd & dosnt read smooth enough but it will do—I am at ease agen & 'a vision of hell' & 'Shadows of Fate' are all laid aside nor do I think I shall go on with the Novel for these things were began as intended helps to my old friends & as they are satisfyd Im the same —I rather feel hipt° at the Village minstrels success the old Vol had gone thro 2 editions ere this & I think a notice in the london agen of a New vol of Poems preparing is nessesary as a stimulant to revive the flattness of these for I am jealous of their ill sucess° at least I feel somthing that tells me they dont go off like the others & I prevent that feeling as much as ever I can from damping my further exertions but I cannot help it doing so at some times—still Im determind in the teeth of vexation to surmount dissapointment by unwearied struggles—under these feelings the dream was written & that is the reason of their explanation—& under the same somthing else shall quickly be with you but I cannot say when nor what—lets have your promise of a notice of the New M.S. poems you have got when leisure suits as it will do me great good—I took this large sheet to insert my new thing 'to Spring'° but its not finishd & perhaps if I give it you as it is I never may sit down to it afterwards —I musnt do no more terrible things yet they stir me up to such a pitch that leaves a disrelish for my old accustomd wanderings after nature—Ill have hold of a love tale that shall have awkard situations in it to give my spirits a rouse & to try ones best—I fear I shall get nothing ready for you this month at least I fear so now but may have 50 subjects ready to morrow the Muse is a fickle Hussey with me she sometimes stilts me up to madness & then leaves me as a beggar by the way side with no more life then whats mortal & that nearly extinguishd by mellancholy forbodings—I wish I livd nearer you at least I wish London w[oud] creep within 20 miles of helpstone [ ] I dont wish helpstone to shift its station I live here among the ignorant like a lost man in fact like one whom the rest seems careless of having anything to do with—they hardly dare talk in my company for fear I shoud mention them in my writings & I find more pleasure in wandering the fields then in musing among my silent neighbours who are insensible to every thing but toiling & talking of it & that to no purpose

yours &c &c
John Clare

P.S. lets have the seal as soon as you can as I am in wants of one

To James Augustus Hessey

[16 March 1822]

My dear Hessey

I got the Mag: safe but have not been able to tell you so & am as little able to write as ever—I have been very poorly in fact very bad all this month but I hope ere long to be myself agen—I have not yet lookd over the Mag: but with the encouragment in your letter shall quickly begin at least as soon as I loose this confounded lethargy of low spirits that presses on me to such a degree that at times makes me feel as if my senses had a mind to leave me Spring & Fall such feelings it seems are doomd to be my companions but it shall not overpower me as formerly with such weak & terrible dreads & fears of dropping off when death comes he will come & while lifes mine Ill make the best of it & have the courage to treat such things as trifles—I take a great deal of Exerscise & try to write nothing which I do as the best way to mend & get better next month I hope to have somthing for you good or bad this month you must excuse me tho I shoud feel happy to be able to get somthing for it & if oppertunity dont come too late I will make use of it—give my respects to Taylor & I remain | yours &c &c

John Clare

To his Family

London [22] May 1822

Dear Friends

I have just written this to say I am safely arived in London° & at present with Mr Taylor & Hessey —my promise° will be performd but I cannot name the precise time nor is it nessesary

My journey up ended very bad indeed we went 20 miles & upwards in the most dreadfull thunder storm I ever witness'd & the rain was very heavy & lashing but as I am safe thats satisfaction enough my respects to all & a kiss for Anna | yours &c &c

John Clare

To his Family

Fleet St 93. [4 June] 1822

Dear Friends

I have at last performd my promise they are both of the same price & both my choise but thats no reason why they shoud please Patty or Sophy° two very difficult creatures on that point as I have before experiencd—but if they dont suit I make no more attempts to please let them remember that—one is 6½ yards & the other 6 yards the first is of course intended for the largest but Patty may chuse which she pleases or at least they may divide their choise between them—Ive done all I can & all I intended—

I hope every thing goes on well remember & take care of the doves I think it odd that no letter comes I have expected one these 3 or 4 days

I have got an invitation to go to Bristol° & shall accept it if nothing requires me at home but if you wish me to desist I will return to Helpstone very shortly somtime next week at the furthest on what day I cannot tell so dont expect till I come the parcel started this morning Tuesday I have directed it for deeping as usual

A second thought tells me you need not write for as I am weary already you may be sure of my coming home next week° & Bristol shall be left for another excursion

yours &c &c &c
John Clare

I shall send somthing else ere I return if my money holds out

To John Taylor

Saturday [22 June 1822]

My dear Taylor

I coud not write to you sooner for I have not been myself till now on monday morning I got to helpstone but how I can hardly tell for I was so 'reeling ripe'° that when I got to peterbro I askd the name of the place & when it was told me I took it to be a hoax & coud hardly be convincd to the contrary—I found an addition to my fortune on my arival in a daughter then 3 days old the mother is perhaps getting better—I am & has ever been since my arival as sober as a judge—give my respects to Hessy I might have said 'farewell' & take it for yourself likewise

Give also my parting regrets to my literary friends which good fortune has provd too many to enummerate so much the better—my sincerity is divided equally amongst them & I do asure you (in spite of their [? punning]) my heart achd as I lost sight of London at the thought of being forc'd away perhaps for ever from the merriest set of fellows I ever met with—tell C[unningham] I left his letter safe at the Inn were the coach stopt but it was too soon in the morning to call my self & we had not 10 minutes to spare—I passd poor Bloomfield° for twas no use stopping in the state I was in & had I been sober I dont think my inclination woud have gone far then to persuade me —I have read Lambs last paper° & think it one of his very best surely his heroes will subscribe an annual feast to his memory at the Beggars Opera° & make him their laureate—hes surely done good to the trade for I shall treat beggars as respectable after this —I have nothing m[ore] to say for my head is as yet v[er]y muddy so | Farewell

John Clare

To Henry Francis Cary

Helpstone Aug: 23. 1822

Revd Sir

I have long thought of writing to you & shoud have done it with great pleasure had I not a fear of becoming troublsome by so doing but Lord R[adstock] in a mysterious hint° some weeks back told me you wonderd I did not this has set me at liberty & I have not written a letter but an attempted one for I have just got over a very bad fever that is now raging from house to house in our fenny villages like a plague its making its progress thro all the family & the two childern with my mother are not yet out of danger—I am on lucks side once more tho in a very feeble state

The two days spent at Chiswick have left pleasant remembrances behind them of friendship & hospitality° I beg to give my remembrances to Mrs Carey & family & to your Curate Mr —— & his lady: I was sorry at least dissapointed to find your pen had been idle last month with the 'Lives of the poets'° its an article that I generally expect to find & my earliest search is accordingly the rest seem to be writing themselves out (as I think) Lyddal Cross° is falling & the others are going off—but perhaps only to catch breath for this month I hope it is so—I expect you heard of the addition to my family in another daughter which I found at my return home

As my poetry has been honourd with your favourable opinion I shall fill up this letter with 14 lines° which I made yesterday morning as I walkd out agen for the first time wether the muse was with me I cant tell but conseit is better then the nine muses together I find it so at least

Morning awakes sublime glad earth & skye
Smile in the splendor of the day begun
Oer the broad easts illumind Canopy
Shade of its makers majesty the sun
Gleams in its living light—from cloud to cloud
Streaks of all colors beautifully run
As if before heavens gate there hung no shroud
To hide its grand magnificence—O heaven
Were entrance een to thought is disalowd
To view the glory that this scene is givi[ng]
[W]hat may blind reason once expect to [see]
[When in] immortal worlds the soul is liv[ing]
[Etern]al as its makers & as free
To taste the unknowns of eternity

I have written some things for a new vol: entitld 'Summer Walks'° but I fear they will not do when I send them up to Taylors I coud wish you woud take the trouble to look over some of them yours & T[aylor]'s opinion together woud set me right on the subject before I [? miscard] them my sheet is wearing short & therefore I must prepare to conclude & with the hopes of hearing from you in return I beg to remain | your

faithfull & Obdt St

John Clare

To [John Taylor]

October 19. 1822

Sir

I shall send you in due time a small collection of poems for your perusal and opinion the longest is a poem on love for nothing can be done without it now a days I have shown it to a friend whose greatest objection is to the Motto which is from Sir W. Scott 'Kissing and cutting of throats' I think it beautifully applicable but obstinacy shall not misguide me be as it may I know a simple tale of love now a days (like a name without a title) is nothing without at Castrophe mine is the 'Suicide' thus much is sufficient tis in your place to read and judge and not in mine to commend but before we part I will give you a Specimen of my abilities which in fact is an address to one whom I soon hope to call 'Mrs Green' and however your opinion may be biasd I cannot say but hers is mightily in its favour I assure you

I am your sincere Friend and well wisher
Percey Green°

Ballad

O throw aside those carless ways
My consious heart to move
Affected anger but betrays
Suspicious doubts of love

That face were frowns at will can dwell
Were cold deciet beguiles
May just as easy and as well
Dissemble while it smiles

Tis cruel when false smiles betrays
The heart into a snare
But crueler when slighting ways
Turns pleasures to despair

Thy face is fair let that suffice
And scorn a meaner power

Truth adds to beautys fading price
Like fragrance in the flower

Yet tho you frown or smile in jest
My folly must declare
A weakness burning in my breast
Feels all in earnest there

P.S. I have heard it affirmed that your predilection for the Northamptonshire Peasants poetry has made you blind to the more high & refined style be as it will I have made the attempt wether it be attended with success or not

yours again &c &c
P.G.

To James Augustus Hessey

[5 November 1822]

My dear Hessey

I certainly like a novelty as early as possible & you have gratifyd me accordingly I know Gilchrist is in Town he was with me at Helpstone last week & he lookd so ill that I dont think him long for this world I hope I am mistaken—I like the last of Autumn very well & will try somthing for your next month—I keep writing on with my love story & think worse & worse of it as I proceed I am likewise finishing the Satire of 'The Parish'° in which I shall introduce the 'Vicar' alredy written—perhaps upon parish oppressors I am to severe—but all the flattery they deserve is a horsewhip—I can do but little at letter writing at present that hell of a pestilence is still amongst us & my mother is fallen agen even worse then before—Dewint never calld well never mind if he wont come he must do the opposite I shall be glad to find you make somthing of the Cottage & shall be happy to see the 2nd Edit:° announcd the sooner the better —My Summer Walks are stopt for the present but I think next summer will bring fresh spirits with it to urge me to proceed—my mind has its ebbs & flows like the tide I wish I coud be settld to somthing but it seems impossible here is 14 lines but wether good or bad I know not & care as little

To the Deity°

Almighty mystery—thou whose power & might
Free as a thought first rob'd the infant earth
That lookd the wakening darkness first to light
& breathd all worlds & heavens into birth
& bade them live neath merceys angel care
Incomprehensible as thou must be
If aught of mortal thought or hope may dare
To be familiar in addressing thee
If calld by earthly names be not profane
Accept o god a mortals worship—free
As natures soul born hopes which are not vain
To hope the best an helpless worm like me
Tho vile—thou hast no pleasure in its pain
—I am but dust—& thourt Eternity

give my respects to T[aylor] | yours &c &c &c
John Clare

To James Augustus Hessey

[12 December 1822]

My dear Hessey

Your note was a little dissapointment as I fancyd once a month had room in it sufficient assuredly for a letter my letter of P. Green was merely a joke for a christmas puzzle which was quickly unriddeld by the parcel as I did not reccolect the seal woud betray me

Taylor I expect is forgot I am living I coud wish however to jog him in memory of the mistake & hope he will give me an opinion of the Tale as I am waiting for it & cannot proceed further till I have it—respecting the Cottage Artis woud do it & I dare say Simpson likewise as you wish but Cowie° an irish Artist by profession is coming to Milton at Christmass whom Artis will get to do it in style his pen-&-ink drawings I understand are exelent—so that will end the job without further assistance tho I heartily thank Dewint for his kindness—I shall be glad when the 2nd Edit: is fairely on the run for a few sniffling knowing ones about me are giving out that I am fallen never to rise agen—this is not pleasant tho it be only the *wisdom of fools*—country booksellers are great critics & meddlers in such conscerns—but I intend to get my friend Drakard to put in a notice about the 2nd Edit: immediatly to choke such consciet tho I thought it best to ask you of the propriety of such a thing—it will cost nothing at all events for he will not deny me a kindness in that way I know—tell Taylor to write me in a day or two if he pleases for I have been expecting a letter ever since the Mag: came—I shall have somthing else for him shortly perhaps I wish some of you woud give us an idea of a subject for a story of love—for I have been reading about for a subject to no purpose tho I often fancyd the book of 'Ruth' might supply me with a model to work on what say you? I have just written to Lamb° to thank him for his books & got it frankd for the india house tell me if it finds him—I shall write to Tomas,° Reynolds, Hood, & Mr Carey ere long—tho Hood has not [ ] as you promised he woud never mind [ ] do somthing first & then things will follow of course tell Taylor to give my best respects to Dewint Hilton & the rest of the family—I have done nothing latley but visit & pay almost a daily worship to heavey wet° to make solitude less irksome which in fact makes it worse my respects to Taylor &c &c | yours sincerly

John Clare

To James Augustus Hessey

[8 January 1823]

My dear Hessey

Give my hearty thanks to Elia for his valuable present° efeth tis beautifully printed & it deserves to be so—what is all this dying about Elia dead & Weathercock dead° if this dying comes in fashion with the contribs: why the magazine must follow but Elias ghost will perhaps contribute somthing still the

Elisan fields have plenty for subjects no doubt & Weathercock tho his name is taught to vanish his hillarity & [?whims] is no doubt as bodily & healthy as ever—my new fangld childern which you sent struck me with wonder & they seemd to know as little of their father as their father does of 'Francis Turner Esqr'° I know of Sharon Turner & Dawson Turner but Francis was a blank to me & is [?just] born in your letter—well but a Lawer working without fee deserves something tis an appendix to the worlds seven wonders & stamps 'good angel on the devils horn'° at once so I have done as you requested but guess-praises written to unknowns like Macbeths Amen rather 'sticks in my throat' but your reccomendation is plenty & I have writ down my hearty respects for I hate pretentions & cold blooded compliments are worse than nothing

I must confess I shoud have done it more pleastly to Woodhouse but be to whom it will my heart goes with it & I hope the gent & you will believe its sincerity & give it welcom—I sent a Letter off on Saturday & got your parcel on Sunday night from deeping let me hear from you ere this weeks out tis nessesity solicits the reply—respecting the cottage Cowie is not come & I shall wait no longer moreover the trees have been [?bound] up like maypoles latly & my hut stands beneath them like a grotto or moss house or the rem[ains] of a London [?whim] a cockney cottage Artis considers the effect spoilt & declines giving an outline saying the old one is better then aught that can be taken now so let it pass & I shall expect to see the second Edit: out directly for I imagine New title pages & a wood engraving will not take long doing—my anxiety increases with the delay—I shall as soon as they are out want to make presents to your London contributors Hood Reynolds Cunningham Weathercock Carey &c to whom give my respects & a newyears welcome give Janus my returns for his farewell remembrance of John Clare who wishes he was lifting up the lid of his [?stringing] tankard° or drinking his health over a bottle of Scotch Ale at this moment —but alas many miles stretch their weary lengths between present miseries & former comforts I am wind bound in my sultry corner drinking now & then a pot of misnamd medly as nigh Ale as shadow is to substance small beers sad reallity or now & then seeking the 'Bell' to be cheerd with the [?silence] of company w[ho] sleep all day with their eyes open or only [wake] to howl about the times books & Authors are as dark & unknown things as if they inhabited the bottom of the sea—this is a fine part of the country for blue devils & low spirits but a damd bad place to cure them—I shall send up the poems with my magazines which woud have come ere now but the last is at Milton Patty was nigh being in danger last friday by the overturning of a Cart in which she went to market the man that drove it dyd the next day from the fall & the jury met yesterday she excaped unhurt—

yours sincerely
John Clare

To James Augustus Hessey

[before 13 January 1823]

My dear Hessey

Here is your books but wether injurd or not I cannot say I packd them up as well as I coud—I have broke the tail piece of my Cremona not by fair means perhaps for it was done by substituting as second string for a first as a makeshift I wish it to be mended if possible as it is a limb of the fiddle & a new one in my opinion woud have but a shallow claim to that character I have written to Tomas & told him about it & sent the thing in the parcel—my bills are now in these are my dog-days I hate arithmetic that proves these sad calculations here is the sum next door in extent to eternity with me £27. 11. 3—I must cut a string from the Minstrel so there ends the whole & live by the loss—£7 from the sum grins at my follys on the greazy mantltree at the bell thats the curse of the Confession

I shoud almost dread to see Taylor more for his small-beer sermons woud quite undo me I will resolve next year to be more respectable & more independant & you shall hear no more confessions till then—I am just getting ready to visit Milton so I cannot fill the sheet—I have written a letter to the Marquis but have not sent it till you see it tis on the subject of a future Dedication as I think I have done wrong in not giving him the Minstrel's but time explains all things & it will mine he is now in france

yours sincerely
John Clare

To James Augustus Hessey

[before 28 June 1823]

My dear Hessey

I have waited this while to send up the Mag: for binding & with it a MSS on 'Spring' but I have been prevented from continuing it by the illness of my 2 childern who are both getting better as I shoud hope but the fate of a neighbour makes me uncommonly uneasy & unable to do any thing who lost a son & a daughter both in one day when they thought they was recovering   it commences with a hoarse cough & ends with an inflamation of the lungs & carrys them off in a moment when death is the least expected   as soon as I find them safe I shall write agen—but what is the reason you dont give your opinion of my latter poems   you must have time now & then to do it if you chuse—as 'there is a time for all things'—do you know any thing of a somthing publishing upon me (a Critique or Essay° for I know not the title) by Murray   I can give no opinion on things I have not seen I can only surmise   I believe Lord R[adstock] & Mrs E[mmerson] 2 of my best & very best friends but I must have consciet enough in me to think they cannot read the world so well as myself & I must prophecy thus much on its futurity if its such an one as to please his Lordship it abounds in praises on my poems which my enemeys will readily conjure up into flatterys: Critisisms overflowing with milk & honey are as vain as those of the reptile uttering nothing but the venom of gall & bitterness   there never was a land of Canaan discovered as yet but it raisd a nest of wasps to share in the spoils   if its impartial I shall give it welcome if not god help me I can but turn back to other days & sigh in vain for times

When friends were needless & when foes were few

I have made up my mind to publish next winter & have written to Lord Exeter respecting the Dedication whom I expect to hear from every day—I turnd it over & over a many times in my mind before I res[   ] for your silence seems determind & n[ot] to be broken but I coud heartily wish you woud say wether I have done wrong or right—yesterday fortnight is helpstone feast   I shall want to settle my accounts as usual before it for that 'doomsday' is nigh agen so I wish you woud send me the half yearly rents as soon as you can—I know were the last poem° is wrong but I cannot correct it now & have no short one to send you still

I am yours as sincerely as ever
J Clare

To the Marquis of Exeter

[January–June 1823]

My Lord

My success with a generous public has emboldend my vanity to request an additional favour to the many recievd from your Lordship tho popularity is often a fading species of merit it urges me to solicit it & flatters me that I shall not be denyd

My request is that I may be alowd to dedicate a vol of Poems (whose publication tho not yet fixd upon the ensuing year may determine) to your Lordship perhaps the last I may ever publish tho such confessions of Authors are far from infallible

My heart tells me its no flattery when I fancy your Lordship my greatest patron tho good fortune blest me early with several illustrious names that became my friends to whom I must be ever indebted tho my humble oppertunitys shall not be neglected in making them trifling returns

I have met with many too that illustrate the old vulgar proverb 'When the childs christend there is always plenty of gossips'

Your Lordship condescended unsolicited to befriend me when I was almost an unknown in the world & had few or none to help me when my forlorn hopes dare scarcly indulge in a pleasant thought & when the voice of encouragment was a stranger the goodness of your Lordship in becoming a friend at such a season speaks for itself how welcome a reception it met with & how sweet it must be to remember & my gratitude will witness an additional pleasure shoud it be alowd to make its humble return

I have only to add that I hope your Lordship will believe that sincerity is the only motive that urgd me to ask what I now solicit

My Lord I have the honour to be your Lor[d]ships obedient
Servant
John Clare

To John Taylor

[before 9 July 1823]

My dear Taylor

It perhaps woud have been more appropriate to have said 'Sir' considering the long silence between us has gone a long way to make strangers but the past is always a poetical name to me & therefore I adhere to it: I write this to tell you that I have got a letter from the Marquis respecting a dedication to the visionary Vol which I wish to publish next winter & which I am anxious for your opinion about the propriety of such a thing I mean the pieces in the London with some new ones woud it be right or woud it be too soon you know I told you in London I shoud bother you the winter after the last remember what you say is law & I hope you will write me & say somthing here is an Extract from his Lordships note 'I am happy to hear that you persevere in your studies & that you intend to amuse the public with a fourth Vol of Poems. I am obliged to you for wishing to dedicate it to me & am much pleasd with your intention of doing so—I beg you will put my name down for 10 Copies & remain your obt St Exeter'—thats all

I hate dedication hunting worse then fox hunting tho I like neither but 'hope' that jilt & 'gratitude' that worrying hussey woud not let me be—whats done is done & cannot be undone—I coud give more reasons for my being tempted to do this but as they are like blossoms on the fruit tree that come ere the Spring in danger of being blighted I shall say nothing of them the last prayer of a malefactor is but a doubtfull sort of repentance & the hope that accompanys it but a fit consort for such a companion but its time to have done with such mysterys—I write about the book & earnestly hope you will gratify me with an answer about it as soon as you can—poor Gilchrist is done° I coud not have thought it woud have affected me so much when I first heard it I was stupified & woud not believe it but its too true—god help us its the 'common lot' & the passage were friendships, loves, hopes, fears, joys, & troubles in oblivion meet—well it must be so & I h[ave] grown to care nothing about it—I have [ ] apathy about me that looks on the powers of hells & heavens as mysterious riddles & Death as an animal consequence I hope its not heathenism—I hope its not worse but so it is—I expect Mr Allens book about me is no News to both I consider him a sensible & clever fellow & I expect you think likwise—with the attachment of old remembrances my dear Taylor believe me | yours as sincerely as ever

John Clare

To [Elizabeth Kent]

[Hessey had sent Clare a copy of *Flora domestica* (1823), but since it was published without the author's name, Clare assumed the author to be male. Elizabeth Kent, the sister-in-law of Leigh Hunt, wrote several letters to Clare.]

[August 1823]

Dear Sir

I have often felt a wish & have now attempted it which is to thank you for the pleasure which the perusal of your book on plants has given me & for the use which it has given to society at large for every body who makes use of that mind which his creator has given him must feel delighted with the study of Botany   it is the book of nature open at every season & every day turns over a new page to amuse & instruct the looker on as he passes from the village pasture to the cultivated field or the wild & uncultivated heath   her pleasures are every where & her profits are ever found in the minds of those who make this delightful study their amusement—I do not mean the mere science for of that I know but little but the reflections it creates to see the various colours of field flowers & the eternal variety of shapes & different tintings of the leaves of herbs & trees & when we notice these things we feel a desire to know their names as of so many friends & acquaintance & the easiest way of becoming acquainted with these is by the assistance of Botany which is so far a very useful system & every one who attempts to render a useful system popular deserves the thanks of those interested in it for his labours & you deserve them in many instances & if I might put in a plea for the future shepherds & ploughmen of my country (as intelect is the heritage or birth right of every sphere of life) I think your abilitys might render Botany popular enough to win their attention by making them acquainted with the flowers of their own country that make gardens in summer of the spots where they live & labour by publishing a Work with illustrations of our British Plants similar to your book of Plants & instead of giving figures of select specimens of plants as you did there I think you might give illustrations of them all & yet leave it acceptable to the purchase of such readers

To John Taylor

[3 January 1824]

My dear Taylor

I recievd the thing safe & am very pleasd with your early attention to my nessesitys°

I am very supprisd that you had not got the M.S. as it was sent to Deeping on sunday last but I hope you have it now & if you have I hope you will skim it over & tell me directly how you like things as I am waiting for your remarks—I have just finishd a tale on a subject given by you somtime ago you remember the yorkshire Farmer going in disguise as a labourer you said it woud make a tolerable subject for a Drama be as it will I have made a tale of it & I think not a bad one a gossip tells it

Any other things that you may think would [make] tales or any pictures you may have noticd in the months of rural scenery woud be very acceptable to me now you know better then me what will suit & I am certain a man of your taste has not let them pass bye without notice

Hessey propossd 'Harvest home'° as a 'capital Subject' but in my mind it is too barren of incident unless it be connected with a story & I am looking over my mind for one to suit it

When I have done with the 'Shepherds calender' I shall make up my mind & publish no more for 8 or 10 years wether the thing be successfull or not

& in that interval I intend to try the Drama in pastoral & tragic pictures & I have made it up in my mind to write one hundred sonnets° as a set of pictures on the scenes & objects that appear in the different seasons & as I shall do it soly for amusment I shall take up wi gentle & simple as they come whatever in my eye finds any [inter]est these things are resolves not merely in the view for publication but for attempts

I have not yet got the Mag: & if it be not sent off ere this arives I wish you woud send me a blank book rul'd & fellow to the former that I may copy the things down in as I write them

Be as soon as you can wi your remarks as I want them to go on with

yours &c &c &c
John Clare

To John Taylor

[Clare had been ill since Jan.; his certainty that he was on the verge of death prompted him to think again about a will, and Richard Woodhouse advised him accordingly. Dr Thomas Arnold, of Stamford, had been treating Clare, and Taylor sent some money to pay his expenses. Clare had been contemplating joining the Ranters (Primitive Methodists), and Taylor offered reassurance that such 'Enthusiasm' was 'far better than Coldheartedness'.]

[after 3 April 1824]

My dear Taylor

I got all safe & Dr Arnold shall recieve his claim on friday I have felt as bad as ever since I wrote you but now I am thinking I feel improving again I think the docters none of them know the real cause of my complaint I feel now a numbness all over me just as I shoud suppose a person to feel when bitten by a serpent & I firmly believe I shall never get over it be as it will I am resignd for the worst my mind is placid & contented & that is somthing for when I was first took god forgive me I had hard work to bare up with my malady & often had the thought of destroying myself & from this change in my feelings I satisfactorily prove that Religions foundation is truth & that the Mystery that envelopes it is a power above human nature to comprehend & thank god it is for if a many uneasy discontented minds knew of the bargain they shoud gain by being good they might still be discontented & I might be one of them besides there is little merit in undergoing a hardship for a prize when we know what it is—the labourer goes to work for his hire & is happy or sullen according to the wages alowd him—I agree with you that the religious hypocrite is the worst monster in human nature & some of these when they had grown so flagrant as to be discoverd behind the mask they had taken to shelter their wickedness led me at first to think lightly of religion & sure enough some of the lower classes of dissenters about us are very decietful & in fact dangerous characters especialy among the methodists with whom I have determind to assosiate but then there are a many sincere good ones to make up & why shoud the wicked deter us from taking care of ourselves when they ought to appear in our eyes as a warning to make us turn to the right way—my opinion Taylor of true Religion amounts to this if a man turns to god with real sincerity of heart not canting & creeping to the eyes of the world but satisfying his own conscience so that it shall not upbraid him in the last hours of life that touchstone of faith & practice carless of what the world may say either for him or against him that man in my opinion is as certain of heaven in the next world as he is of death in this—because we cannot do wrong without being conscious of it—& if no dread overweights us at that hour it is the surest proof of innosence—I feel it impossible for me to copy offr° my rough things so I have sent you them to do what you can with them yourself

the *marks* will lead you were the *outslips* are to be inserted I know you have but little respect for after thoughts but these are not such it is the way in which I always compose & you will see most of them nessesary for corrections sake the Pastoral is my idea of one but if Popes difenition° be true that everything in nature is vulgar & every monstrous fancy out of it a past[oral] then mine is grossly wrong your judgment is my sta[ndby] & if I live I intented to write 11 more in [that] way & had begun another 'Love & Flattery'° your approval or condemnation if I am ever able to write agen will settle the matter—I believe with you that there is quite plenty for a Vol & a respectable one likwise so consider of it & act just as if it was your own you have now every poem in your possession that I am worth what is left are but outlines or shadows & not fit for your eye at present—this book is the only copy in existance so take what trust you please of it—the sooner the book is begun the better so I shoud think once but Im in my way feel anxious about anything now—I coud wish if you thought it proper not without that you woud write to the Marquis to explain the delay

I have not answerd Hesseys last letter   I delayd it to have some doubtfull passages in our dissenters creeds here explaind but I can see thro the vulgar errors that blinded them & correctly find their origional notions myself   it was respecting their ignorant notions of tenets which they stile 'Free Grace' 'Election' & 'Predestination' things that are far better kept out of the way of the ignorant who interpret them to suit their own purposes & make religion grossly rediculous by such abuses

yours &c &c &c
John Clare

To James Augustus Hessey

[20 April 1824]

My dear Hessey

I have not written to you a long while   I waited partly thro indisposition & partly to get some doubts explaind which I do not want now   I feel resignd & quiet & thats enough   as to my health I can give you but a bad account tho I have gave up doctering save the taking opening pills occasionly   I am as stupid as ever & blood comes from me often   my insides feels sinking & dead & my memory is worse & worse nearly lost   the sensation as if cold water was creeping all about my head is less frequent now tho it comes on now & then in the evening for at that time I am always worse   I have joind the Ranters that is I have enlisted in their society   they are a set of simple sincere & communing christians with more zeal then knowledge earnest & happy in their devotions   O that I coud feel as they do but I cannot   their affection for each other their earnest tho simple extempore prayers puts my dark unsettld consience to shame this is how they keep the sabbath   at 7 o clock they meet to pray at 9 they join the Class at half past 10 they hear preaching at half past 2 they meet agen to pray & at 7 in the evening preaching again   thus passes the Sabbath with the Ranters making an heaven on earth   there is a deal of enthusiasm in their prayers & preachings & manners but as it is real & not affected it is not to be found fault with but commended   my feelings are so unstrung in their company that I can scarcly refrain from shedding tears & when I went church I coud scarcly refrain from sleep—I thank god that he has opend my eyes in time & let all scoffers remember this line of Young° 'They may live fools but fools they cannot dye'—I shall never forget the horror that I felt in reading this line but enough—I feel desirious Hessey of having Dr Darlings advice & woud feign get to london if I coud but I am so fearful of the way lest I shoud be taken for the worse & unable to proceed on the journey & I have made such an expensive doctering at home that perhaps I ought not to come to you to increase it but life is sweet & I feel feign to get better tho I am next to hopless—what shall I do°   if I thought Dr D. coud do me no good I woud not come for I cannot enjoy no pleasure & am loath to leave home but if I knew he coud I woud try for it tho double the distance it is   I am able to come up outside if the weather suits & if it does not I can wait   I cannot reconsile my own m[ind] what to do for I think my disorder incur[able] because I feel as I never felt before in my li[fe] & further I cannot feel much better   if I do its only for a day or two & then I am as bad as ever—give me your advice as to what you think woud be best & I will abide by it   you did not send the Mag: this month   you might for I can read betimes tho very little & I have not as yet lost my relish for the things of this world tho I feel my situation very awful & often [?lingering] on the brink of another   well we must all come to it at last tho some has more trouble in getting there then another

yours &c &c
John Clare

To John Taylor

[8 May 1824]

My dear Taylor

I wrote to Hessey a long while back when in a very bad & restless state respecting coming up to London but he never so much as noticd that letter—an old post horse when he has done all he can is laid bye   perhaps that is my case but I woud not willingly think so   however there is one comfort left me I am still in the land of the living & as experience is a wise teacher I may if I shoud recover get more knowledge among the mysterys of men——

I recievd a letter from Revd Mr Brooks° written as he says at your request   I cannot answer him at present but his views of religion are the same as mine   he appears to me an enlightend & what is far better a good man & I heartily thank him for his kindness tho I fear I shall neither be the one or the other for doubts & unbelief perplex me contin[u]aley & now I think seriously about an hereafter I am more troubld in my thoughts then I was before & I much fear that I shall never feel a sufficiency of faith to make me happy   the sincere & enthusiastic manners of the methodists in devotion puts my glimmering consience to shame—there is a preacher of the name of Blackley° comes in our circuit whose voice is just like your own   I never heard such a similarity in my life   I mean he preaches just in the tone & manner which you read in   it struck me the moment I heard him & seemd as if you was addressing me   he is a favourite of mine but the people dont think much of him   his persuasive tenderness of speech is not deep enough for them   they like shouting & ranting far better— he has been a printer & is a good scholar having a knowledge of several languages & likes to talk about books of which he has a general knowledge   I felt an affection for the man the moment I saw & heard him—Dr Skrimshire has been 4 or 5 times I dont know which but I am almost sure it is no more then 4   I have now done with him & perhaps it woud be as well settld   as to Mr Walker he was sent by Lady Milton at first & pretends that he sent in his bill to her & started on my account when Dr Skrimshire came   I have reflected on this & believe he had no business tho I have no desire to make a disturbance but he shall dress me no more for it looks like quackery & I woud as lieu have been without him as with him for I think he has managd the matter with Lady M. so as to injure me for she woud doubtless wonder why her assistance was not needed any longer   if I get well I shall sift the matter & serve him accordingly

I wish now to hear that the book is going on   its high time to start & I am satisfied there is enough & more then enough for a Vol   I shall wish to hear from you about it   I have been written to about a little Vol of descriptive Poems for childern in plain language without provincaliasms   I have not been able to answer it yet nor shall I agree further then that I am wi[lling] to attempt one but not to have my name to it [?unless] it be sanctiond by the public & then to be sure I shoud own it for when one trys to be simple one is apt to be silly & thats what I fear but its far out of my power at present to produce either exelence or folly—a poor fellow a farmers son° who thinks himself a poet & in that comfortable selfopinion has publishd a Vol: has written to me to use my interest for him & to tell him wether it woud be of use to send a copy to the Editor of your Magazine & they are such lifless things that I coud scarcly have patience with the mans egotism & self consiet he may do as he pleases with your Editor but he gets no favour from me I have long been troubld with these sort of gentry & am sick of them—lets hear how you think of the Calender for I want it out now as I feel a little revivd tho I know its not for long continuance for my head & feelings are as dead in apathy & my insides as sore & out of order nearly as bad as at first—what the complaint is god knows I do not I know one thing that I am very anxious to get better because I know when a family looses its father the provider is gone & I have a little consern about my fame because I think I can do better then I have done if I am sufferd to remain a little longer

yours &c &c &c
John Clare

To James Augustus Hessey

[19 May 1824]

My dear Hessey

I shall start on thursday morning with gods leave & tho I like the outside best I must go inside on account of my head for I fancy its worse since I wrote you I shall make use of the Draught for my coach fare & little expense on the road & bring up the rest my family are very loath to let me come but I have so great an opinion of Dr Darling that I must start tho I feel very difficult my self to encourage the resolution—as for Company I know not I do not feel a desire for company but what ever Dr D[arling] advises as the best that I shall be willing & anxious to do my desire is to get well I forgot to say that the 'Boston Coach' is the one I come by it goes to 'Snow hill' I think the

'Kings Arms' or 'Head'—their is one thing I feel a great antipathy against & that is noise nor can I bear merriment of any kind anything quiet & mellancholy suits me if I coud get my head right I shoud do for if I coud read or write or even remember what I have done or know & feel as my self I shoud do but to be in this walking dream is almost unbearable I am certain its somthing more then nervous that there is a portion of that likewise connected I can write no more this time | yours

&c &c

John Clare

To Henry Francis Cary

Helpstone Sep 18. [18]24

My dear Sir

As a friend of mine° has taken a journey to London I have taken the oppertunity of conveyance to write to you I am getting worse & worse & what my complaint is I cannot tell—I wrote to you before I left London but I know not wether you got it you mentiond a particular sort of school book° as the most suitable for childern when I was with you at Chiswick & as my eldest daughter is able to learn I am desirous of knowing what thoses books were which you reccomended & shoud be thankfull if you woud take the trouble to inform me

You must excuse this scrawl for I am ill able to write or do anything else I thought I was getting well° once but Ive not a hope left me now I have empolyd myself when able since I came home at writing my own life which if I live to finish it I shoud like to trouble you to read it & give your opinion of it for my own judgment in such matters is very often faulty your Life of Chatterton° turnd me to read his poems over seriously I was very often struck with remarkable passages & happy expressions did the reading strike you as such I hope in your lives of the Poets you will think of Bloomfield he is a great favourite of mine—Give my kindest remembrances to Mrs Carey & family I must end this letter for I can get no further my head is so stupid & my hand so feeble & trembling | I am

yours affectionatly

John Clare

To Henry Francis Cary

Helpstone Dec 30. 1824

My dear Sir

I shoud have written long ago if I had been able for I always feel a pleasure in writing to those I esteem but had I been well I shoud have had little to say worth reading for our parts are very barren of news I have not yet finished my life for like everything else I do I have left it unfinished but my former listlessnes has nothing to do with the present cause: I have been utterly unable to write or even read this 6 or 7 weeks my mind is numbd & dead like my body & my memory is broken but as soon as I am able I shall resume it as I feel anxious to finish it & I feel also anxious that you shoud see it & I shall be greatly obliged for your opinion of it as I mean if I live to publish it I have gotten 8 chapters done & have carried it up to the publication of the 'Poems on rural life' &c—I feel it rather awkard to mention names as there are some that I cannot speak well of that is were I feel an objection I cannot flatter over it & I woud not willingly offend anyone I have made free with myself & exposd my faults & failings without a wish to hide them neither do I care what is said about me but if you shoud see anything that might be against me in speaking of others I shall be thankful of your advice & also your remarks on the thing all together for it is written in a confusd stile & there will doubtless be found a deal of trifling in it for I am far from a close reasoner in prose & rather fall under the censure of Popes 'period of a mile'° when the thing is done my three Vols of Poems (& the Shepherds Calender if out) will accompany the parcel as trifling tokens of my esteem & a small recompence for the trouble given besides as a keep sake for remembrance for I seriously think & feel I shall not recover this stupid & stubborn complaint—I have not strung a dozen ryhmes since I was first taken & never shall any more I always feel as if I was dreaming & my legs & thighs will dye up to my body very often & when they come to themselves the sensation is as if they had been asleep—how is Mrs Carey & your family my wife & my youngest daughter has been very ill but the first is now well & the child is much better & to make up my list of calamitys the small pox is in the village & I am in daily expectance of some of them falling the eldest was innoculated for the cow pox but I fear it took no effect—we must abide by providence who by the bye appears but an indifferent obse[r]ver of troubles by times but we are not to play with destiny—I am anxious every month to see the continuation of your 'Lives of the Poets' & always meet dissapointment, for there is nothing so entertaining to me as the Biography of literary men—I met with a poem full of tender & touching passages a while back in a collection of Poems which was lent me calld 'Distress' written by a Robert Noyes° I suppose you have seen it there was some other very beautiful pieces in it of poets which must be familiar with the reading world tho they were strangers to me till now I was most pleasd with 'Lewesdon Hill' by Crow° the 'Four Seasons' by Brerewood° the 'Parish Clerk' by Vernon° a rather hard straind imitation by the bye of 'the Schoolmistress' A Song 'Dear Tom this brown jug' by Fawkes° a trifle sufficient to immortalize any one & a Sonnet on Goldsmith by Woty° there were a many more of merit in the Vol but my judgment led me astray to make choice of these—I have been also much pleasd with a poem calld 'Walks in a Forest'° & with some little things written by (I think) Greaves° particularly one entitld 'An Invitation to the featherd race' but why need I gossip over these names to you when doubtless they are all as familiar as the day—I know nothing of the new things of the day but when in London I was uncommonly pleasd with some passages in a Vol of poems written by [ ] L[aetitia] E[lizabeth] L[andon]° 'the Improvisatrice' &c but I am to [b]reaks the eighth commandment too often—a Vol of Poems by an A. A. Watts° was much spoken of by the reviews but I never saw it—I can always find more to say when I get at the end of my sheet & when I begin I often feel as if I had nothing to write about—give my kindest remembrances to Mrs Carey & family & whenever you have an hour to throw away a letter will give great pleasure to | yours sincerely & affectionatly

John Clare

P.S. I forget to tell you my present occupation when my illness alows me to join with any you woud not guess it—I have always had a great fondness for wild flowers—& I am now passionatly bent after collecting 'English Ferns' & whenever I am able I make journeys about the woods in the neighbourhood I have discoverd 8 sorts already about us

To his Children

A Letter of Advice to my Childern

[1824–5?]

My dear Childern

Before this meets your knowledge I may be unconsious of your welfare & the laughing schoolboy may be gathering the spring daisey from the sod that covers me with unconsious pleasure yet it matters not good counsil is always in season come when it will

To Edmund Tyrell Artis

[7 March 1825]

My dear Artis

How are you getting on nay I may be like the Irishman & ask were you are for I dont know were to find you nor know wether you are at London or York as I write at a venture & the purport of this is to beg your kindness to get a frank for the enclosed letter° if in case the pencil marks be rubbed out the Direction is to '*Mrs William Wright Clapham Surrey*' how are you getting on with your 'Fossil Plants' & 'Antiquitys' I have found some more fragments [of a Rom]an pot in Harrisons close near Oxey w[ood & a]m now convinced myself that there is som[e mo]re worth the trial one of the bits had the letter 'V' on it a mark of the potters I suppose I have saved them all for your inspection when you next come to Helpstone—have you been to see Hessey° I suspect you have as they have began printing the New Poems—lets hear from you—a little news of any sort is acceptable here—did you see the poem° in Montgomerys Iris I think you heard me talk of it when you was last here

I am dear Artis yours very sincerely
John Clare

To Joseph Weston

Helpstone March 7. 1825

Dear Sir

In answer to yours of the third I am sorry to say that I posses but little of the corespondence of my departed 'brother bard'° what I do posses you are welcome too & as to my letters to him you may do with them just as you please & make what use of them you like I deeply regret that ill health prevented our corespondence & that death prevented us from being better acquainted I sincerely loved the man & admired his Genius & had a strong anxiety to make a journey to spend a day with him on my second visit to London & I intended to have stopt at Biggleswade on my return home for that purpose but my purse got too near the bottom for a stoppage on the road & as it was too great a distance to walk home this with other matters prevented me from seeing him as one of my family was very ill at the same time & hastened my return—Whatever cause his friends may have to regret the death of the Poet—Fame is not one [of] them for he dyed ripe for immortality & had he written nothing else but 'Richard & Kate' that fine picture of Rural Life were sufficient to establish his name as the English Theocritus & the first of rural Bards in this country & as Fashion (that feeble substitute for Fame) had nothing to do in his exaltation its neglect will have nothing to affect his memory it is built on a more solid foundation & time will bring its own reward to the 'Farmers Boy'—I beg you will have the kindness to take *care of the M.S. & return it* when you have done with it as I wish to preserve a scrap of his handwriting—the Copy on the other side is a note which accompanied his present of 'Mayday with the Muses' I gave the origional to Allan Cunningham the Poet who has a high respect for Bloomfields genius & whose request on that account (to posses a scrap of his writing) I was proud & happy to gratifye—soon after the Poets death I wrote in a mellancholy feeling 3 Sonnets to his memory I was not aware that his 'Remains' woud have had such insertions or I shoud have sent them to his daughter—I shall fill this sheet with them for your perusal tho I expect they will come out in the Volume now in the press that will be published this Spring: with my best wishes that your kindly labours for the memory of the departed Poet may meet with the success it deserves | I remain yours very faithfully

John Clare

Three Sonnets on Bloomfield°

1.

Some feed on living fame with conscious pride
& in that gay ship popularity
They stem with painted oars the hollow tide
Proud of the noise which flatterys aids supply
Joind with to days sun gilded butterflye
The breed of fashion haughtily they ride
As tho her breath was immortality
Which are but bladder puffs of common air
Or water bubbles that are blown to dye
Let not their fancys think tis muses fare
While feeding on the publics gross supplye
Times wave rolls on—mortality must share
A mortals fate—& many a fame shall lye
A dead wreck on the shore of dark posterity

2.

Sweet unasuming Minstrel not to thee
The dazzling fashions of the day belong
Natures mild pictures field & cloud & tree
& quiet brooks far distant from the throng
In murmurs tender as the toiling bee
Make the sweet music of thy gentle song
Well, nature owns thee let the crowd pass bye
The tide of fashion is a stream too strong
For pastoral brooks that gently flow & sing
But nature is their source & earth & sky
Their annual offerings to her current bring
Thy injurd muse & memory need no sigh
For thine shall murmur on to many a spring
When their proud streams is summer burnt & dry

3.

The shepherd musing oer his meadow dreams
The mayday wild flowers in the summer grass
The sunshine sparkling in the valley streams
The singing ploughman & hay making lass
These live the summer of thy rural themes
Thy green memorials these & they surpass
The cobweb praise of fashion—every May
Shall find a native 'Giles' beside his plough
Joining the skylarks song at early day
& summer rustling in the ripened corn
Shall find thy rustic loves as sweet as now
Offering to Marys lips 'the brimming horn'
& seasons round thy humble grave shall be
Fond lingering pilgrims to remember thee.

To John Taylor

[The printing and publication of *The Shepherd's Calendar* had become a contentious issue, as delays continued and no proofs appeared. Taylor sent an irate letter on 18 Apr., setting out his side of the case, even suggesting that Clare might prefer to seek another publisher: 'At all Events it is better to terminate the Connection at once than to continue it in Distrust.—' The quarrel simmered on, and the volume did not appear until Apr. 1827.]

Helpstone May 5—[18]25

Dear Taylor

I delayed to answer your letter till a proof arived to prove that you had not forgotten the promise of sending one & getting on with the book but as nothing of that kind come I must write without it—I had hopes when I recieved your last that your resolves to get on with the poems were in earnest—it is not for the mere gratification of seeing it out that makes me urgent but it is for more substantial reasons which I shall not lengthen the letter to explain—for I am weary of writing or talking about my conserns—Anticipation is a pleasant feeling but it borders on dissapointment which is a very unpleasant one therefore I have waited & hoped for the best & as I hate offensive correspondence I pass over the unpleasant part of ours as well as I can I might be under a mistake & if so the feelings they excited woud be irritating yet I feel now that the negligence in getting out the poems woud make any one complain & whatever harm may come from complaining of matters that appear to claim no commendation I am sure no good can come from speaking in their praise—when I feel any thing I must speak it I know that my temper is hasty & with that knowledge of my self I always strive to choke it & soften hard opinions with reasonable interpretations—but put yourself in my place for a minute & see how you woud have felt & written yourself & if you feel that you shoud have acted otherwise then I will take it as an example & strive to correct my failings & be as perfect in an imperfect world as I can

I have no desire to seek another publisher neither do I believe any other woud do so well for me as you may do much less better but when obligation is sought or offered it sells the kindness therefore I will go no further on that head & if I did drawing comparisons from others woud not be adding praise if the complaints of authors are to be noticed & why shoud they not have cause for their lamentations as well as Jeremiah—all I have to say is that if you want to get out of the job of publishing my poems you may tell me so & I will seek another & trust to providence but if you have no desire to turn me adrift the speedy publication of my poems will gladly convince me that I was mistaken & I shall be happy to prove that you are my friend as usual—here with me ends the matter I shall say nothing further I dont like to write under such feelings & I wish to get out of them as soon as I can

I beg that miss Taylor will accept my kindest remembrances & I am heartily glad to hear that she recovers so much—as for my part I cannot get rid of my complaint at all it leaves me & returns again as virulent as ever last week I was much worse & this I am much better agen but I have little hopes it is not lasting I shall be very happy to recieve Mrs W. Wrights kind present of the flowers which she so readily assented to give me & will as gladly send her any thing that I posses in return I wish you woud tell her so—I dont think it woud be too late to send a sucker of the White Province Rose provided it were lapt up in wet moss & not kept on the journey the Tiger lily too woud not hurt if sent in the same manner moss keeps the wet like spunge & if this is not to be had fine hay well wetted woud do nearly as well I hope you will tell her as I have been expecting them this 3 weeks I shall send my flowers to her in Hendersons parcel to Milton House for I fear they will be too bulky for any other conveyance & not worth the expence of carriage

I will conclude with the hopes of seeing a proof [of] the Shepherds Calender in a few days—I told Hessey that I was ready to join the Young Lady° in writing the History of Birds but I have heard nothing about it & I have such a fear of my own inability to do any thing for such a matter that I cannot enter into it with any spirit as I find that I dont know half the Swimmers & Waders that inhabit the fens & I understand that there are a many of them strangers to the Natural History bookmakers themselves that have hithertoo written about it

I am dear Taylor your sincerely
John Clare

To James Augustus Hessey

July 7—1825

My dear Hessey

I recieved your letter of the 30 of June enclosing my sallari[e]s of £15 safe but in my letter to Taylor I told him that I shoud want £10 more then my half yearly dividend & therefore I was dissapointed in paying off my accounts as they exceed the present means so far as to make it useless to begin to settle them till I get a sufficient supply—so if Taylor thinks it impolitic to supply my present need I wish that he had said so for in that case I must make a breach on the principal some were or other but if he will let me have the £10 I shall feel obliged to him as I can get no further at present without such assistance—the proofs have grown into a standstill again I doubt I keep expecting them every day lately & am expecting on I feel very anxious to see the end of it & have strong hopes that I shall get paid for the dedication or I shall be curst mad if I am dissapointed—I shall always be glad to correspond with you & if the alterations°

between you & Taylor had made any difference in that much less broken it altogether I shoud have felt a great dissapointment but when business is out of the question you must not plead so often busy to get off with short letters for I like plenty of news & a sheet full tho I am not in the situation to demand it for tho I am not busy I am not able to get on with a long letter for I am very dull headed & very ill not far short of being as bad as I was this time last year with you & I am so far from my old assistance that I feel in a delicate situation of telling my complaints on paper too often tho Dr D[arling] always kindly bids me write him how I am when ever I feel worse which I have done several times since I wrote him last but I wait & wait to see if I get better & somtimes feeling or fancying I am so I delay it a little further my family are all pretty well just now   here comes the blank in my head & I sit gaping to see what I can say further—I can find little or nothing so I must give my remembrances to Mrs Hessey | & remain your debtor for a [   ] & better letter next time | yours sincerly

John Clare

To John Taylor

Helpston Sepr 15. 1825

My dear Taylor

I recieved a letter from friend Hessey last week saying that you had been very ill but I had not such an idea of its severity till my friend Emmerson° told me & I have taken the oppertunity to convey this letter by him (for himself & Mrs E[mmerson] has just been to helpstone to see me) to offer you my regret for what you have been suffering & to say that I am happy at your recovery   for I begin to feel a desolate sort of conviction that all my old friends will go off before me   two of them are gone & a third I find was very near departing but I hope I shall see you agen & that you will yet be able to give me another call at Helpstone & seek for fresh roman bricks & saxon castles   I am in no sort of feeling for letter writing but I coud not let this oppertunity slip of saying that 'auld lang syne' had not left such apathys with me as to make me forget her & her acquaintance tho I am almost weary of myself as well as the world & feel as if I shoud be glad when my time comes to join those that are gone—health is the root of happiness & like the plant called 'Barrenwort' it seldom produces a blossom   diseases spread such continual winters about it   I have been much better these last two months then I have ever been since I was first taken & the last prescriptions that I had from Dr Darling set me up as I had hoped in earnest   but this last five or six days I have been alarumd with fresh symtoms of that numbness & stupidness in the head & tightness of the skull as if it was hooped round like a barrel but it is only by times a few minutes & somtimes longer—I feel sorry the book has met with a fresh stoppage in its progress but I cannot complain further then feeling a regret for the cause & I hope that you will soon be able to proceed & I doubt not but that we shall both feel glad when it is done with

I cannot write further then wishing you to believe me my dear Taylor | your sincere friend & faithful servant

John Clare

give my remembrances to Dr Darling & Hes[sey] & all others that enquire after me—you will find my friend Emmerson a very sensible plain unaffected & unpretending man in fact I have found him just the sort of man that suits me & he has a large share of my confidence & esteem

To James Power

[Hessey warned Clare (22 Sept.) that Power would be writing 'to ask permission to publish one of your Songs, the Maid of Bromsgrove, which a Mr Barnett has set to music & has offered to him'. Hessey told Clare to ask for 5 guineas at the least. Power sent Clare £2.]

Helpston Sepr. 24 1825

Dear Sir

I hasten to answer your letter of the 22nd to tell you I have no objections to what you require in publishing my words to the music which the gentlman has set to them but as I have always recieved a trifle for such permission for those that have been already put to music before & as my circumstances make such acknowledgements however small very acceptable I cannot give them away for nothing lest I may forfiet by such permissions any benefits that may arise in future from such publications & this is the only reason in the present instance why I require a remuneration for such permission for I am convinced that the setting any Song to good music from a Volm. of Poems goes a great way to make the book popular. & to convince you that no other is my object for asking it then what I have above stated I will leave the remuneration to be just what you think proper to give & as I do not attach a great value to such things a trifle will be thankfully recieved by | yours respectfully

John Clare

To James Augustus Hessey

Helpstone Decr 8. 1825

My dear Hessey

I write to you earlier perhaps then I shoud have done (tho not earlier then I ought to do perhaps) to know if Taylor has retur[n]ed from the country for I think him very long & am all anxiety to hear of him—I told Mrs E[mmerson] to get Mr E to call at Waterloo Place to hear if he was returned so that I might write to him but I have heard nothing from her so that I am at a stand still I am uncommonly troubled about getting out the book & shoud like to hear how he is getting on with it & when it will be ready—if Mrs E makes any thing more of her errand for I know she is rather full of officiousness I wish it to be understood that I did not say any thing further then what I have above written I do not like to be worried myself & I do not like that others shoud be worried either where I am the cause so I wish you woud tell me as I may write to him or else tell him that I may hear from him I have got a great deal to say & a great deal of lumber for his inspection as I shoud like nothing better then what you propose in letting him see all I write—but hither too his carlessness has been so excessive that it woud be of no use what ever for the things that I did send up for his opinion I never heard of afterwards not even a word of good bad or indifferent—I wish he woud shake off this lethargy he coud do me a great service with but little trouble to himself if he chose as I can find no bodys judgment so agreable to my fancys as his own but 'words are idle' & if I was to send up Magazine articles for his opinion they woud be thrown bye & forgotten so I must jog on with my own taste as well as I can but I dont think I shall trouble the 'European Magazine'° much more with my contributions as the pay is but poor & the insertion very uncertain as to the Poetical Almanacks they may all go to Hell next year for me for I can get nothing by them & my contributions are so mutilated that I do not know them again—the 'Ballad' in the 'Souvenir' I will send up to you as I wrote it at least to Taylor & then he may see the *improvements*°—I shoud not have written for such matters at all for I do not like it but nessesitys has troubled me so terribly that I thought I woud do somthing to get out of them if I coud & many of my friends held out such profitable reprenstations of them that I was tempted to try & the result is that my hopes are broken & I am as deep in nessesity as ever nobody pays half so well for pereodical trifles as you & Taylor did & I find its a useless barter for profit but I was glad of trifles for it payed for my medicines of which I take a great many this leads me to my illness I am somthing better since I wrote Dr Darling whose prescriptions I find now [give] me instant benefit in a far different & more direct manner then they did when in London for which I cannot account why or werefore the reason—I feel now I owe to Dr Darling my present existance & I am grown into such a stubborn opinion of his skill that I can believe in none other in fact they are very poor creatures here & I make no doubt kill as many or more then they cure & I feel now that they woud have speedily done for me had I not met with a better remedy—give Taylor & Dr Darling my kindest remembrances & tell Taylor of my anxious expectings about the 'Shepherds Calender'—my youngest girl is very ill alarmingly so & I am very uneasy in consequence—give my respects to all enquiring friends—I am glad you liked the Gipsey Song & the Popularity I have some other things scattered about in different pereodicals that I shall acquaint Taylor with bye & bye as I fancy they are among the best I have written

I am yours very sincerely
John Clare

To John Taylor

Helpstone Decr 19—[18]25

My dear Taylor

You & I are such strangers now that I hardly know wether I may write to you or not I did write to Hessey a few days back to enquire if you was got home but I got no answer in return & since then Mrs Emmerson has told me that Mr E[mmerson] has seen you & her account of you has much pleased me tho I do not like that any one shoud forestall me in my intentions° I did neither wish nor authorise him to make any further inquireys then about your being at home that I might write to you & if I knew that any other use was made of my desires I shoud be mad I like Mr E. very much but Mrs E. is too intriguing in her friendships & dwells too much on show & effect to make me feel that it is not one of the first value neither do I admire her opinions & judgments often for they are of the same kind & if I loose by the openess of my opinions I must generally speak as I think—with you I have nothing to find fault with but your delays & seeming neglects for I must confess that they not only injure my temper but hurt my mind very often but I hope that we shall become better correspondents & that your health will be the cause of better dispatch in getting out my poems for I often fancy that it is a burthen to you & that notion makes me loath to trouble you with things that I am obliged to trust to the judgment of others who mangle & spoil them very often & the Ballad that I wrote to the 'Souvenir' is so polished & altered that I did not scarcly know it was my own I shall trouble you with a copy of it just as I wrote it I feel a disgust to write for such things but I did it for the sake of making a little money which is so little that I shall not attempt to get it by writing for such things agen if I remain in the same mind I am in now as to the European Magazine they only give 12s/6 a page but the[y] promise better pay after awhile—will you correct my things for me for the Magazine—I attempted to venture in prose there & they tell me such favourable opinions of it that I shall venture agen it was not written for the Magazine it was an episode taken from the Life I am now writing of myself which is not yet done to my mind tho I have taken great pains—I often think that 'Essays' upon common every day matters & things of Life m[a]y take I feel very anxious to expose the cant & humbug of the days fashions & opinions but I am unable now to do any thing for I have been uncommonly ill agen & am very little better now I feel so very stupid & chill & cannot get out of the house for exescise—I shall want my sallaries as soon as I can get the[m] & I almost feel afraid to tell you w[hat] I want besides for I shall need as much mo[re as] they to get me descent if not straight with my creditors but if the 'Poems' had been out I shoud have been able to have done without any at least I think so—I shall feel very anxious to hear from you & to hear that the proofs are coming for I feel as if I was writing to a stranger & a patron & am almost in an uneasy suspence as tho my hopes might fail of success for you have been in my memory so often that you are almost [never] forgotten excuse this scrawling letter in lieu of a better & believe me my dear Taylor | yours very sincerely & affectionatly

John Clare

let me hear from you quickly I have gotten to tell you about some things that I have written in different pereodicals latterly under feigned names & what I have done for other matters but I leave it for another letter as I woud not wish to trouble you for your opinion about them if I did not think you woud be interested in knowing of them

yours &c &c

J. Clare

To John Taylor

[The delays over *The Shepherd's Calendar* continued. Taylor reacted to Clare's promptings with indignant fury, refusing any more to take the blame: 'I must now frankly tell you, that for the principal part of the Delay & for the present total Stop again, you are alone responsible.' The MSS were illegible, the poetry feeble; 'July' was particularly hopeless. Clare refused to 'continue this paper war', and mollified Taylor by sending a revised version of 'July'.]

Helpstone Jany. 24. 1826

My dear Taylor

I am very much aggitated & alarmed at your long silence & delay with my earnest applications for the £15 which I am in wants of directly & must have from somewere or other therefore if I do not hear from you on or by Sunday I must be under the nessesity of writing to Mr Emmerson to request him to lend it me till I am able to do somthing to get it myself—really I cannot wear my patience for such expectations for promises of this kind are like lawsuits in Chancery tho I dont say that you feel that they are so—so keenly as I do because you have so many things in town to attract you[r] attention while mine has nothing but one point to look at every day till the same repetitions make me half mad with additional dissapointments—I hope you will write to me to say wether or not you will send me the money & I shall then know what I must do—I have recieved a very pleasing letter from Miss Kent° & I shall answer it as quickly as possible & give her all the information about birds that I know of for I have abandoned my own intentions of writing about them myself as I think she will be able to make a much better work of them then I shoud—I think I shall not be long before I see London agen for I cannot rest here with such delays & cross purposes that keep continually upsetting me for I cannot hear a word from any body scarcely—I am all anxiety about the book tho I almost fancy now it will never come out at all the words that have been spent about it are idle ones & proves that promises & performances are not near neighbours by a wide difference but I will end this letter as I have nothing further to say then an anxious request that you will write to me—I am just going to Milton for a few days were I shall write to Miss Kent

I am yours very sincerly
John Clare

To Edward Villiers Rippingille

Helpstone May 14. 1826

My dear Rip

I have thought of you the oftener for not writing to you the sooner & my reason for not writing was to see how matters would turn out with me for I thought of coming to London this Spring & then if I did not meet you there I hoped to get to Bristol° if possible but I have now gave up all thoughts of going to London or any where else this time so I have laid my old hulk up into winter quarters till a better oppertunity occurs & the moment I found what my destiny was I sat down & wrote to you—so I must haste to tell you that I shall be more then happy to see you here & that you shall be heartily welcome to such providence as you find & that is a poor mans welcome & if you do come (for I think you had not the humbug about you when you wrote it to say one thing & mean another) to prevent dissapointments I will describe the spot & the sort of company & cheer you will meet with here with us—you know of our scenery our highest hills are molehills & our best rocks are the edges of stonepits yet we have a many woods on one hand & a many nightingales but no Chloes or Phillises worth the mention we have brooks & wild bowers for Poets but no piping shepherds 'the walls of Jerusalem are desolate' of these pastoral beautys—the village itself is a 'dead letter' in life it is a large straggling place for a village but there is nothing in it of character the 'better sort' that imagine themselves gentry are dull money getting panders ignorant of the world & all that constitutes its glory genius & talent & merit are greek words to them the men of greatest merit in their eye is those that have strength to do the most work & can keep from troubling the Parish the longest—as to books they know as much about them as I do about the Talmud or the Koran they are exactly what Goldsmith fancied the Dutch to be 'Dull as their lakes that slumber in a storm'°—now if you think you can keep away the 'bluedevils' & the other humbugs of misery in these terribles & can drop your spirit into so low a mood as to venture to visit a brother poet not in a Pallace on Parnassus but in a Hut two storys high whose top windows you may reach with your walking stick & whose door you cannot enter without stooping whose chimney corner is open to the sky where the sut falls plentifully to remind me of storms & the storms pepper me so teazingly betimes as to make me wish for better shelter even in a hovel now if you can stoop your mind to these reallitys come & see me I have a snug cupboard of Books to amuse you & very pleasant walks in the fields & a Public house next door to kill time where they keep tollerable Ale & where I can procure you a clean lodging if not a handsome Landlady & where I can promise that you shall steer clear of the Itch & London Bugs let what else will betide you & I am sure Patty will be as happy to see you as my self—my Study is not thronged with the Muses but with the melodious mischief of 3 Childern & my Pastoral Mistress is on the eve of bringing another into the world to add to the Band which is looked for every day° I shall like you to come here about the beginning of August as the scenery is then in its greatest beauty the fields will be alive with harvest & the Rides through the Woods will be left to quiet & the lovers of Solitude as will the Heaths & all my favourite places for I shall like to show you my favourite haunts when you do come—at my back door I have a little garden which I cram with Flowers for I am foolishly fond of them & am now ambitiously striving to be a Florist tho with but little success at present now I think I have told you sufficient so come & find out the rest yourself & besure let me know wether you really will come or not—I have been doing little or nothing latterly save a few odd things for Magazines for Taylors neglect in not getting out my book makes me very heedless about ryhming I have nearly finished my life having brought it down as far as our last visit to London & as soon as its done I think of offering it for sale°—I attempted an Essay in prose sometime back which was published in the 'European Magazine' & thought very well of—it was on 'Pop[ularit]y in Authorship' did you ever see it—I think of writing a series of such things after awhile & have a many more projects in my head which would be of little interest in telling you of what may never be done—how is it that you seem to be so out of humour with the world & your bretheren the Painters is it because you could not get the first letter in the Alphabet for a title I should think not I do not like to appear to flatter any one but by g–d I cannot help saying that I would sooner possess such merit in painting as I think your own possesses then have all the tagrags & flourishes at the end of mine the 'As' & 'R.A's' & 'F.R.S's' & G.L.S's & all such humbugs as Cant & fashion has created—it would seem very droll & unnatural to me to see 'E. V. Rippingille R.A'—Royal 'A's' must rot as well as Royal carcasses but merit will live with eternity let fashions prate & flatter as they may—they are but so many flies teazing the sunshine of summer for a season & to regard them as any thing more then such trifles is doing them too much service—Silks & Maoganys° will dye their natural deaths after awhile & may do for shrowds & coffins for their admirers when they are found good for nothing else but I have chatted along while & must prepare to bid you farewell write to me whenever you get an oppertunity & believe me my dear Rippingille | yours very sincerely & affectionatly

John Clare

P.S. you never mentioned Elton° in your letter how is he & where is he if you know remember me to him & dont forget

To John Taylor

Helpstone July 15. 1826

My dear Taylor

I hasten to acknowledge the reciept of the £20 Check & thank you very kindly for sending it down so speedily I will see if I can do without the £5 more & if I can I shall feel very happy in not having to trouble you further but if I cannot I must—I do assure you that I live as near as ever I can & tho I did not tell you I have been out to hard labour most part of this summer on purpose to help out my matters but the price of labour is so low here that it is little better then parish relief to the poor man who where there is a large family is litterally pining I know not what will be the end of these times for half the Farmers here will be broken again this dry summer & I think that low rents & no taxes is the only way to recall a portion of their former prosperity but I am no Politician & know little or nothing about such matters

I have not gotten any tale by me of any sort to send you but I am very willing to have the Magazine Poems inserted & like the idea much & if there is not room for all of them you may take which you think best but I must have one opinion in the Pye if youll alow it & that is I shall like to see the 'Superstitions Dream' in for one & I think it would be better to call it there simply '*The Dream*' you know better when to publish the Vol better then I do & I shall leave it wholly to you but I shall thank you for a copy for the Marquis as soon as you can send me one & I should like it very plainly bound with very little gilt on it he ordered me to send him 10 Copys but I think they should not be sent untill it is Published—I have often tryed at a Dedication for him & cannot get one to my mind I want one simply honest & out of the beaten track of fulsome dedications one very short & very plain & I think if I set it down here in my own way you will soon make one out by it properly in your own I want somthing in this way I expect I must call him noble—To the Most Noble the Marquis of Exeter these Poems are Dedicated in remembrance of unmerrited kindness by his Lordships faithful servant the Author' or 'John Clare' as you please—I dont like to puff nor I dont like to flatter so if you dont like it put a simple straight forward thing down in your own way—Drury has not sent me his Bill° he only hints demands of payment from me & speaks as if he was not far from troubling me for it but I know now he cannot I saw the Bill at his shop some years back & told him then that it was extravagant but I cannot say as to what it was now he took hold of every oppertunity to get me in his books & then made a boast of it I shall tell you a few facts in explanation of what I have said in another letter as to its extravagant 'Notchings on' & then you can judge yourself as I wish to reserve all the room here for other things I am very pleased with your idea of 'Visits of the early Muses' as a Title for my *old* Poems & shall keep adding to the number as I feel inclined & I shall not publish any more of them in pereodicals now you have past your opinion of them so favourably for I only did it to try the opinion of those which I thought superior to mine but I am greatly at a loss for the want of seeing some of the Best pieces of the old Poets I have a Copy of Spencers Poems & Cowleys Poems lent me by a friend but I wade about them untill Im weary & my mind cannot rest to feel their best spirit & manner but when I see their best selected by others I take it for granted that it is their best & muse over it till a thought strikes me how to proceed—I should have liked to have seen these old poems at the end of my present volume but I like your title so well that I will reserve them all for a future volume as you suggest & shall send you them up from time to time as I write them which will be but very slowly as I feel anxious and almost certain that they are to be my best the Winter is my best time for them for I can sit in my corner in the long evenings when the childern are all abed in peace which I cannot do now I am sorry you have troubled yourself so much to procure 'Ellis's

Specimens' for I dont suppose you can readily meet with it I sent to the Library at P[eterborough] for to Borrow it but they had it not tho they kindly sent a Vol of Specimens by Campbell instead it is a new work & by Campbell the poet I fancy but I dont like it much as the Specimens dont seem to be selected for their exellence often but for their novelty in not being collected by other editors & this would mislead me—I will get Henderson to have a good hunt in the old Library at Milton the next time I go & perhaps he may succeed in finding somthing useful there & if he can I can have it & replace it before they return—give my respects to Hessey & all friends & believe me my dear Taylor | yours very sincerely

John Clare

To Henry Behnes

Stamford July 23. 1827

My dear Behnes

You performed the task I imposed on you of delivering my letters so speedily that I feel tempted to indulge in giving you the additional trouble of transmitting a greater number of letters to the care of friend Franks° parcel for your kind delivery but I have not the time to do so for Frank is determined to send off your parcel to day & I am with him scribbling away to you as fast as I can for if I wait for the inspiration of pointed sentences & witty thoughts you will not have a letter from me this fortnight at least so excuse all together—I have accompanied F.s beautiful Drawing of our Cross with a trifling trifle the best that the spur of the moment alowed me—to do somthing towards fulfilling your request I wish for Franks sake & my own that it were better—I thank you kindly for the Toys sent to my childern as nothing could please them better then the 'Village' & 'The Huzzars' but I fear my little trooper will make as great havoc with them bye & bye as they met with at Waterloo—I am very happy that you have found out VanDyk° for me for he is a friend that I heart[i]ly esteem tho his late absence does not deserve it yet I will write to him to know the cause of it the first oppertunity—I recieved Mrs Emmersons letter safely & if I cannot get time to write while here at Stamford I will trouble you in the meantime to give her my kindest remembrances for I need not tell her of the pleasure it gave me in hearing from her in so unexpected a manner by your conveyance to Frank—I will strive all I can to take your advice but I have an awkard timidity about me that will not & cannot wear or grow out of my nature I have a passionate fondness for Solitude & would much rather avoid then court the notice of my superiors when I say superiors I mean men of titles wealth & fashion with nothing or little of impartial feeling towards an inferior who wants all three of these grand matters to reccommend him to their notice the proudest feelings I posses in becoming known to the world arise from the lucky accidents that introduce me to men of genius these I consider the most fortunate incidents of my life & I would always as I have done strive to gain the notice & esteem of such men & under that feeling I indulge in the desire of becoming a regular correspondent with yourself & I hope you will not construe that desire into either flattery or compliment—for I am proud (& it is the only pride I possess) to think I have not that shallowness of feeling about me to possess neither the one or the other

I think you will be delighted with Octaves Drawing° it is well done & the first sight of it realy astonished me for I had no idea of his doing such things in the style & manner he has done it—I fear I am tireing you with my disjointed Epistle so give my kindest remembrances to your Brother | & believe me my Dear H. Behnes your very affectionate Friend

John Clare

To John Taylor

Helpstone August 20 1827

My dear Taylor

I recieved the Five Pounds safe & take much discredit to myself in not writing to say so before but I have not had much time untill this wet Day—I feel much hurt at the odd conduct of the Marquis° for he still remains as silent as ever & all the money I have gotten for the 30 Copies is £1 19s 6d I have calculated it up & that is the truth & an agravating truth to me it is I am sorry too that I should have been forced to ask you for money but urgent nessesity forced me & I could not help it & I feel very dissapointed at the bad sale of the new Poems° but I cannot help it if the public will not read ryhmes they must still read Colbourns Novels° until they are weary for he will never be weary of being a quack & puffer till he gains by it—to tell them what they ought to think of poetry would be as vain I fear as telling the blind to see the age of Taste is in dotage & grown old in its youth—as to the Accounts I am sorry I have so overshot them but I am sure I have never been extravagant but on the contrary kept striving & fancying I was illustrating the annals of thrift & keeping within bounds & I hope for your sake that the Poems may turn the tide & sell better for Novels & such rubbish were in as bad repute once as Poetry now & may be again as matters turn out I dare hardly remind you of an old promise much less request a new one however I must tell you that I never recieved the 4 copies each of my Poems which you told me you intended sending along time ago if you did I never recieved them & as I am at a stand still from writing to a Friend or two which I cannot make up my mind to do without accompanying them with the Poems I should feel greatly obliged to your kindness if you would do me this favour—Darleys Play° I make no doubt is a good one & I shall feel anxious for its publication & happy at his success for I esteem him both as an Author a Poet & a Friend tho I almost fear that the paradoxical truths of Mathematics will do somthing [? flat]tening the visions of Fancy but perh[aps] they may sharpen it—I shall write to [ ] directly I recieved the letters from him when I had not the power to reply & worldly vexations often take the advantage of time to damp the spirit & obliterate the early feelings of friendship for when I think of days gone bye & the hearts that are cold some in the world & some in the dust & every other assosiation connected with them I am often affected even to tears give my best regards to Darley &

believe me my dear Taylor | yours very sincerely

John Clare

To Peter De Wint

Helpstone [14] Octr 1827

My dear Dewint

You will be supprised perhaps to meet with this but I have determined on the matter ever since the New Poems were published & that is to give you my thanks on paper for your kindness in drawing the Frontispiece for my new Vol & I hope a time is not very distant when I shall be able to thank you personaly it is a very beautiful thing the figures are well grouped & the maiden with the face fronting is a beauty but the bottle in the reapers hand is too big for the company in fact it appears too big for a bottle at all in my eye but thats perhaps its own fault & not the bottles I think the engraving is done uncommonly well & that altogether it posseses attractions that aught to have pushed the book into a good sale but I heard from Taylor a good while back that the contrary was the fact & that comparitively speaking it did not sell at all & turn out in the end as it may we cannot help it I am sure its dress is sufficient to win even the hearts of the Muses tho they scouted the rest but ryhmes is gone or going out of fashion for a season & Mr Colbourns Novels by new unknowns & little great knowns coming in—so bye & bye its to be hoped things will come round agen—I had intended to have accompanied this with a Vol for Miss Dewint but thinking it would be scarcely worth the cost when at the end of its journey I desisted till a better oppertunity offered to send it a cheaper way & I ought to have said at first what I have left unexplaind till now which is the reason for my not thanking you sooner & that was occasioned by my waiting in hopes of getting a frank but the Milton family have been out all the summer & have not yet returned so you must excuse the postage—how is friend Hilton he has been in a rare way with his painting latterly if accounts be true & it seems that the scriptures have showered on him some fat benedictions for his conversion from the heathens which are as good perhaps as fat livings to the clergy tho efeth they may not be so certain of durability—I have seen mighty praises of his Picture for a Church at Liverpool° in our papers & I expect bye & bye that the next news is of his being a Sir William of the Academy well I heartily wish him more luck then he has met with & more luck then that give him my kindest remembrances as also to Mrs Dewint & your daughter & as I have nothing in the way of news to fill up the sheet I will leave it & save you the trouble of reading my scribbling trifling further then that I beg to remain my dear Dewint | yours very sincerely

John Clare

To Henry Francis Cary

Helpstone Novr 4 1827

My dear Sir

I was pleasantly informed by Taylor that you told him I was two letters in your debt I was heartily happy to hear that you still remembered me & I was glad for my own credit that you had made a mistake for I am but one as I answered every letter but your last which illness made me neglect so long till I was almost ashamed to reply & before I go any further let me give my kindest remembrances to Mrs Cary as a step towards good manners is a step towards amendment & I am sure it is good manners & amendment both to seize the first oppertunity given to remember those we esteem after so long silence but I ought to have known before I got so far that self-praise is no reccommendation so I will go on Taylor told me a long while ago (for he writes seldomer then I have done latterly) that a direction to the British Museum° would find you but gave no other reason so wether it will find you there now I cannot tell I hope it will however

I think my new Poems has been published since I heard from you & I should like to know how you like them if you have seen them & if not I shall feel great pleasure in begging your acceptance of a copy—your opinion will do me a service & therefore I hope you will tell me what you think of them—the things that I am attempting now are I fear only attempts after the manner of the olden Bards in the reign of Elizabeth & the Muses I have not done much but one of the things has gained me an high compliment from Montgomery the Poet for I dare hardly believe that I merit it as praise tho I feel its value & hope that it will stimulate me to further exertions that shall better deserve it

I am often very anxious to know how you proceed with your 'Lives of the Poets' & think it long ere it makes its appearance for it is a work much wanted & I was so pleased with those that appeared in the 'London Magazine' that they were generally the first things I looked in & they always left me a stronger desire to see them continued in the next number then any thing else connected with it & I heartily hope you have not given them up—Mr A. A. Watts is going to publish a series of the living ones° & those latterly deceased which has been advertised so long as in a state of forwardness that almost makes me fancy it will never come forward at all but the bankruptcy of his Booksellers° I believe extended the delay further then he anticipated

I have latterly read a good deal of Darwins poetry° & I am astonished to think why he is neglected so much for I am sure there is passages of uncommon harmony & beauty in them particularly his descriptions of nature or scenery more properly speaking—& I am highly pleased with them tho I am no Critic & my judgment goes no further then being pleased in itself not having the confidence to feel what is likely to please others—I think many Poets only want to be more known to be more esteemed & admired & that the neglect is only owing to the Publics finding no path that leads to their beautys—it is something like the case of the 'Sleeping Beauty' that had remained so long unknown in her pallace of Solitude that the paths which led to it were all choaked up & over grown with trees & brushwood that took the knight errant even a number of years to cut them down ere he could get at his prize & break the spell of solitude that bound her beauty in its almost impenetrable veil—I think it is so with once popular poets they only want to be known agen to be esteemed dont you think so & if it is so I [am] sure you will feel a pleasure equal to the labour in bring[ing] them again under public notice in your Lives of them—Let me hear from you as soon as it will give you pleasure to write for I feel Ive no room to claim of you a quick reply & I am sure it will be a great pleasure for me to recieve it at any time tho I must say the sooner the better—I ought to have said ere I ended that I have waited much longer then I intended

for a Frank & am now obliged to send it without one so I hope you will excuse the postage | & believe me My dear Sir | yours very sincerely & affectionately
John Clare

To Henry Behnes

Helpstone, Decr 30 [1827] Sunday

My dear Behnes

I did indeed think you was lost to us totaly if not to the rest of the world for I could not hear a word about you from any where or any body & now I met your letter I fancied I was going to be edified with a Sermon instead of being amused with an Epistle of gossip the only Epistles I like & I am glad that I have been gratified in both matters & am only sorry that I cannot make you a better return then this dull scrawl of mine for I live in a nook of the world where it is next door to living out of it where any occurrence of literary News is as scarce as a Famine—but what has left you in distress is it illness or what is ten times worse hypochondrical imaganings what we call here the 'Horrors' & 'Bluedevils' be as it may you went to the right book for a cure for after all it is the best I have been reading 'Job' myself this winter & 'Solomons Song' both of which I have been uncommonly struck with the simple sublimity of the poetry is more then beautiful tho in some parts I confess I have been puzzled wether or not I should call them beautys or b[l]emishes of such is the following conclusion of a sublime sentence—'Who can number the clouds in wisdom or who can stay the *bottles* of heaven' Job but to turn critic in such matter would only be 'Multiplying words without knowledge' such as the following are the essence of sublimity & beautiful simplicity—'With God is terrible majesty'—'His eyes are like the eyelids of the morning'—'He esteemeth iron as straw & brass as rotten wood'—'Darts are counted as stubble he laugheth at the shaking of a spear'—'Upon earth there is not his like who is made without fear' but we may have too much of a good thing so I will stop yet I know of nothing in point of Poetry after the Bible that is so worthy of being placed by its side as Shakspear they are two books that I think I should first snatch up from a fine gilt & lettered library in the last conflagration if I had the power—I do assure you that if days had had the power of speaking & also of knowing my thoughts they would often have whispered in your ear that you was not forgotten at Helpstone or at Stamford either I agree with you that the old country custom of 'how do' & a shake by the hand altho on paper is heart stirring & comfortable friendship in fact it is friendships 'peace offering' & sign like a free masons but more openly & hearty—Patty is not well but what she aileth I cannot say tho I hope it is nothing worse then a cold my Father & Mother are well & my Childern all noising round me in bustling happiness & Fred & John are bowling you[r] kind presents about the floor with more noise then fair Play while Anna & Eliza are aranging their domestic minatures in more order & less noise & I will put their thanks all under my Pens point together which are as hearty & sincere as mine Patty also desires to thank you kindly for your kind attentions to her tho it had the misfortune as friend Frank tells me to be broke in the Parcel & in fact it gave proofs of its 'waste of sweetness' for the Parcel was so perfumed that I could not tell what was the cause of the insence untill I read Fs letter & the Box of Utensils was very much injured by the crush° but how I cannot tell & now it comes to my turn to thank you & that very kindly for the Almanack & our fair friends 3 Songs° 'The Red Rose of England' is good as is the Nightingale tho the first is best & the 'Chickweed for birds' is worst in fact I like not those popular theatricals whose fame is a claping from the pit & whose life a nine nights [?wonder] in a play house the 'Buy a broom' & the 'Cherry ripe' are nothing in my taste & to judge of the Music I cannot for we have no musical ladys at Helpstone & if I take them to Stamford I shall not be able to hear their best for our friend Miss Simpson is far from a Nightingale in fact she has no voice at all but she plays well—give my remembrance to Mrs E[mmerson] if you see her before I write—& I had forgot to thank you for the interesting account of a brother Poet in the Table book° poor fellow he is deserving of better luck but there is many a Milhouse 'wasting his sweetness in the desert air' at this moment in fact they cannot make room thro the many to be heard there is so many of us that waiting for a turn to be heard is like waiting in Chancery for the coming on of a cause—what is your Poetical friend doing I was much pleased with one of his Poems in the Ladys Album & wish him success—your kindness in offering me the perusal of the 'Examiner' is more attention then I dare believe my early acquaintance deserves altho I cannot help accepting it & if directed for me thus will besure to find me. 'J. Clare Helpstone near M Deeping' when I will preserve them & send them back with every oppertunity that offers   the paper I know is one of great merit in literary matters & thats enough for me—I have not forgot the Orchises but have often wondered wether you realy wished for them or wether it was a compliment to my fondness for them by expressing a fondness for them also—you shall have them as soon as the first will suffer a removal   I will send you the 'Flye' 'Bee' & 'Spider' with an account of the soil that suits each sort—& now let me remind you of your promise which I have not forgotten either & that is that you would make me a sketch of our friend E[liza] L[ouisa] E[mmerson] do you remember—my paper is now growing to a conclusion & my news is grown out already—so I will fill it up with some little matters conscerning self & in the first place I am very unwell & what ails me I know not but my head is horribly afflicted with a stupid vacancy & numbness that is worse then hell itself & I have done to the uttmost of my malady to write thus far without flinching for if one is ever so ill it is a pleasing task to write to a friend & I have felt pleasure at every step till I hoped to lay down my pen in health but its no use for the horrors are upon me & will have their will or humour out before they leave me   I have not yet seen or wrote to Friend Simpson tho I hope to do so to morrow

I am my dear Behnes yours very sincerely
John Clare

To Patty Clare

[Clare's health had been failing for some time, and in Feb. he went to stay with Mrs Emmerson in London. He did not return home until the beginning of Apr. 1828.]

20 Stratford Place | Oxford Street | London | [25 February 1828]

My dear Patty

According to promise I write to you today to tell you that I got up safe to London & that as you know I am now at my good

Friend Mrs Emmersons & I have not been any where else as yet

But I ought first to have asked you how you are I hope you are better then I fancy you are & how is my dear childern—my Anna—Eliza Frederick & John kiss all & each of them for me & tell them I shall not forget my promises of their little books &c when I return Mrs Emmerson desires her kindest remembrances to you & the childern & their grand father & grandmother Mr Emmersons Docter a Mr Ward told me last night that there was little or nothing the matter with me & yet I got no sleep the whole of last night but I hope for better success to night I have as yet taken no medicine & perhaps I shall not but I shall most likly see Dr Darling befor long for satisfaction & I think I shall go to Taylors tomorrow I shall not trouble you with a long letter but merely desire my remembrances to Baxter & Royce° & to you all make your self perfectly easy on my account tho I cannot exactly feel so on your own for I am in the midst of my best friends & if kindness & friendship can make me better I shall come home well where I shall hope to find you well but if that cannot [be] Gods will be done & not mine but well or ill I am my dear Patty | yours sincerely & affectionatly

John Clare

To William Hone

[In June 1825 Clare had written to Hone, under the pseudonym James Gilderoy (the famous Scottish highwayman), sending a poem purporting to be by Marvell; the poem was published in Hone's *Every-day Book*. Another attempt at deception ('Farewell & Defiance to Love'), sent under the name of Frederic Roberts (the name of a servant at Milton Hall), failed to impress Hone, but it appeared, unsigned, in the *European Magazine*. Although there seems to be no extant reply from Hone to this letter, Clare's library contains a copy of *A Tale of a Tub*, presented by Hone on 2 Mar. 1828.]

20 Stratford Place Oxford Street. [29 February 1828]

My dear Sir

I hope you will excuse my troubling you with this letter the reason why I write it is that a Lady a Friend of mine° has in her possesion 2 letters which I addressed to you for the Every day Book one of which the 'Helpstone Statute' was never inserted & the reason why I thought you would not insert it was that you thought it not worth it therefore I took no notice as I would not set my face against your judgment   but if I understand right another reason for which there was no foundation was that you thought it a forgery & what is a heavier charge a *Plagerism* & that you thought that you had read it in an old Magazine   I say that you thought so tho' it was asserted positively that you had read it but as that was impossible & such a positive lie I will not believe that you ever did say so for it was from an admiration of you[r] honest & independant integrity as a man & you[r] talents as an Author that I attempted to assist your entertaining Work with my trifles & tho I felt the desire to do so stronger then the ability to accomplish it yet my sincerity was real & I feel now that I ought to tell you that the doubtful Poem in question was wholly my own both its defects & merits (if it had any)   I did attempt to decieve you in one instance or two which I was gratified to find won your approbation but it was far different to the one of which I was accused & rather then take another persons writings to insert under my name I sent them under the name of another & that might be the means of winning half your praise of which I do assure you I had the vanity to feel proud one of the Poems so sent was entitled 'Death' & offered you as the production of the honest & illustrious Marvel for which offence & blasphemey to his genius I humbly crave pardon tho it won from you more praise that I dare feel that it derseved to meet with before I sent it so I was pleasantly dissapointed—I told you I think that I found it in a Vol of the Spalding Society of Antiquarians & if I mistake not I fatherd that lie on an imaganery personage whom I identified as being a John or James Gilderoy of Surfleet Lincolnshire   another which you did not insert was sent as from F. Roberts of Milton with a poem a 'Farewell & Defiance To Love' but this appeared afterwards in the 'European Magazine'   these two letters with the two letters in question make up my whole correspondence to your valuable publication for the one signed 'J. Billings'° was mine & now I hope you will excuse my troubling you with this confession & if ever you undertake a Work where any thing of mine might be found worthy of insertion I shall always feel happy to send it   therefore my dear Sir

I hope you will alow me to subscribe myself your faithful

Friend & Obt Servt

John Clare

To Alaric Alexander Watts

20 Stratford Place March 12. 1828

Dear Sir

I thank you kindly for the 'Souvenir' & I assure you that the one you sent before never reached me & for the abscence of it I cannot help confessing that I felt dissapointed

I also thank you as kindly for your liberal offer in paying me for my contributions & tho I would not have requested it if I could have done without such means of bettering my condition yet my Publications have brought me so little real profit (tho a good deal of words have been wasted to the contrary) that for my increasing needs I am obliged to seek out other rescources.

& I shall feel heartily glad of contributing somthing worthy of your next years anual & as I am now in London I should be happy to call upon you & make arangements to that effect

I am dear Sir your faithful Servt
John Clare

To [Alaric Alexander Watts]

20 Stratford Place March 16th [1828]

Dear Sir

I wrote to you a few days back but recieved no communications—& I now send a MS Poem for your approval one which I reserved on purpose thinking it would suit you & as my stay in town is limited to a few days 3 or 4 at furthest I hope you will let me know wether or not it is worthy of your pages as I shall then be enabled to make offers to some other publication my object being to realize some little benefit for my increasing family claims & all I require is to be remunerated as you pay others—my Poem is accompanied with two contributions from my friend Mrs Emmerson who begs if they do not suit your pages that they may be returned

I am dear Sir yours respectfully
John Clare

To John Taylor

Helpstone April 3rd—[18]28

My dear Taylor

I waited till I had made somthing out respecting the 'Roman Coins'° ere I wrote & I went yesterday to Milton on purpose & my friend Henderson says he will send you all he has gotten as a sample & if you like them at the price he gives for them he will become your collector & get all he can tho he says they are not brought to him so plentiful now as they were—he gives a penny each for the common ones & as much as 6d for such as he thinks good but seldom or ever more he has made several out which he will send you among the rest he would have put them into my charge for you but I told him to send them himself & then he & you could explain matters about them better as to what may suit you best & what he may collect—so much for antiquity—Tho I have not as yet opened any prospect of success respecting my becoming a bookseller yet I still think there is some hopes of selling an odd set now & then & as you are so kind as to let me have them at that reduced rate when I do sell I shall make somthing worth while for a trifle which I thought so in my days of better dreams becomes somthing considerable now & even trifles are acceptable for I do assure you I have been in great difficultys & tho I remained silent under them I felt them oppress my spirits to such a degree that I almost sunk under them for those two fellows of Peterbro° in the character of docters have anoyed & dunned me most horribly by times & tho ones claims are unjust I cannot get over him by any other method than paying—but my coming up to town has aleviated me a little & by next latter end of the year I hope to be half set up I have got 4 pieces into Ackermans forget me not for which he has paid me already after the rate of 20 guineas per sheet which is the utmost he gives & with which I am well contented & I am going to write for the 'Spirit of the Age'° for which I am to have a pound a page & more when it becomes more established—but promises tho they produce a plenteous seedtime generally turn out a bad harvest—& be as it will I am prepared for the worst I have long felt a dislike to these things but force puts no choice—'Interest makes strange friendships' White the

Naturalist says & I feel its truth & its misfortune but thank God I am once more in my old corner & in freedom I am as great as his majesty so a fig for the Babelonians

Will you be so kind as to send me the half dozen sets of my Poems as soon as you can with an extra half dozen of the Calenders & I shall take it as a great favour by your enclosing those little books as you promised me the Virgil & Homer &c &c as I should like the whole of them with the portion of the Bible & I hope you will compleat the Virgil

I went to A A Watts but I did not feel at home there for there was a party of literary men & painters all entire strangers to me I was very unwell & rather in the situation of a fish out of water struggling for my own element but Watts himself behaved very well to me & was quite a different man to what I expected from the first sight of him yet our opinions of Poetry do not agree & I shall never attempt to write for his Souvenir any more as I sent him one which I fancied my very best but he did not like it—I shall now advertize my Books in Drakards Stamford News & if I succeed in selling them all well & good if not it will not be the first dissapointment I have met with & now my dear Taylor I will as a man of business say what I have long neglected as I never liked to refer too but it is a thi[ng tha]t must be & it will never interfere in our friendship be as it may—so I should like to know at your leisure how I stand with you in my accounts & my mind will be set at rest on that score at once for if there is any thing coming to me it will be acceptable at any time & if there is nothing I shall be content   the number printed of the three first vols I have known along while by Drurys account but wether I have overrun the constable° or not since then I cannot tell & that is what I should like to know the first oppertunity & I hope you will not feel offended at my mentioning the matter as I do it for no other wish than to make us greater & better friends if possible then whom no one my dear Taylor has a sincerer claim to yours than | Yours affectionately

John Clare

To Frank Simpson

Helpston April 9 1828

My dear Frank

I have been obliged after a good deal of hammering to give up all trials as dissapointments about the Epitaph° for they are cursed dissappointments to myself more so then they will be to you for I wished to accompany your monument yet its all no use I can do nothing for the more I try the worse I am & the reason why it is so is I believe that I never knew Mr Friar & therefore I cannot feel the subject at all so here I give it up with much reluctance for Patty went over to Wilsons° on wednesday with a letter but more for a Vol which I much wanted & delayed writing to you by her in hopes that I might be able to do somthing by friday so you see instead of getting better I get worse & such will be the attempts I doubt at Behnes's Princess Vittoria° which I am most anxious to attempt as he has flattered me to desire it but thats all against my success & I have but little time now to try I expect as Mrs Halls Evergreen° the Work in which it is to appear was to go to press on the 6th of April for so she told me her self & I imagine it will not be far from a first article so I have as good as gave it up entirely—I have also a commission to write feth stop thats too much a trade word for friendship the fact is I am to write a Poem for one of the anuals To my kind friend E[liza] L[ouisa] E[mmerson]° it is to be called Wreath or Chaplet I dont know which & wether it will ever get any further than the title I cannot tell—yesterday Mr Ryde called on me & told me he was going to London in a few days & wished for my friend Mr Emmersons address which I told him & he told me about his sons attempts to find out a Publisher for me but really this is a thing that only one word expresses better then the rest do you reccolect Mr Burchell in that immortal Bard of Erin's Vicar of Wakefield when the ladies were promising the daughters of the Vicar so much & so many idealitys of successes in life & fortunes this said Mr Burchell stood rubbing his hands by the fire & uttering rather audibly to their patronage pomposity—'fudge'—& tho I have never uttered it I have often thought of it when Mr Rydes sons stories meet my ear for how can it be expected that a man can further a poor Authors interests in reccommending a publisher when he has a commodity going the rounds of the market quite as unsuccessful as the one he would pretend to help for I have not yet tryed any thing of my own for fear of a refusal any further than small things which have never misst the success they were seeking its plain that if Mr Colbourn is his friend why the d——l is it that Mr Colbourn does not publish this Classical or heathen Dictionary I can see thro this Farce of Folly & mock patronage this play at chuck ball & catch it between Mr R[yde] & Mr R[yde] the son & egad Ill be a ball no longer so here the Farce ends for I must tell you my dear Frank I dont like them at all & I never shall like them that is as friends & I do not wish to have indeed I shall give them no cause to be enemies their pomposity & fudge I dislike most damnably & never wish to cross it any more & neither will I so you must manage matters as well as you may for my likes & dislikes are past all cure I feel vext at myself often but I cannot act the flatterer well at all & if one does not lay it on thickish its no use but I like such folks who are too honest to be flattered those John Bull sort of fellows they are the sort for me & shall you take me for a flatterer when I say that the people I prefer are somthing after your own way & that of your family to whom I beg to include my kindest remembrances & to none more sincerely then to yourself while I subscribe myself my dear Frank | yours most affectionatly

John Clare

You must have the sincerity to believe my failing in the d——d (poh that is not the epithet for an Epitaph they are always sacred) as a sincere failing that is of no other cause than inabil[i]ty to please my self or others for that is the cause & none other

yours &c &c

J.C.

To John Taylor

Helpstone April 12th 1828

My dear Taylor

Having advertized the Books yesterday I write agen to you for the parcel & hope you will send it directly as I have 3 orders for them already 2 for the Calender only & one for the set & 3 ladies came this morning wanting them & are to call agen tho I did not ask how many they wanted but I hope to succeed so do let me have them quickly I do not like to give you trouble by this additional letter but I feel anxious about having them & you may as well write to Henderson of Milton in the parcel as he has got some very curious roman Coins such as will suit you if you really wanted them as you expressed you did & he will think perhaps I made all the talk about nothing if you make no enquirey however be so kind as to forward the Books as soon as you can if you please & I shall write no further this time then being | yours sincerely

John Clare

Here is another of those Imitations of the Psalms & this I did this morning look at the origional & tell me if such will do as Imitations°

By Babels streams we sat & sighed
  Yea we in sorrow wept
To think of Sions former pride
  That now in ruin slept

Our Harps upon the willows hung
  Cares silenced every string
Our woes unheeded & unsung
  No hearts had we to sing

For they that made us captive there
  & did us all the wrong
Insulted us in our despair
  & asked us for a song

They wasted us of all we had
   Inherited by birth
& as if ruin made us glad
   From us expected mirth

They bade us sing with taunting tongues
   & rude was the demand
How could we sing gods holy songs
   In his revilers land

Jerusalem if I forget
   Thee thus may my right hand
Forget my Harp that never yet
   Was played in such a land

Yea ere we cease to honour thee
   May our unruly tongues
Grow dumb nor longer leave them free
   Than while they love thy songs

For when we had no fear of them
   & joy was on our brow
That joy was thine Jerusalem
   & shall we mock thee now

No they that humble thus our pride
   Do only make it strong
Them for our ruin we deride
   & leave to God the wrong

So cease exulting Babylon
   Nor triumph in thy powers
A sword shall waste thy land anon
   As thine hath wasted ours

To John Steward°

Helpstone April 23. 1828

My dear Sir

My uncourtious behaviour you must pardon in neglecting to answer your kind note but I did not give it the thought at the moment therefore you will I hope excuse it—I am sorry you took so much trouble in providing me a conveyance to get over to see you but the fact is that I am such a bad horseman that I would much rather walk two miles than ride one & I dare not have hazarded my neck on the one you sent had nessesity been ever so urgent for it appeared two spirited by half for me nor do I think you are aware that the waters are out which was the only obstacle that prevented me from coming for I have lived too long at Helpstone to be frighted at dirty roads so I shall be very happy to take another oppertunity to accept your kind invitation & if its not objectionable I will come on Tuesday next so that it be fair above head & the flood in the meadows be gone in the meanwhile I remain | My dear Sir yours very respectfully

John Clare

To Samuel Carter Hall

[Hall had written on 6 May: 'You do not send anything for Westley & Davis for their Magazine [the *Spirit and Manners of the Age*]. I hope you will do so, in time for the next.—My wife is anxious to see the Grasshopper.' Anna Maria Hall thanked Clare in Oct. for 'The Grasshopper', which appeared in her *Juvenile-forget-me-not* (1829). 'Impulses of Spring' and 'Pastoral Fancies' appeared in the *Spirit and Manners of the Age* (1828), but the poem Clare sends with this letter was not published in his lifetime.]

May 13. 1828

Dear Sir

this Poem has been written out a long while for Mrs Hall but I was prevented from sending it by some tormenting & distracting matters that are always occurring in a family mans affairs—Dissapointments I have met with so often that they cease to be any thing but the name & so it is with the Magazine I did not write to them time enough but I did send to them a Poem within 3 days of Publication which I wrote out under such inability that I was obliged to send 2 days after that a corrected copy with a desire that they would cancel the other it was 'Impulses of Spring' which I fancied not much amiss I wish you would request the Publishers to send the Magazine direct to me as I have not got the others yet and per[haps] they would let me have the back Nos to compleat it as I shall wish to write for it in earnest & I wish to hear as soon as convinient how Mrs Hall likes the 'Grasshopper' when you can tell me if [not] then insert the Poem mentioned above in this Month

I am yours &c
John Clare

Verses

Tho winter comes dreary
In frost & in snow
A sun shall come cheery
& bid them all go
The spring it shall greet with
Its songs & its showers
The summer shall meet with
Its dancing & flowers

But alas for the lover
Thats loved not again
No art can discover
A cure for the pain
Full dark is the token
Of pleasures adieu
The heart that is broken
No hopes can renew

The star falls in darkness
To be no more seen
& leaves a blank markless
Where splendour hath been
On the shore speedy drying
Noughts seen of the wave
So the heart for love dying
Sinks into the grave.

John Clare

Helpstone. Septr 13. 1827

To John Taylor

Helpstone July 2 1828

My dear Taylor

Will you have the kindness to send me my little money as soon as you can & excuse my abruptness for I have nothing good to communicate to make up a letter & bad is not worth talking about   my bookselling business° has not succeeded much for I have only sold 2 sets & got paid for one & that perhaps is better than I could expect   I am fearfull that I shall not be able to make my money cover my expenses in fact I am sure I shall not so I am at the nessesity of being forced to trouble you as usual for an extra £5s & I hope to hear from you as soon as possible

did you get the Coins   I saw Henderson last Thursday & he said he had sent them   an old man in our neighbourhood has a copper medal° struck in commemoration of Admiral Vernons Victory over the Spaniards—on one side are two men & a Ship with this insc[r]ip[tion] 'The british glory revived by Adml Vernon: Comr Brown' on the other the Devil leading a man into Hell with a halter round his neck & this inscription 'Make room for Sir Robert: no excuse' which I take to be a satire on his political capacitys a sort of minature model of the present day—if its worth it I can get it for a trifle but as I am doubtful of that Im loth to purchase it at all—give my respects to George Darley my best respects & thank Mess[rs] Dewint & Hilton when you see them for their prompt acknowledgment of the reciept of my Ryhming ambitions in the shape of 4 Vols for I dare not say my Works   but I shall trouble them both with a reply some oppertunity or other as I shall Darley directly for we have a Londoner here now & a Friend of poor Van Dyk° who I hear is gone

I am my dear Taylor yours sincerely
John Clare

To John Taylor

Helpstone Octr 15 1828

My dear Taylor

Will you have the kindness to send me 6 more sets of my Poems compleat & 6 of the Calender as I have sold every one & not got a Vol: left by me now & I have another set ordered to go to Boston° where I have been on a visit & met with a very kind reception the Mayor of the Town sent for me as soon as he heard I had come & treated me in a very hearty manner & wished me to procure him two copys of my whole poems & desired me to insert his name in every Vol: he also lent me Leigh Hunts Memoirs of Byron° the first time I had ever seen it the Portrait of Lamb is like him as far as a portrait but the life & vivacity of his countenance is lost the one of Keats I know not what to make of its bad the books interesting & not so abusive as I was led to believe from the accounts in the journals &c—have the kindness to send the books as soon as you can as I wish to return my thanks with those I send for the loan of this Book—when I got to Boston I had another invitation to go to Hull but they looked on me in a character that I could not fill up without making myself very ridiculous for several young men in Boston had made it up among themselves to give me a Supper at an Inn where I was to have made a Speech &c &c but as soon as I heard of it I declined it in the best way I could & told them if they expected a speech from me they need prepare no supper for that would serve me for everything & so I got off of the matter—I felt the kindness but I could not tell them I felt it & now Ive got home agen I must write them my feelings—& realy this speechifying is a sore humbug & the sooner its out of fashion the better—I heard that Dequinceys Mother had been on a visit to Boston some time back & that he has been expected having relations there—Lamb is a great favourite there as Elia—& Dequincey too as the Opium Eater but the worst is that many of the bookeaters laud it as the production of Lamb & you cannot convince them to the contrary—give my remembrances to Hessey Darley Dewint Hilton &c &c bye the bye Hilton was at Lincoln I heard when I was at B[oston]

I am Dear Taylor yours sincerely

John Clare

I had forgot to tell you that I cannot procure the Coin without giving more than its worth for the mans been told its worth much more than it really is Artis gave me good advice respecting the purchase of old coins which I mean to abide bye & that is never to give silver for any thing but silver unless one is sure its gold (for doubtful gold & silver too is very current among antiquarian fancys) & then one cannot be far wrong the coin I told you of is copper & if I can get it for copper you shall have it but the fellows got it & if he cannot find a customer elswhere I shall have it brought back for a quart of Ale at least I expect so

yours &c

J.C.

I have read over those Books you were so kind as to send me the Translations° I mean & I like Virgil best & I should like to see Darley undertake the whole version & without the latin for common or universal reading for the interlinings bothers ones eyes terribly

You never sent me Darleys later Mathematical publications°

I should much like to see them—Lord Milton has sent me 13 Nos of the 'Useful Knowledge Library' which I expect he intends to continue for there will be no end to it

To Henry Behnes

Helpstone Decr 20. 1828

My dear Harry

I have been so long absent in the way of scribbling that I dont know wether I am the debtor in a letter or you but it signifys not for I have oftener thought of you by not writing then if I had written mechanically once a fortnight or less & the reason why I write to you now is that I am apprehensive that some of the News papers you are so kind as to send me get lost on their journey for last spring after my return from London there was several weeks past without bringing any paper so I thought that you had given up sending it untill it again reached me after 5 or 6 weeks absence & since then only one has been missing which was the *23rd of Novembers Paper* & I felt rather uneasy thinking that you would fancy I had lost it when on the contrary I am very careful of them for they contain matter worthy of russia backs & corners° & a place in any library it is most assuredly the best paper I have ever seen—I wish you would say wether you sent them or not & if you did I would rather for go the pleasure of reading them then you the risk of loosing them & so spoil the collection I shall return those I have with the first oppertunity that offers—our friend Frank Simpson wrote to me a long while ago saying that you wished me to write somthing for more 'Albums' & I must confess that I have nothing but what would spoil them & therefore I cannot send any thing the rage for Autographs & Albums is getting a very foolish rage & its quite time it was out of fashion—Mr Hall has as usual paid me in part for my contributions & *promised* me the rest which I expect is somthing like the 'sinking fund' neither can I get any thing for my latter contributions for the 'Spirit of the Age' tho I have just urged my request for the third time & as I shall feel the wants of it in a few days Christmass being the time of my half yearly payment I should hope that they will favour my request & send it—I am now attempting a long Poem on 'The Pleasures of Spring' but get on very slowly & have very little hopes of succeeding above the usual way tho as to description I think the thing will do as to action there is none at least as I can see applicable to the subject

have you been to Stratford Place laterly I heard from Mrs E[mmerson] somtime back & she was much pleased with the Annuals of which I have as yet seen but two tho I believe I am in all I have written for excepting the 'Souvenir' & Alaric Watts wrote to me a short time before it was published & said he should insert one of the things I sent him—I have been on an excursion to Boston & brought home a terrible illness which has gone thro the house but we have all of us recovered the youngest child & myself suffered the worst & yet I am well without so much as a doctors pill being thrust down my throat for I was not able to swallow the large bill that would have followed it so I took the main chance & found it answer—give my best respects to your Brother William & to Charles & also to Mr——I forget his name but you do not so give him my respects | & believe me dear Harry yours sincerly

John Clare

To John Taylor

Helpstone Decr 21 1828

My dear Taylor

Will you have the kindness to send me my little money as soon as you possibly can for Christmass is nearly here & I want to get straight as near & as soon as I can—I began very abruptly but having got the business over which caused me to write I shall now fill up the sheet with somthing or other—I should hope you are well as to myself I have had one of the severest fits of sickness I ever remember to have had I was taken soon after I recieved your letter with the books & was ill six weeks it was a very bad Fever & I expect I brought it out of the Fens home with me for it went thro the house & my wife & childern were all ill but myself & the youngest child were worse than any of the rest & thank God we are all recovered & well & what is better I never took one dose of phisic tho a kind man a stranger to me heard of my illness & kindly sent me some medicine last week gratis & at a venture but I was well & have been well this 3 weeks or month past I daresay yet the kindness was the same & do you know I am taking the medicine regurlarly till its gone to prevent a return of the malady which I understand is often the case & then it ends in a consumption & finishes the matter so say the wise folks of the fens & it shall be a long while ere I visit them again tho when I wrote to you last I felt as well as ever I did in my life & I had not the least idea of illness tho the friends were I was at fell very ill before I left

I have written to Darley which accompanys this & I have written to him for advice as I am trying for a long poem & my present intention is a poem on the 'Pleasures of Spring' I had some desire to try one on 'The last judgment' but expecting I shall be on the wrong side in this world as well as the next by so doing I dare not—I shall write to Mr Cary also for his advice & I should like to have yours as to wether I had better go on with short pieces in the manner of the old poets or attempt somthing long—I like Darleys Companion very much indeed & think it far better than if he had enlarged it & I think it would have been more popular if both Treatises could have been compressed in a Vol

The vol *was charged* against me in the accnt with my books but I should suppose without your knowledge for I cannot afford to buy a mathematical library & yet am very anxious to see any thing which Darley writes as there is always somthing to interest me—Henderson of Milton came over to see me about 5 weeks back & I asked him about the coins when he said he paid *10* or *12* shillings for them & I am going over to Milton when I will pay for them but my opinion is that he was over charged & I think if I make enquirey I can get coins cheaper the best way is to offer those who hunt them so much a dozen did he tell you the charge when he sent them if he did not I shall desire him to insert it on a scrap of paper as you may know there is no extra charge of mine—I dont doubt but they might cost him that in the lump neither have I a doubt but our friend Artis has had [a f]inger among the best of them & 3 or 4 out [of] that quantity underrates the value to an antiquarian for I know there was some among them which he thought very good indeed I told him that you wished for more & he said none of those who gather them had brought any to him latterly nor did he say he would enquire for I was ill at the time & could not pay much attention to any thing

I am my dear Taylor yours sincerly
John Clare

To Henry Behnes

Helpstone Decr 29 1828

My dear Harry

We recieved your very kind Presents° safe & without any occupation for apology in not writing a few days sooner or without adding more words to the matter I that is *we* the whole of us thank you very kindly for every favour & I make no doubt but you are enjoying a happy christmass as for me I have no amusment but looking over my few Books by the fireside or walking out into the Fields & thinking about my Friends—I have drank your Health often Harry over heavy wet from the Bell & since then over that lucious juice of the grape which you sent me or rather Patty but I must be honest enough to confess that I did not sit up untill 12 oclock for I could get none to keep me company & I never passed a more solitary christmass in my life & never possesed better means of making merry with it but contrarietys are the regular occurrences of life & so it would seem by our letters crossing each other on the road & none waiting for the others arival—I dont know what I said in that letter or wether you got it nor do I hardly know what I am saying here for my mind is very muddy but I shall expect your answer as quick as possible remember & as full of gossip as you can muster literary & all sorts for you dwell in the heart of it which like Shrimps in a seaport is brought out fresh every morning—& you know I have a sort of taste for the Fancy° & my Father too is a most determined Gossip in its affairs who as soon as he knew I was writing to you reminedded me to be sure & ask you to tell us who wins in Curtis's & Jones's Battles to day & if you take in any of the daily papers which contains the fights we should be very much obliged to you for the loan of one—do you often visit Stratford° & who do you meet there give me all the News you can & I in return will give you all the enquir[i]es you ask after if I am able—on Sunday our friend Frank & Mrs Simpson his mother came over to see me with an Album of yours in which I inserted a trifle on the Bust as I promised—it has been published (as I imagine) in the 'West of England Magazine' for I have not seen it tho the Editor wished me to write for it & also to reccommend it among my Friends Maunder I believe is the Publisher & therefore if you wish to know further about it you can for I cannot recommend what I have never seen—how do you get on with your Bust° or more properly speaking your humble servants & how do you get on with the Portraits of our good Friend of Avon—I expect they are just as they were when I left you Fye on ye Harry a pretty [?'froy'] you (as the jews would say) to preach sermons on broken promises as you did to me on brown paper last summer & for gods sake or at least sombody elses take them back carefully to Mrs E[mmerson] for I expect all the blame lyes with Jonas tho Ive heard not a word latterly about them—I have a glass of your Brandy dashed with a little water at my elbow so heres your Health & happiness Harry & success in the Arts & I hope ere I am much older to hear of a Venus in marble by Behnes carrying away both the palm of beauty & art from somerset house & not the humbug & puff that is so often carried away without either of the former requisites to make appology for the latter I am now getting to the end—what I have crossed out shall be said hereafter when Ive more room so Ill bid you farewell | & believe me Harry

yours very sincerely
John Clare

Has Mr Watts inserted any thing of mine in his 'Souvenir' Mr Ackerman° has not favoured me with a copy of his 'Forget me not' or Mrs Emmerson either is it not usual with him to do so as the rest do so

To John Taylor

Helpstone Jany 3 1829

My dear Taylor

I recieved the Anuity quite safe & the check from Lord Spencer also which I have got changed I know not why his Lordship sent it thus (tho it is quite as well & much better then sending a bill by letter) for I have never wrote to him to do so nor did I ever send the last Vol as he never took any notice of the 3 first Vols which I sent some years ago so I thought I was intruding by so doing & that his Lordship might think it was a fresh apology to his kindness—I believe my illness was caused by the journey & not by any irregularitys while there tho I one night took a little more liquor then I was in the habit of doing & felt ill two days with a sort of fever while there it was at the Mayors of the Town he was a very jolly companion & made me so welcome while a lady at the table talked so ladily of the Poets that I drank off my glass very often almost without knowing it & he as quickly filled it but with no other intention then that of hospitality & I felt rather quere & got off almost directly after finding myself so but I was nothing like disordered yet it was wine & I was not used to the drink & tho it made me ill for two days or at least helpd to do so for I had a sort of cold at the same time it was nothing of that kind that caused my illness after my return which was a bad fever & it is a mercey I am here now tho I did not feel the danger of my illness untill I had got over it & then I felt it a miracle that I escaped & a greater that all my family did the same for every one of them was ill tho myself & least child was worse then the rest—I dont think I have drank a pint of ale together this two years in fact I can drink nothing strong now in any quantity & as to spirits I never touch & yet without them I feel hearty & hale & have quite recovered from my last ailments & hope to prolong the lease of life for a good season—tho I dont think I am much qualified for an old man—your opinion of my intended Poem is in some instances correct for the same images must certainly occur of which I have written before yet if I could succeed others would be added that would do away the impression of repe[ti]tion° but action is what I want I am told & how action is to get into the pleasures of Spring I cannot tell

I think many of the productions of the day that introduce action do it at the expense of nature for they are often like puppets pulled into motion by strings & there are so many plots semiplots & demiplots to make up a bookable matter for modern taste that its often a wonder how they can find readers to please at all I shall do as you say & go on with little things I feel pleased with your opinion because I feel you speak as you think these Annuals are rather teazing to write for as what one often thinks good the Editors returns back as good for nothing while another gives them the preference & what one thinks nothing of they often condescend to praise—Allan Cunninghams is the best Annual° of the whole & a piece by Procter & one by Allan are the best in the book Darleys I do not like so well as some of his earlier pieces but his Play° the more I look at it the more I like it there is certainly somthing very happy & clever about it & it will be read of that I am certain for a neglected poem in these days is almost a sure sign of its merit—I have paid Henderson & orderd him that is wished him to collect you more coins & he will seek out for all he can find

I write to Hessey to day who has kindly offered to send me the Nos of his New Work on Religion° which will either be entertaining or else very dull from its intended magnitude but if the prospectus is followed up with the spirit it professes to set out with it will be a very entertaining work & I have no doubt command a good sale I thank you very kindly for Darleys Book but your kindness only urges me to increase it by reminding you that you never sent me his Trigonometry° which at some oppertunity I wish you would as I wish to see every thing he writes in english for I feel a great esteem for him & believe he will produce somthing ere long worthy of better esteem then mine & meet it also—I have wrote a long letter & so farewell | My dear Taylor yours sincerely

John Clare

What a dreadful Tradegy I have just read in the Trial of that Burke of 'Modern Athens'° the terror seizing descriptions of Shakspear are mere farces of horror compared to the simple narration of this dreadful Trial—the party dancing & drinking till midnight as the prologue of the Tragedy—Hunt & Thurtells° was nothing in comparison

To Allan Cunningham

Helpstone Feby 22. 1829.

My dear Allan

Here I am agen with lots of rhyme both for your reading & Anniversary also—Of the three Vols I beg you will accept them as the completion of my intentions when in London last spring as I had not the oppertunity to do so then & I shall be glad to hear your opinion of them some time or other—not the humbug of fashionable flattery for we both of us hear enough of that I dare say at times but your honest likes & dislikes that are ever the best & most profitable to correct ones errors for we seldom 'see as others see us'—as to the things for your Anniversary I have sent the 'Statute'° thinking it not amiss & the other° was written & sent by *request* so if you like them both they are at your service for I do not write as if I expected pay by the foot or page either but I like to give good measure & throw in an extra gratis—you gave me too much for my last & I hope you will keep that in mind next year & not do so for I never feel the loss of independance worse then when I cannot serve a friend without knowing that I recieve a reccompence in return for more then the labour is entitled to—tell me if you get the packet safe & how you like the two trifles—

I am my dear Allan yours sincerely

John Clare

I forgot to ask you wether you recieved my last letter which I sent under a frank soon after I recieved the Copy of Anniversary & in which I gave my opinion as you requested I have to add that the Poem to the 'Glowworm'° by Mr Fergusson is very good as I think for it pleases me much—write as *soon* as you can to say you recieve this if you will have the kindness as I shall be doubtful of its arival tho I have addressed it as particular as possible

yours &c &c
J.C.

To Samuel Carter Hall

Helpston March 7th 1829

My dear Sir

I recieved yours this morning & in reply I must beg leave to tell you that as to writing for the Manners & Spirit of the Age° I must in justice to myself decline doing so any longer for Messrs Westley & Davis have not paid me a farthing for any of my last things since July which amounts to *6 guineas* in all—& for which I have not only written myself several times but have requested some of my friends in London to have the kindness to make application for it & they have repeatedly done so but all to no purpose for the publishers never returned a word in reply & under such circumstances you my dear Sir must feel there is little encouragment for me to write again but if you will have the kindness to talk with Mr Westly about the matter I have no doubt but he will send me the little money for my trifles according to agreement for I have a letter from the Editor who tells me that Mr Westley did not wish me to write more then a page for the guinea a month & that he himself thought that I wrote too much for the money alowed—I wish also you would have the kindness to send me the £2 which you intended to transmit to me the first oppertunity in addition to the sum sent for your Annuals for money is a welcome visitor to me at all seasons & I have been so dissapointed this year with the delay & neglect of some of those for whom I wrote a few trifles in expectation of payment that I almost came to the resolution of never writing any thing of the kind again but for those who paid me punctually & you will I hope give my respects to Mrs Hall & tell her I will send her somthing for her 'Forget me not' & also for your 'Amulet' & I hope you will have the goodness in the mean time to speak to Mr Westly &c & I shall feel myself accordingly | your much obliged & very faithfull Servant

John Clare

I forgot to say that I have no objection to write for your Magazine at the price you state for I want no more then other people for such things & I wish you would or could procure me the last Nos of 1828 from July to Decr as I have the others

yours &c

J.C.

By making up a parcel of the numbers above mentioned the money due to me would come safe in it directed thus—John Clare Helpstone *left at the Bull Inn* Market Deeping

To Eliza Louisa Emmerson

[after 6 April 1829]

My dear Eliza

Did you think I should ever write agen I hope you did for I have been head over ears at hard work for the last 3 weeks in the field & this last glut of wet has given me a day or twos leisure for writing & the first letter I have written since I recieved yours is to yourself I also waited to give you all the literary news I could respecting the annuals but I have as yet heard little I got a letter from friend Cunningham° yesterday who tells me that my trifles suit him one of which are the verses to E[liza] L[ouisa] E[mmerson] of which he makes a strange mistake by fancying they are writ to Miss Landon & flatters me much by praising them & also by thinking them worthy of the Poetess so I wish that the first oppertunity you have you would correct the mistake if you feel the matter too delicate to write upon you can tell the Miss Frickers° when they next call upon you for he will most likely transpose the 'E L E' to L[aetitia] E[lizabeth] L[andon] which I shall not be able to rectify if he does not send me a proof sheet & I would much rather that they should stand as written & proud as I am of Brother Allans commendation &

proud as I should be of Miss Landons commendation also I feel much prouder to know that they were deemed worthy the acceptance of yourself to whom they were written   I will give you the quotation from Allans letter relating to the verses—'I have placed your contributions in the approved box marked with my hearty approbation   your verses to Miss Landon are the very best you ever composed after all a flesh & blood Muse is best & Miss Landon I must say is a very beautiful substitute for these aerial madams   I shall show it to her'—how Allan should mistake E L E for L E L I cannot say but in his hurry he has over looked it & I hope you will rectify the mistake   I did not tell him to whom they were written because I thought it was not nessesary but I wish I had now to prevent the mistake that may get into the proof sheet & remain there if not corrected before hand   so much for this matter   I have not heard a word from Mr Pringle° to whom I have sent a trifle for his annual & I wonder how he could refuse the sonnet of yours as you say he did for I am sure it was much better then those he inserted of my own last year but there is no accounting for Editors—I am very glad you like the Bust as I thought myself it was a good one but Frank Simpson tells me he thinks Harrys last touches in my absence did not add any improvements to it but rather injured the freshness of the likness that he so happily caught in the model & as it was when I last saw it

To Eliza Louisa Emmerson

August 1st 1829 | Helpstone

My dear Eliza

To get out of debt in the way of our correspondence is one reason why I write now & having an idle hour to spare another but which of these reasons can make apology for a bad letter I cannot tell so I leave it with you—yesterday I saw Artis at Milton & he spoke very highly of the reception he met with at your temple in Stratford (for I presume you are now at Brighton) but he did not speak so favourably of the *Bust* as I had anticipated   he says it struck him too forcibly at first sight of being a copy of Hiltons picture & he left it with a stronger impression of its being so now of this I can say nothing   I thought it good for Hiltons picture is good & they are two good things together & thats all I care about the matter most of my friends are desirious for me to attempt somthing in prose° as verse will not sell & I am looking round for a subject as Cunningham anxiously urges me to it & he anticipates my success so friendly & earnestly that I have determined *to try* at all events but wether I shall produce a novel or a prayer book I am sure I cannot tell Fashion is a fine dog but a very false one it barks at shadows & lets monsters of every description pass by to its ladys library without a growl so if I can manage one of these successful abortions I must as that success is a much better payment then after praise will you excuse this half sided epistle° as I have nothing more to say & as I am in but little spirits to write my wife being at this moment dangerously ill & in bed & the childern noising round me in all directions I hope next time I write I shall be better provided for a longer epistle hoping yourself & Mr Emmerson are well I remain my dear

Eliza | yours sincerely
John Clare

To Henry Behnes

Helpstone August 1 1829

My dear Harry

I shall not make any apology for not writing sooner further then saying that I have not had the length of a sheet of papers time to spare for this last four months excepting on sundays & wet days for I have taken up my old occupation of hard work & feel quite as happy as I did when 'Hope told a flattering tale' the fact is we only live to hope the best & to be undecieved by meeting the worst & then to hope agen as usual & perhaps it is good that hope should thus be an evergreen—I cannot imagine how you feel dissapointed in not finding me writing oftener when you write so seldom yourself for I 'take no note' of those *notes* of yours further then mere nothings in correspondence when paper is plentiful in a time of scarcity they might tell a little more then cyphers my eyes are not so bad but I can read a sheet full from you by candle light if I have no time by daylight so remember—I have got settled with Westley &c & I am now writing to Mr Hall as to the 'Spirit of the Age' the present price is a too near neighbour to nothing to be of much use writing for—I think I shall be in town before winter now but only for a few days as I want to get some matters settled which I feel impossible to do without coming up—Your Examiners are all safe as you send them but I am sorry to say that some of the Times are destroyd for paper is such a useful article in my house & considering the Times papers as waste Time to read after present time had done with them I let patty use them as she liked untill your last note checked me from doing so & I shall take the earliest opportunity to return them all—give my best thanks to Mr Hone for poor Humphry° & believe me my dear Friend

| yours sincerely
John Clare

To William Sharp

Helpstone Octr 1829

Dear Sharp

On next Tuesday or Wednesday I shall start off the packet of flowers & having taken so much care of the paper on which you inserted those you wished for as not to be able to find it after many searches I am obliged to send you a selection by guess & to insert as many of those as you liked as possible I shall send you portions of almost *every perrenial* I posses—I send small bits of each to make the parcel as small as possible for flowers ought never to cost much for if our amusments get too much hold of our pockets those amusments are far from being pleasures in the end which is only considered as another name for pleasure therefore to make the fact consonant with the maxim I have compressed as many sorts in as small a parcel as I could make & if you water them when you plant them they will all most assuredly thrive for they are perfectly *hardy* for all weathers & those that were not I declined sending on purpose that their loss by frost should not dissapoint you—I shall send the names both Botanical & English as well as I can make them out for altho I know wild flowers tollerable well my knowledge of garden flowers is very limited but I have made out the list as well as I could & the number on the plant refers to the corresponding number & name on the paper—I shall wait untill I hear from you before I send them because I wanted to trouble you & the packet with the care of a few letters if *I dare* or may do so for as I wish to do nothing against existing laws that may get either of us into trouble I ask your advice first wether I can do so or how I may do so I can send them open if that will be any difference to the matter tell me & I shall act accordingly

I never sent you any thing for Mr Hall because I have had no time having been at work in the ground in which you found me untill now but if Mr Hall will advance the money in *your hands* or his publishers either will do so for twelve months writing for the Magazine at the rate of two pages per month I will take care to supply them with somthing either in prose or verse every month but upon no other terms will I do any thing for the very trouble in getting the money is as much as the trifling pay is worth—*what money* will they advance on a volume of poems does Mr H state what, when he says he can get me a publisher on those terms the fact is I would rather take a small sum for the volume altogether then a large promise in 'half profits' because I have been disappointed at that game already with Messrs Taylor & Hessey—I shall send you a copy of their accounts° very soon which I shall wish you to show to Mr A. A. Watts for his advice as nobody knows more of Booksellers & publishing then he does & he behaved so kind to me when I was last in London that I dont think he will refuse to give his opinion about it

To Edward Bell Drury

[In Aug. 1829 Clare had received a copy of the accounts covering his first three publications; he was incensed by what he took to be a series of mistakes and inaccuracies, and he drafted letters to Drury and Taylor, carefully working out the best way to express his sense of having been wronged. But he was to get little satisfaction from either. See Appendix II.]

Helpston [before 15] Novr 1829

My dear Sir

Having recieved a statement of Accounts from Mr Taylor I was astonished at finding an Item in them of which I had not been apprised & *in addition* to the debt you claimed & was paid for it is the following statement '*Paid Mr Clare for Copy right per*

Drury £20' now *you know* that I never recieved a farthing extra from you beyond the debt which you claimed & was paid for & that the selling of the copy right was all fudge which you desired me to accord with merely as you said to prevent Mr Taylor from depriving you of your share as you feared he would do in the end but how ever well grounded your fears might seem to be at the time is best known to your self for you have since found them groundless by having your share of the profits granted you in the same ratio as he alowed himself & I should hope my fears respecting the loss of this £20 may be as groundless as yours were for whatever tricks may have been played with my ignorance I cannot think that this was a plea of yours to cheat me out of that sum but that it is a mistake which you made in making out the accounts for you well know that I never recieved a farthing beside the debt you claimed which was to be temporarily considered as the price of copyright merely for your own interest as you desired to defend you from your supposed enemys who turned out your friends so far as to grant your dues in the end & I hope that by expecting the same treatment from you I shall not be dissapointed for there are a set of people who profess a great deal about character & religion & honour & all that who are often found to want the very possesion of common honesty

I understand from Mr Taylor that the publishers of those Songs of mine made you a remuneration for them & tho I was to have had a remuneration also you know I have never had anything & tho they may not have made much yet a portion of that little as my right would have done me some good & you no harm as it would tend to show you to the world what we always wish to be considered a fair dealing man you also posses a quantity of my writings & a folio sort of Tax shaped book in parchment covers which you only borrowed to copy out the trifles it contained & which you never returned & tho they are of little worth either to yourself or me yet you know they are mine & if you would have the kindness to return them at the same time that you show your willingness to correct the above mistake & comply with my just rights in the other matters you will prove by so doing what you often professed to be my friend & I shall feel the proof as warmly as you often made the possesion [*for* profession] of considering myself your very obliged friend & Serv[ant]

John Clare

P.S. you told me when you & Taylor disagreed that 5000 Copies of the first Vol was printed   in my accounts there is only 4000   I suppose this is a mistake also of yours

yours &c
J.C.

To John Taylor

Helpston Novr 15 1829

My dear Taylor

You have no doubt wondered at my long delay in answering your two last letters & the long accounts that accompanied them but the reasons were that when they reached me I was beginning harvest & have been at work with short intervals of intermission eversince—& having leisure for the first time I replye & you must excuse my enquireys if I make them where none are nessesary for my ignorance in such matters must be my innoscence of any impertine[n]ce that may appear to be so—as every wish in making the enquirey is to be satisfied of things that I do not understand & not one uttered with the intention to offend—so where I am right I feel convinced that you will alow it & where I am wrong I hope as strongly you will excuse me of any other intention then that of wishing to be right—The Account 'A1 & 2' is I think not far from right tho in comparing it with my own some of the different sums of money are not only set down under wrong dates of the month but in several instances of the year also to that in which I recieved them—And you have not accounted for my writing for the Mazagine you know I was to have twelve pounds a year while I wrote for it which was three years but if this be considered too much for the trifles inserted you may pay me by the article for I am not a bargain hunter only pay me somthing—Hessey also had in his hands in 1824 seven pounds given to him for me by a Duchess & I never recieved it neither is accounted for as I expected   I want that which is right & nothing more & if you tell him he will remember it at once—In the Account 'C.' Drury led me to believe that there was 5000 copies of the first Vol printed & tho it was at the time he & you disagreed yet I imagined it was true   but he has made such a false charge to you on me in these accounts that one who could claim the one may easily be alowed to assert the other it is the following '*Paid Mr Clare for Copy right pr Drury £20*' now you will be astonished to hear that this is a lye—for mind I never recieved a farthing extra beyond the debt which he claimed of me & which you settled—the selling the copy right was all fudge & pretence he persuaded me to agree that it ought to be so merely as he said to prevent you from hurting him in the end yet what ever tricks he may have played with my ignorance in my acquaintance with him in those hours of hillarity with which I frequently indulged at his house I cannot now remember but this I can say that the selling the copy right is all fudge & that I never had nothing but small sums of a few pounds to the extent of that debt & nothing else & I have written this day to desire an explanation of the matter & I shall then if he persists in the falshood *prove* to you that it is a false charge—it seems that instead of getting any thing by the first Edition I am the looser by £20 from drurys mistake or cunning artifice I cannot say which yet

I think Mr Woodhouse rather hard with me in his charge of £7 for a deed of trust is he not? & I see also another Item of which I do not understand the import or the meaning viz 'for transfer 2s 6d' I have no knowledge of its meaning or nessesity—There is also the portrait charged for which I did not expect would be an item in the way of my half profits when it was painted for you & at your desire—& respecting the copies of my poems which I had from you these are overcharged for in the account a great deal beyond what you voluntarily offered them to me for on my last visit to London viz 10s the set that is 2/6 each for that was what you told me in Waterloo place—& now the matter is got thro so far I am heartily glad tho dissapointed for in loosing hope I have cleared the prospect to see a little further as to how I must proceed for the future & my intentions are to get a small farm or cottage as soon as possible & I have written to Lord Milton for that purpose but have recieved no answer as yet from his Lordship for my family is large & my means small to support them & all I regret is that matters were not settled sooner but when I expressed a desire to have a settlement years back Hessey urged me to patience & told me to wait & that I should be in the end 'rich & happy' I am not amiss off for happiness but the other part of his prophecy is badly fulfill'd but I am contented

I long to have a scrap of Dewints sketches for a frame to hang up in my cottage & if you would alow me to posses the painting he drew for the 'shepherd calender' I should be exceedingly pleased & when I was at the Bishop of Peterbros this summer Mr Herbert Marsh his eldest son told me he admired some of Shelleys Poems very much & on my asking him if he had read any of Keats he said not & I much wish to present him with a copy of the 'Endymion' yet not at the same time be left without one myself so as you owe me 12s for the Roman Coins perhaps you will send me a copy down & that at *trade price* & there is another book I should like which is the 'Guesses at truth'° but if the money will not b[u]y both at the price send the first only & never mind the overplus money & if you will spare me Dewints Drawing you can place it in the parcel the book makes excuse my freedom

Poor Hesseys failure astonished me much because I always thought that his constant attention to business would have prevented him from being caught up in the tempest that destroyed the more inconsiderate portion of the trade but I hope he will yet meet some success for his family as like me he has a large one—I always thought Hessey a cautious monied man give my rememberances to him—& poor Mrs Wright° what a breach Death makes in our acquaintance every time he pays a visit among them & what an imperceptable impression such visits make with the world the newspapers are read by thousands & the thousands of deaths in them are passed over as matters of course but the loss is only felt by the few—I am almost happy that I knew her no better yet I knew enough of her warm attachments to her friends to regret the accident of her loss & to feel what a loss it must be to others the fact is we never know half the esteem which we ought to have felt for a friend & little of the value we possest by such friendship untill it is too late to show our sincerity when every one hears it but one who would have been most interested in our esteem yet even these sorrowful reflections are not without their satisfaction for to feel sincerity for friends that are gone is a sure proof that we esteemed them when living or at least feel that we ought to have done so I am sure nobody respected the kind hearted friendship of Mrs Wright more then I did

You threaten me with a visit to helpstone but had you not said it so often & never proved your doing as you say in the matter but once I can feel it in no other way then that of a complement if you *mean so* I shall be most happy to see you give my best remembrances to Darley to whom I shall write soon & believe me dear Taylor | yours sincerely

John Clare

To Edward Bell Drury

[after 18 November 1829]

Sir

I am sorry that you have gave my enquiries so little satisfaction respecting the mistake of the money but I am not dissapointed in your explaining the matter against me because when I saw it inserted in my accounts from Mr Taylor I knew that the impudence that claimed it would not be without an excuse to justify it

As to what you say respecting settling the accounts (at the time you executed the instrument not I) this is a lye for you never gave me any account at all all the reccolection I have of the matter is this that you wished me to say that you had bought the copy right for £20 & you wished me to write that down in your account book one evening which I did remarking at the same time that you should cross out £20 of the accounts & not trick me into an additional debt by my agreeing to your desire

I now find I acted foolish in the matter but thats no use all I know [is] that your explanation of the matter is as utterly vound [*for* void] of foundation as the instrument you talk of was of honesty for Mr Taylor declared he never saw a more impudent attempt at imposition upon my ignorance in his life

I should not have written again to you in reply had not you chose to be very pathetic towards the conclusion of your letter respecting me & my affairs all I wanted from you was what I considered my just rights & as you have denied them all I have nothing further to [say] on the matter only that I am happy my affairs are out of your trust & heartily I had been out of it sooner as feeling such an occurrence would have been a benefit & I earnestly hope that I may never encounter such zeal as yours again

I never entertained the least idea of your [*gap in MS*] with my comfort & happiness I do not think you have much to do

Mr Taylor said right I think in respecting that he did not consider you were entitled to participate in the latter publication & its my intention that you should not have any further conscern in the earlier ones

You forget that your two insolent letters did not deserve answers tho they demanded them I demanded my right & had you not determined to sacrifice every thing to self interest you would not have answerd mine which only demanded what I considerd right & my own & instead of which you got over them by stating explanations which are not true & not any of your pathetic pretensions about of my welfare & making out & whining commendations of your past actions which you please to call 'trusts' which I neither asked for nor wanted they are always bad commendations you have denied that which I considered as right & therefore I must endure the loss & you may enjoy the triumph at your leisure as you will hear no more about the matter

To Peter De Wint

Helpstone Decr 19 1829

My dear Sir

Nay I will not be so fearfully polite as fashionable policy urges people & friends of cold blooded etiquete to be for I hate it so I will say at once My dear Dewint (a much better commencement to an old friend & I am sure I have known you long enough to be one & you see I have not waited to enquire wether you will alow me to call you so but have taken french liscence for the liberty without asking it)—but to proceed your Daughter flattered my vanity in asking me to find time to become one of her (that is one of your family) correspondents now I feel such a respect for the young Lady & her family & am so proud of having an oppertunity of being acquainted with one of the first Landscape painters of the Age that I will not let slip either time or oppertunity to become correspondent with either yourself or family & tho by the way I have taken an odd oppertunity to commence with I know you will forgive it at least I will hope as the Irishman did that you will grant the favour first & forgive the liberty afterwards

The favour requested & the liberty taken to request it being neither more or less then a wish to posses a bit of your Genius to hang up in a frame in my Cottage by the side of Friend Hiltons beautiful drawing which he had the kindness to give me when first in London what I mean is one of those scraps which you consider nothings after having used them & that lye littering about your study for nothing would appear so valuable to me as one of those rough sketches taken in the fields that breathes with the living freshness of open air & sunshine where the blending & harmony of earth air & sky are in such a happy unison of greens & greys that a flat bit of scenery on a few inches of paper appear so many miles for so some of those beautiful little things appeared to me which you so kindly indulged me with a sight of in your study 8 or 9 years back—alas that it is so many for time has made a sad gap in my little catalogue of friends since then I dont know how it is but nothing in the Royal Academy & other Exebitions struck me so forcibly as representations or rather fac similies of *English* scenery as those studies of yours—now I think many Painters look upon nature as a Beau on his person & fancies her nothing unless in full dress—now nature to me is very different & appears best in her every day disabille in fact she is a Lady that never needed sunday or holiday cloaths tho most painters & poets also have & still do consider that she does need little touches of their fancies & vagaries to make her beautiful which I consider deformities tho I should have given up the point in fancying that they might be right & I wrong if I did not feel that your sketches I speak of illustrated my opinion—The reason why I dared to take this liberty of a request is that on hearing you had the kindness to make a drawing for the frontispiece for nothing I felt heartily anxious to thank you for the kindness & having done so (excuse my vanity) I felt as heartily hopeful that I should one day posses the drawing but never having those hopes gratified my dissapointment has at last grown up into a determination above timidity to request somthing of the kind which would give me a pleasure to posses & having done so if I thought it needfull I should ask your pardon but feeling it otherwise I shall ask nothing about it but go on in begging you will kindly remember me to Mrs Dewint & to your

Daughter to whom I shall take the liberty to write first oppertunity also to friend Hilton & Mrs H [to] whom my respects are not less sincere from being strange & unfamiliar—Miss Dewint asked me when I came out again in the shape of a vol: of Ryhmes in fact I cannot answer the question but being strongly urged by my Friend Allan Cunningham to try somthing in prose I am doing so but wether I shall succeed or not I cannot tell I hope on as usual & with the assistance of these hopes I scribble my leisures into the bulk of a sizable volume & if it be deemed worthy of reading so much the better I shall most assuredly solicit Miss Dewints earliest opinion of it as soon as published if it ever arives at that honour—if you see Mr Herbert Reynolds now give him my remembrances for I shall never see him perhaps to give them myself

I am dear Dewint yours very sincerely
John Clare

To [John Drakard]

[after 21 December 1829]

Dear Sir

In answer to your flattering request° for my becoming a correspondent to your new paper I only fear that you overate my poor abilities in thinking they will be of service to such an undertaking but such as they are they are most certainly at your command—I can wish you success as heartily & as sincerly as a Scott or a Cobbett altho I cannot bring powers into the field to assist you to gain it as they could—theres all the difference & a mighty difference it is—I have not forgotten your kindness to me in early life when you used to let me have a few books on credit to the amount of a few shillings at a time when no one else would have trusted me for a halfpenny ballad these kindnesses assisted me materially to come at a knowledge of the world & to be what I should not have been without them & tho you fancy you are not personally known to me time has only forgotten these little [?circumstances] which I am fain to remember always feeling that one good turn deserves another there fore I am much at your service tho I cannot promise weekly contributions as I shall be unable to fulfill that promise if I do for altho I write a great deal I bear such a poor opinion of what I do write that I cannot believe it worthy of public [*gap in MS*] untill some friend has given his opinion upon it or I myself have laid them aside for a season the better to overcome partiality & to distinguish errors—which is no easy task for a man who writes for aprobation as every one most assuredly does to[o] few have the honesty to acknowledge it

To [Eliza Louisa Emmerson]

[after 21 December 1829]

You speak of publishing in the country° I dont reccolect ever saying I was going to publish anywhere—I only told you what was told me in a letter my friend Mr Sharp of the General post office who had it from Mr Hall that is all I either know or care about the matter

do I write intelligable I am gennerally understood tho I do not use that awkard squad of pointings called commas colons semicolons &c & for the very reason that altho they are drilled hourly daily & weekly by every boarding school Miss who pretends to gossip in correspondence they do not know their proper exercise for they even set gramarians at loggerheads & no one can assign them their proper places for give each a sentence to point & both shall differ—point it differently

to be sure I do not often begin a new sentence with a capital & that is a slovenly neglect which I must correct hereafter in my Essay pretentions for I fear they will be nothing else

To Henry Francis Cary

Helpstone Jany 25 1830

My dear Sir

As it has grown into such a wide breach of time since I either heard from you or wrote to you I cannot say wether I am a letter in your debt or wether you are one in mine at all events I value your correspondence & friendship so much that I will not loose either the one or the other by any neglect on my part therefore tho I have little or nothing to communicate I will make out a letter to ask how you are & to beg you will give my kindest remembrances to Mrs Cary & to your son & all the family which I know & friends also that you may fall in with & whom I may never chance to see again I am often sorry upon that account that the Magazine dropt into oblivion it took so many pleasant meetings along with it

Do you ever see or hear any thing of Wainwright that facetious good hearted fellow I long to hear somthing of him agen & where is Charles Lamb° I have never seen him since the year 1824 what a season—where is Charles Lamb do you ever see or hear anything of him now or do you know where he is to be found if I could procure his address I wanted to write to him but nobody can tell me where he lives now further then that it is 'some distance from London' which is a bad direction to find him with—I have had a settlement with Mr Taylor & feel so far dissapointed that if I had known I would never have had any thing to do with 'half profits' for it is certainly called by a wrong title—do you ever see him now I heard from him a few weeks back when he was ill of a cold he somtimes speaks in his letters of having seen you but he has said nothing latterly—I do not know how times are with you in the city but with us 'sales & bankrupts'° form the general conversations among all classes & conditions of men how it will end I cannot imagine but it does not seem to be much felt in your loyal city as the newspapers give accounts as usual of your pulling d[own] [pa]llaces only as it would seem for the happiness of building them up again in spots where a husbandman would scarcely think it suitable to errect his cottage but taste now has nothing to do with such things where fashion is every thing & royal fashions too° they must be excellent or it would evidently be considered radicalism to think otherwise—again I beg to be remembered to Mrs Cary & family & hope at your first leisure that I shall have the pleasure of hearing from you

I am dear Sir yours sincerly
John Clare

I have just heard of the Death of Sir Tomas Lawrence° it is a pity that such exellence should be born to die

'When a monarch or a mushroom dies'

the blank is so easily filled up that we scarcely percieve their exit & very seldom their loss but it is not so much with the Laurences the Hiltons & the Ettys° of painting when they go the loss is irretrievable & that they must go is a very melancholy feeling to reflect over when we have been made so happy by the beautys of their immortal creations

To William Robertson

Helpston Jany 29 1830

My dear Sir

I think the *weather* has brought you sufficient apology for the neglect of my travelling gossip in answer to your kind invitation which I am sorry to say I am unable to accept just now for I am confined to my corner chair with a cursed bad cold & quite unable to get out any where but I am otherwise as happy as misfortunes can make me yet if I did not think there was 'a few more rainbows in my sky' I should be cursedly down at heel with my present comforts let me tell you—but spring is a coming & I shall be reanimated with the other insect animacule worshipers of sunshine & flowers

Since I began this lazy letter the blast has decamped & still I cannot make up my mind for so long a journey so you must excuse me & if I had nothing more then excuses on my part to keep me away I should not wish you to do so I assure you

Will you have the kindness to thank Mrs Robinson in my behalf for her beautiful verses°—altho I have not sufficient vanity to think I deserve such praise yet I feel the compliment paid me & the more so in its coming from a Lady & if 'Dan apollo' had any thing of the gentleman in his godhead he would show mercy on my innabillity & assist me to return the compliment but we have discarded his beautiful mythology & it is nothing but right that he should discard our petitions & this is the reason perhaps that we have so few Homers & Shakspears in this *golden* age of canting & tract-vending—the mores the pity

What do you think by the bustle & bother of this country meeting mania when every village is metamorphosed into a Forum & every Giles into an Orator but the strangest metamorphose of all is these out-of-place tory folks becoming radicals & brawling in every corner of the country about reform

Are these the signs of better times I much fear it—yet it is strange to turn round for a moment & see these proteus assemblages—*self* being the only thing that sticks to its own colours for I have not the least doubt that Lord Balmerinos° reasons for joining Prince Charles may be at this day universally applied to these our reformers—'As for the two Kings & their rights' said he 'I cared not a farthing which prevailed but I was starving [ ] God if Mahomet had set up his standard [ ] Highlands I had been a good Mussulma[n] self interest & stuck close to the party'

I have not used that awkard squad of poi[nts] called commas colons & semicolons—feeling y[ou] able to make my scrawl out without [i]t is for this very reason that I have not [ ] them for altho they are at drill hourly daily & weekly—yet they do not know their proper exercise for they even set grammarians at loggerheads & no two can assign them their proper places therefore how should such a novice as I do it—for give each a sentence to point & both shall point it differently—so I have omitted this awkard squad that you may drill my sentences in your own way & understand me the better—give my remembrances to your friend Mr Nell° & alow me to subscribe myself | yours respectfully

John Clare

To John Taylor

Helpston Feby 1 1830

My dear Taylor

I ought to have told you long ago that I got the annuity safe & thank you for sending it—& the reason why I did not do so is that I have fell in with a very violent cold which is now getting better—otherwise I have been well & hearty for a long while—

The times as you say are bad & the worst is that I fear all this bother about 'country meetings' & other rigmarole pretentions will not better them—tho there are many voices mixed up in the cry commonsense is seldom among them for self interests &

individual prosperitys are the universal spirits that stir up these assemblages of reformers

The Farmer as usual is on the look out for 'high prices' & 'better markets' as he stiles them altho these markets are always known to be curses to the cottager the labourer & the poor mechanic

The Parson is now stirring up to radicalism (which some years ago he cryed down as infidelity) for a reduction of taxes merely because he sees that somthing must be done & as he wishes to keep his tythes & his immense livings untouched he throws the burthen on government

The Speculator is looking out for a new paper currency which placed a false value on every species of his trafic & thereby enabled the cunning to cheat the honest & the unprincipled to ruin those who had a principle for so long as country banks are alowed to accumulate their three farthing bits of paper on the public as money without any other check then a trust on their honesty—so long will a few build their prosperity on the ruin of thousands

Yet I cannot help thinking that a paper currency founded upon *just principles* would still be a very commodious way of traffic much better then gold—but I would have every bank issuing one pound notes (which is but a shadow of a promise for a substance which the promiser has pocketed) dependant as branch banks on the Bank of England (many of the other banks are not worth a capital letter) nay every bank issuing paper at all ought to have that check upon them as I think to prosper the general good of the community rather then to encourage the knavery of individuals—but you are a better politician then I am—yet I feel as common sense dictates & I think that a universal reduction of tythes—clerical livings—placemens pensions—& taxes—& all renovated & placed upon a reasonable equality suitable to the present decreased value of money & property is the only way to bring salvation to the country

I know such thoughts sometime back would have been considered as proceeding from a Leveller & a Radical—the meaning of the last word being indefinite like Wig & Tory I cannot say what it means tho I have often heard it bruted in ministerial papers—but I am sure I am no Leveller for I want not a farthing of that which belongs to another—all I want is to keep the little that fortune alowed me to call mine but if government goes on thus partially taking a little from those who have only a little & leaving the wealthy untouched I cannot help but think I shall quickly be what I have been—but times must change & they cannot right[ly] get worse—heavy burthens with proper assistance become light ones—& when there is so many idle lookers on who have no burthens to bear & immense strength to bear them they ought to assist with the rest wether they belong to church or state thats my political creed & if the ministry will for the first time attempt real good to the country this parliment I shall say 'God speed em' but I have no faith in believing impossibilitys becoming possible

I am delighted with Dewints intended kindness° & shall look for it with delighted anticipations—Sir T. Lawrence is gone I hear—he was a kind hearted man & the reccolections of his kindness to me when at his house affected me greatly to hear of his death—

If merit has any thing to do with the choice of the next as it had with the last—Hilton & Etty will be very prominent names in the contest & if the first happens to win it I shall be heartily delighted for he is every way worthy & if Etty gets it I cannot help thinking but he deserves it—both are kind hearted fellows who seem to have nothing in their composition but good will to others & a carless indifference to themselves—I had many things to say but have no room—remember me to all friends

| yours sincerly
John Clare

To George Darley

[January–February? 1830]

My dear Darley

How are you & where are you° in the land of the living or among the monuments of the worthies in 'Westminster Abbey' for it is so long since I heard from you in the shape of a letter or otherwise that I cannot tell where you are or what you are neither can I say wether you are a sheet of paper in my debt or wether I am one in yours & the very reason why I write is to clear up the mystery & come to a correct conclusion as soon as possible for I hate that any obstacles should lie in the direct road to friendship most d—d—ly they are as troublesome to me as those tollbar creeds are in the road to heaven or the hereafter which you please

How the times have altered the opinions & views of the people even here we have our villages mustering into parliments & our farmers puffing themselves up into orators & there is scarcley a clown in the village but what has the asumption to act the politician & I hope this general stir may produce general good but the farce of the thing is that our tory folks should be grown into radicals & be brawling after the reform which they alone have so long & so obstinately prevented—what is the reason—it is a known fact in natural history that foxes will do all they can to drive badgers out of their holes—that they may get in themselves—& I think there is a parrarel in this matter true enough to alow the comparison—such ridiculous inconsistencies in public characters make us ready to exclaim with Mrs Winnifred Jenkins 'O Molly these sarvants at Bath are devils in garnet—they lite the candle at both ends'°

I heard from Taylor a little while back & he says he seldom or ever sees you now—I have had a very unpleasant business to settle with him which thank god I have nearly got over & that was to settle my long pending accounts of 'half profits' which taking every thing into account is I think a bargain that goes under a wrong name—in the first instance I was so far taken in by a Drury of Lincoln (a trafficing hugster after self interest rather then a book seller) as to loose entirely the profits of the first edition of my trifles which is past John Taylors power to prevent or remedy & I cannot expect him to loose it so I must—& all I am sorry for is that such a fellow as Drury should be found professing every virtue under heaven & wanting even that of common honesty—& I am happy so far to find that altho in the first instance I mistook Collins' Ready Reckoner for a Treatise on Friendship John Taylor is not among the number of those professions for I should have been very down at heel indeed to find at last that he had not been a Friend & I am happy to find that I am not dissapointed for dont you think that the situation of booksellers is somthing like that of lawyers & that the mystery of a many of their Items appear rather more consistant to custom then to fair play

Where & how is our friend Allen° give him my kindest remembrances as soon as you see him as also to Mrs Cunningham & all I hope is that you & they are all well—Sir T Laurence is gone I understand & the loss is attempted to be filled up by Mr Shee° did they forget in the hurry that there was such names as Wilkie° Hilton & Etty or was it deliberately considered—Mr Shee may be a great Artist as far as I know but of the others I did know as the opinions of many confirmed that of my own—I am at the end of the sheet & beg to remain dear Darley | yours sincerely

John Clare

To [Eliza Louisa Emmerson]

[March–April 1830]

Had I not recieved your letter to remind me of my errors I should not have been with you in the shape of a letter untill the day after tomorrow for I was indulging in the gossip you desired° of me & wishing to make it more commendable by variety I determined to speak in parables & that in past moods & tenses for I am growing out of myself into many existences & wish to become more entertaining in other genders for that little personal pronoun 'I' is such a presumption ambitious swaggering little fellow that he thinks himself qualified for all company all places & all employments go where you will there he is swaggering & bouncing [*gap in MS*] in the pulpit the parliment the bench aye every where even in this my letter he has intruded 5 several times already who can tell me where he is not or one of his family thats his brother or from how many pen points he is at this moment dropping into his ambitions on humble extances he is a sort of Deity over the rest of the alphabet being here there & everywhere he is a mighty vapour in grammer he grows into a pedantical nuisance & often an O would be a truer personification in philosophy a juggling gossip in oratory a consequential blusterer & in fashion a pretender to every thing—next to points this 'I' is the most consequential in correspondence but he surpasses points he keeps his place but they ramble any where & change places as often as they change writers so that no two puts them in the same posts of honour—where one points with a colon another will afix a semicolon & where another thrusts in a comma another will deprive him of his consequence & put nothing in his place showing that he was a nothing there so much for the pomposity of gramarians but in such a place he cannot be ambitious—he is an absolute Paul Pry°—I wish there he is agen—for varietys sake the english language like some of the oriental ones had no present tense & to come at this variety was the very cause of my delay & to show you that my letter was began I (once more) copy the beginning from the spoilt sheet knowing no more then you do what would have been the end of it tho certain I am again that it would not have been either a poem or a sermon & what is worse feeling a conviction that it would not have been worth reading so altho' the sheet is spoilt your dissapointment is not therefore all is well

To Henry Behnes

Helpstone Aprl 25 1830

My dear Harry

I am ready to shut my eyes to hide myself from the sorry excuses that my pen is preparing to make for my long silence & being so utterly averse to shuffling excuses of all kinds—I paused—shook the ink out of my pen—dipt it again—& again paused but came to the resolution at last of making no excuses at all—so take me as I am & like a good christian I promise to mend not only my pen but my correspondence—& if that does not suit you I shall have the satisfaction of a dissapointed gossip in having the last word with ye—so be offended & silent if ye please Harry or like a mercey loving christian write that my sins are forgiven me—having an oppertunity of sending a letter post free by a friend a Mr Gascoyn who if he has time will deliver it at your door & if not will drop it into a twopenny post so that it will reach you by as cheap an invention as ever the Usefull Knowledge society could devise on this side of 'working for nothing' therefore I could not let the oppertunity pass bye without sending an enquirey after you not on a card or a sheet of *note paper* but a good honest quarto sized sheet imperial measure—I dont like half laughs of any sort nor half letters either so here is one double the size of yours which as a plumper I will cram full of somthing even if it be nonsense to fulfill my intentions of devoting myself to your service untill I have worked myself out of the bondage of idleness in correspondence—I was at Stamford Fair enjoying myself with the fun & humours of your London exebitionists who while they set the country flats° gaping at the extravagant unaccountables of what they transacted on the show stage & of more that they would do within—performed some modern miracles on the pockets of those who had more money then wit & so extraordinary was their power in that particular science that altho the farmer felt he had lost his purse he was ready to swear by the merit of his own knowledge—that nobody did it—altho it was done—another sold a cow & altho he placed the soveraigns securely in his fob with the kind assistance of an unknown friend who had the politeness not only [to] caution him to keep it safe but [ ] to help him to make it safe—yet when he got home & began to look for his purse he found that by some miraculous process the whole of his soverigns was turned into half pence! Miracles have not ceased with us you see as yet—I did not go to Mr Simpsons but I saw Frank in the Fair—& that was all—I should have sent back your 'Newspapers' but dare not saddle the parcel on the bearer of this letter for fear of its being thought too much trouble I have written to Mrs Emmerson & have heard from her also & am going to write again to day but she says nothing of you—do you go there I should hope you have not made such bad use of your evenings as to omit spending some of them in stratford place—remember me to your brothers & all friends & if you are still disposed to condemn me have the kindness to look into yourself & be charitable for remember you have made promises & never performed them as yet & if I even thought you never would I should still be disposed to excuse you

& subscribe myself | dear Harry yours sincerly

J Clare

To John Taylor

July 1 1830 | Helpstone

My dear Taylor

In this *half yearly* correspondence there is always somthing very gloomy & melancholly stirred up with former reccolections—it is now a matter of nessesity that forces the communications—but it was not always thus—& whose fault it is I dont know but I think it is not mine—however time makes changes among us all—from the throne to the cottage there is no difference° he proves us all nothings at last—I cannot hear of any of our old acquaintances now except by accident even George Darley cannot condescend to remember me—no not so much as for a moment even to answer my last letter—nor Dewint tho he promised you he was sending the picture & altho I have from that scircumstance reminded him of it—he is still silent—well what is to be must be—I hear from one friend still the amiable english Dante—Cary—he is still the same—still possesing that calm quaker like urbanity that is never ruffled either by prosperity or adversity—& still a Curate I dare say to the disgrace of Bishops & Patrons of Church property—but merit has nothing to do now a days even with matters of godliness—cant chicanery cunning & hypocrisy are the only candidates that shuffle into success

> 'We know the things are neither rich nor rare
> But wonder how the devil they get there'°

from Cary I have heard of Charles Lamb & Wainright the Painter who has fell into good luck & I am glad of it many very many are destined to illustrate the old adage—'It is better to be born fortunate then rich'—& I am sorry that with many more worthy I am not of the number

I began this letter with an intention that memorys of other days have displaced & might have done so to the end of the chapter & that is to desire you to send me my little money as soon as you can—how I am to stand these dockings I cannot tell—for my family increases & my income diminishes & I have this year written for none of the Annuals save one—Mr Dales—° for some of them paid me by promises & promises only which was of no use to me & others having refused what I sent without any reasons at all (& as I thought inserted much worse things in their places) that I came to the resolution to write no more let the consequence be what it might & so I am left in an awkard dilemma & providence alone is the hope that keeps me in spirits—I asked of you last year Keats Endymion for Mr H. Marsh & 'Guesses at Truth' for myself but you took no notice of the matter—where is Hessey he has been to see Mrs Emmerson who tells me he is a dealer in pictures—remember [me] to him & to all friends especially Dewint & tell him of the picture—write quickly with as much news as you can

yours sincerely
J Clare

To John Taylor

[before 15 September 1830]

My dear Taylor

I have not been able untill now to write to you—for I have been dreadfully ill—& I can scarcely manage even now to muster courage sufficient to feel myself able to write a letter but you will excuse all—I have been bled blistered & cupped & have now a seaton in my neck & tho much better I have many fears as to recovery but I keep my mind as quiet as I can—& am able to read a Newspaper—all I regret is that I cannot describe my feelings sufficiently to benefit from our friend Dr Darlings kind advice in whom I always had the greatest confidence—my fancys & feelings vary very often but I now feel a great numbness in my right shoulder—& the seaton tho I cannot bear it to be dressed for 3 or 4 mornings together discharges so much that I fear I shall fall into a decline at last—but thankgod my head is now relieved tho it stings now & then as if nettled I cannot describe what I have suffered but all I now dwell on is that I am getting better—I thought once that I should never have met health thus far so as to be able to write or read any more I can do both & I am thankful to that power who gave me the means to think & be happy & who can take both away when he chuses—how is Hessey I often thought of his kind attentions to me in my first illness when I could think—& tell him I desire to be remembred to him—I have got another addition to my family a Girl° a few weeks old there is now six of them—& all I want is a cottage & a few acres of land but do you know I cannot get any thing of the kind either for love or money—I have sold all the copys of my poems & I wish you would send me down another packet of them as soon as ever you can for I have several copies spoken for—so send me *6* copies of the first Vol *6* of the Village Minstrel & *12* of the Shepherds Calender & dont forget me there is nothing that would give me more pleasure then the revival of our correspondence but as the fault is not mine I cannot mend it—still my old feelings have never forsaken me & I look upon the early acquaintance which my ryhming trifles procured me as constituting the happiest period of my life I wish nothing had broken in upon those asociations for they had grown as dear to me as my own fireside—but some are in the grave yet death shall not have the warmth of their memorys that lives with me untill this hand is as cold & insensible as the moulds which cover them—where is Darley he never writes & Dewint tho I have written two letters to him [he] never noticed them—did I offend him if I have done so I cannot make out how I did it because you told me he intended to send me the drawing which emboldened me to repeat it—thats all I can say about the matter I have felt the dissapointment long & have not forgotten it yet

I am dear Taylor yours sincerly
John Clare

To James Augustus Hessey

[after 15 September 1830]

My dear Hessey

I recieved your kind letter with great pleasure that accompanied the parcel & was very glad to hear from you & also to hear that you was so well & the account of your healthy catalogue as a first attempt pleased me as much but I had long heard of your success° by my excellent Friends Mr & Mrs Emmerson (then whom two of kinder intentions & warmer feelings never existed for time hath made no change in them) & the success of so old an acquaintance could not fail of giving me pleasure which next to my own interested me as much as any thing could do & I was as sorry to hear of your late struggle but honesty is proof against every thing but misfortune—& poverty never disgraces it—it only leaves it to its own lustre & shows its value—As to religion my mind is compleatly at rest in that matter my late deplorable situation proved to me that I had read the Bible successfully for it was an antidote to my deepest distresses & I had not the least doubt on my conviction of its truth—but I recieved a relish for reading it from some Numbers of Scotts Octavo Bible which is a most excellent Work & it also gave me a relish for thinking—I studied the Bible often & found it long before my illness the one book that makes the carnallitys of life pallatable & the way to eternity pleasant—the one & only book that supplys soul & body with happiness—I also found in it the beautiful in poetry in perfection—I had read Homer but a greater then Homer is there—I found in it gems of the oldest excellence in sublimity which the greatest & oldest poets had borrowed to enrich their own lustre & what astonished me most was that I found beautys that I had never met with before tho I had read it over time after time when I was the happiest fellow in extistance when I had no particular friends & no enemies at all neither wanting the one or fearing the other—it was then the cottage book the only piece & part of the cottage furniture in the shape of a book which I could lay my hands on & tho I read it with the customary reverence instilled into my mind by my parents I read it with a lack of reflection & rather more for amusment then profit—I am glad to hear that your family are well & to Mrs Hessey & all you will remember me—& I am as happy to tell you that mine are all well & hearty & as to Patty she is never or so seldom ill that she forgets from time to time what illness is & I have heard her declare that she never knew what the headache was in her life untill within these last few years—she has been of much comfort to me both in illness & health & I always feel happy that I met with such a fortunate accident that brought us together for 'an honest woman is the honour of her husband'° & Solomon who said it might no doubt have given his whole inheritance of riches for such unpurchased sincerity (as the poor man posseses) & been never able to meet it—my childern are comforts in their kind but the thoughts of their future welfare often makes me uncomfortable about them I wish to make them all good common scholars & wish also to instill into all their minds the innestimable value & the upright integrity of common honesty Mr Mossop our Vicar has been uncommonly kind to me in my illness & he wrote as kindly while I was ill to Mrs Emmerson to ask her to get my eldest boy Frederick into a school°—& he has told me to mention it again to Mrs E but the shock that his success will give m[e] in being obliged to part with him (if the attemp[ts] of his friends are successful)—will be so great that I never have had the courage to alude to it—tho the Boy says that he will go if he can get in & often aludes to it with childish satisfaction—the names of our old friends which you mention I am extreemly happy to hear of & Charles Lamb I want to write to will you tell him so when you see him that he may leave his address with you poor Miss Lamb° I hope she will recover—there is hopes & there is mercey to hope it—Hazlitts death° I saw in the papers I read it twice over before I dare believe it was Hazlitt that I had met & whose writings I had read with so much gratification & it shocked me much to think another acquaintance had made a blank in our memorys & in our esteem for the tallents of Hazlitt was of no every day matter—what I have read are the works of a man of origional Genius & it seems that he died in the character of Genius—neglected & forgotten—when will the cant & hypocrasy of trifling be put aside & the sterling merit of superior minds be so valued as to be considerd worthy of universal reward & the humbug of party cavils & party interest be done away with—I doubt never give my respects to all friends & believe me dear Hessey | yours sincerely

John Clare

To John Taylor

[24 January 1831]

My dear Taylor

I have waited with some dissapointment the arrival of the Parcel & as it containd my fund money I am very apprehensive that it may have met with some accident by the way for altho I have sent four times to Deeping & have desired people to call twice that number no parcel was found there & therefore I thought it advisable to write at once & tell you & I wish you would send it directly as I am in wants of it—that government security is a very precarious one & I expect that they will keep drilling my little annuity untill they get it all into their own awkward squad & leave me a cypher for interest at last for they keep making out one act after another & injuring every bodys interests to keep up their own—& still I have many hopes of the present ministry for I think if they can find out the way to better the unbearable oppressions of the labouring classes they will do it—that Lord Althorp° is an excellent sample of honest intentions & if he ends his course as he begins it wether he looses or wins he will wear an honour that becomes the Gem of all nobil[i]tys & remains the most noble—without which titles & stars & garters are merely baubles—& distinctions nothings—pride is growing into its own proper stripe a 'motley coat' for common sense to laugh at—but pride has done a host of mischiefs that will take much time to remedy & get over—we are quiet in our neighbourhood° but as a spark dropt in gunpowder—the least impression either of oppression or imaginary oppression would burst into a flame—& yet the 'people' as they are called were a year or two back as harmless as flies—they did not seem even to be susceptible of injustice but when insult began to be tried upon them by the unreasonable & the proud their blood boiled into a volcano & the irruption is as certain as death if no remedy can be found to relieve them God forbid that I should live to see a revolution it is bad enough to be under the apprehensions of such a matter but every day convinces us that a hazardous change of calm or tempest is approaching write me *directly* to say *when* the parcel will arrive as I am uneasy as to its travelling in these freebooting calamitys

I am dear Taylor yours &c

J Clare

To John Taylor

[7 March 1831]

My dear Taylor

I must trouble you with this request & I hope you will speedily answer it—for you are of late some letters in my debt—

but as to that I never minded when entertainment was all—it is now nessesity for I am ill & very ill & as I cannot get a frank soon enough (for Lord Milton is not in parliment)° to write to Dr Darling I trouble you to tell him & I hope you will write to tell me you have done so—I was taken 3 weeks back or more with a pain at the stomach which would not go off & as it affected my head very much I felt alarmed & took a part of Dr Ds last prescription which checked it & subdued the humour in some measure but whenever I attempted to walk friction brought it on as bad as ever & the pain at my stomach started again as bad as ever & I then finished the packet of powders & on last s'aturday night by the reccommendation of Mr Mossop (having nothing left of my last prescription) I took a blue pill & on Sunday morning I waked with a dreadful burning humour in my lesks° & a contraction so as almost prevented me from making water on monday I commenced a second course of Dr Darlings medicine & the humour tho abated is not subdued—for I awoke this morning with a burning heat in my fundament where the humour again made its appearance with prickly pains in my head arms & shoulders & they are as bad just now—I fear I shall be in the same state I was in last summer—for untill last night I got tollerable rest but the pain at my stomach was more frequent in its attacks & I awoke in dreadful irritation thinking that the Italian liberators were kicking my head about for a foot ball—my future prospects seem to be no sleep—a general debility—a stupid & stunning apathy or lingering madness & death—my dreads are very apprehensive & uneasy I dislike this prickly feel about the face & temples worse then any thing & a sobbing or beating when I lay my head down on the pillow was first felt last night for a long time—my appetite was gone & from monday to this morning 4 Eggs & a bit of bread have been the whole of my food—it never attacked my appetite before as I know of & I am so alarmed & so anxious to get better that if I cannot in no other way I will draw upon or sell out my fund money (if it can be done without extravagant loss) & take lodgings in an humble way as near Dr Darlings as I can & the Steam baths in great Mar[l]boro Street which did me uncommon benefit in 1827 & would do me as much benefit agen I write this not as a resolution but for your *advice as a friend* for I want to get better & Dr Darling in his letter to me orderd a steam bath but there is no such things here—at all events write by return of post with Dr Darlings advice   I shall wait with impatience for it—I have been favoured by a friend with a sight of the Quarterly Review for January in which is an article on some poems of one Jones° which Mr Southey has published & th[e] poem which induced him to do so is so mu[ch] like a facsimile of a trifle of mine publ[ished] in Pringles Friendships Offering for 1830—To the Autumn Robin & as most of Mr Jones Images are the very same—I should like you to see mine & if you have not got a copy of Friendships Offering—I will write out the verses for your opinion—the coincidences as such things are called might be construed into imitations by many & as mine was first published I like to be correct on that point tho in trifles—for Mr Southey seems to hold uneducated poets in very little estimation & talks about the march of mind in a sneering way—as to education it aids very little in bringing forth that which is poetry—& if a mans humble situation in life is to be the toleration for people to praise him I should say such admiration is worth but little   the whole review for a leading journal exceeds all the twaddle I ever met with—there is a line or two in Italics° about a bell not being rung & a silence pervading at dinner time—are these—beauties—I feel anxious that a selection of my fugitives should appear the earliest oppertunity—as the best things I have written are among them & I wanted to get them written out for your opinion but I cannot—

I am dear Taylor yours sincerly
John Clare

I had intended a good while back to send you some sonnets viz Poesy a Maying° but you are a matter of fact man now in literature & may deem such fancys intrusions

To Marianne Marsh

Helpstone July 6 1831

My dear Madam

I return the Essays with many thanks for the use of them & I am really ashamed to make an apology for keeping this book so long but I kept putting it off from one oppertunity to another untill an almost unpardonable neglect grew up from the omissions—yet my inability to write without much trouble was the cause why I delayed to send it this spring—& in the winter it was dangerous for any lone person to go even a journey to Peterbro—such was the state of feeling among that useful but ignorant class of people our peasantry that mischief became so predominant & daring as to threaten the peacable even in their cottages & I hope for the sake of my own feelings never to see such another threatning winter again—for I fear there is even in our day a class of desperadoes little or no better than the rabble that made up the army of Jack Cade

'a ragged multitude
'Of hinds & peasants rude & merciless

. . . .

'All scholars lawyers courtiers gentlemen
'They call false caterpillars & intend their death'°

the universal wish of such ignorance is 'that henceforward all things shall be in common' & surely when such a desperate flood gathers into strength—the mind must feel terror at its threatning destruction—their passions are not softened by reason or guided by common sense—the mob impulse of the moment kindles their minds into mischivous intentions & reflection never stays their course for a moment   brute strength is all they possess & it is as dangerous a monopoly in the hands of a mob as it is in that of so many savages & I may say I never saw so terrible a threatening of rev[o]lutionary forbodings as there was in the maschine breaking & grain destroying mania of last winter—& I am sorry to say they had too much apology for joining in such disturbances as their wants had been so long neglected as to be entirely forgotten untill it burst out into the terrible jepordays—& these were the chief reasons for my keeping this book so long which you was so kind as to lend me—The Essays are very good   there is some trifling perhaps treated in a more serious manner than a mind of more extensive intercourse with human life would have thought nessesary yet sterling good sense & a common honesty of feeling are their chief characteristics

In point of excellence they should have commenced the volume—but the book that has given me most satisfaction since my late illness has been Horn on the Psalms° & it is one of the very best books I have ever met with—I am sorry to say that I feel very ill at times but I bear up with it as well as I can—feeling confident that whatever befalls me in sickness or health will be for the best & without that feeling I could scarcely bear up with life much less enjoy it—I beg to give my best respects to all your family & to remain dear madam | yours sincerely & respectfully

John Clare

To John Taylor

Helpston July 24 1831

My dear Taylor

I recieved the parcel & thank you for sending it for I assure you that I was troubled in consequence of not being able to meet my expences & even now I cannot get clear of them by a long way but I must make the best shift I can—I will mark out the passages which I fancy sublime or beautiful in the Vols you sent me° with remarks &c at my future leisure & then I will send them to you to do as you please with—as to what you say respecting the Poems I cannot say any thing in the matter further than that you may act with them just as you would do if they were your own property for I know you are my friend & I see no fear in what you may get for them or do with them—for it appears that they are of slow sale—but why do you think they will fetch no more than one shilling per copy°—if that is your opinion as you know such things better than I do I repeat use your own liberty & do as you like in the matter but at the same time I should like to get out a new Vol with some one if I could & I have long intended & am now resolved in putting together what I have at different intervals written for that purpose viz Letters of Advice to my Childern & Essays on common place matters in life & when I get them in a form I will send them to you for your perusal—In the Vol of old Poets I very much admire those of William Brown° there is a freshness & beauty about them that supprised me & with which I was not acquainted—there is much english landscape about them & the second Song of Brittanias Pastorals commences with one of these

'The Muses friend grayeyd aurora yet
'Held all the meadows in a cooling sweat' &c &c

altho not of the beautiful but Surry° is beautiful

'The sunne hath twise brought forth his tender green
'Twice clad the earth in lively lustiness
'Once have the winds the trees despoiled clean
'& once again begins their cruelness' &c &c

Surreys Sonnets are tender & very poetical there is a breathing of Shakspearian healthfulness about them that is evergreen—& there is much more to say about this Vol which at my earliest leisure I will look over & make notes as I go on—but I think it very slovenly edited thats all & many names left out that ought to be in & some that occupy much room m[ight] have oc[cup]ied less by abridgment but after all what [a] dissapointment to see Wither° in little only filling a few pages—

I am my dear Taylor yours very sincerely
John Clare

To John Taylor

Helpstone Octr 1831

My dear Taylor

I have again been very unwell & unable to write or read or in fact to do any thing—but thank God I am now well & mean to keep so if I can—I have not been able to read the old Poets with any intention to select & there is no room on the margin to make any remarks so that I shall be forced when I do start to pass them without any—how is it I cannot find the sublime & beautiful which I expected & I wish I had you by me to read to me for the defect must lie in my imperfect way of reading them but if Mr Southeys judgment as a collector of the beauties of old Poets be correct I am sure mine must be very imperfect for it appears to me a most imperfect collection & would rather seem as a sample got together by a printer as chance directed rather than by the judgment of a poet & that Mr Southey—where is Suckling & where is Herrick & twenty more that ought to have been there for the Lyrics of Suckling have never been surpassed & only equaled by Shakspear

All I want to go on is a stimulus an encouraging aspiration that refreshes the heart like a shower in summer—instead of that I have nothing but drawbacks & dissapointments I live in a land overflowing with obscurity & vulgarity far away from taste & books & friends poor Gilchrist was the only man of letters in this neighbourhood & now he has left it a desert—I see things praised that appear to me utterly worthless & read critisisms in the periodicals when I do see them that the very puffers of Blacking & Bearsgreese would be really ashamed of—& I lay my intentions aside having no heart to proceed but I am resolved to show them I can judge for myself & what ever remarks I make on the ryhmes of others they shall be done honestly & with as little vanity as possible

& now respecting 'self' have [you] made out any thing respecting the publishing my Poems because I now want to try to get them out as I am going to leave here & commence cottage farming° & therefore I shall want somthing to begin with & as I am rather unwilling to interfere with the fund money if I can help it I should like for you to use your interest for me & do all you can for that I am going is positive & I that I want somthing to start me is positive & these two cases make it nessesary that I must do somthing therefore I trust to you for advice & I hope you will write to me immediately—of one thing I am certain that if health keeps on myside I shall become an independent man & care a fig for nobody but friends—I shall have a good Landlord & I am told the place is a good one & therefore it is all on myside furthermore I shall have fewer regrets to leave this old corner where I now write this letter the place of all my hopes & ambitions for they have insulted my feelings latterly very much & cut down the last Elm next the street & the old Plumb tree at the corner is blown down & all the old associations are going before me—I can send for your inspection all the poems I have written for the present Vol—I thought of you very often in my illness & wished then to say what I now can say which is that if you outwear me that every thing I have written may pass under your observation & nothing be published without your opinion—I find that true friends are scarce—illness has not shaken my confidence in yourself but confirmed it

How is Hessey & Hilton & where is Dewint have I offended

him that long promise has never reached me—How is Carey you have another Ed: of his Dante I see in the popular size & it will be popular—where is Charles Lamb are 'Album Verses'° his own publishing or the collection of a Bookseller—I have not seen any thing but the title which I thought in bad taste

yours sincerly
John Clare

To [Sir John Trollope]

To the honourable Sir J°

[1831–2?]

Sir

Altho I am a perfect stranger to you my love for old times & my veneration for antiquity emboldens me to write my wishes which are the wishes of antiquity herself (as she seems to have got out of the worlds way into every nook & corner to be at rest)—In a wood of yours in your Lordship of A[*gap in MS*] there are some fragments of an old castle or some other vestige of ancient shadows & I frequently in times past paid it a visit as a favourite spot but on last seeing it I was very dissapointed to find that the hand of modern improvement (whose thirst for change is eternal) had found it out & commenced its utter destruction to supply materials for mending the road through the wood—& as I satisfied my own mind that you knew nothing of the matter—to please my own feelings & that of antiquity by rescuing the remaining fragments from the intentions of the road menders I came to the resolution of taking the liberty to write to you—feeling in no fear that I shall offend by the intrusion but a pleasant hope that the spot will be saved from the levellers who on a second visit will leave nothing but the level on which it lies—It is in the wood called the 'Lawn' at the south east corner & close beside it in the neighbouring close is a portion of the moat that used to suround it

To Marianne Marsh

[early January 1832]

My Dear Madam

I recieved your note of this morning with great pleasure as it gives me an oppertunity to say that my family are all in a fair way of being well although they are now troubled with the hooping cough or chincough as for myself I have just fell in with a bad cold & I cannot shake it off sufficiently to get out for I have been so subject to illness laterly that I dread every hazard that may tend to renew it & under that feeling perhaps incur more danger of illness than if I had no fear of it—I am going from Helpstone at Spring to a cottage at Northbro'—where I hope that exersise will keep me in health & then I shall have a pathway to contentment & I think these ingredients are a sufficient receipt for happiness—but I have much ado to work myself up into a resolution to leave a spot that is so familiar to me—but in thinking of my family likes & dislikes were thrown bye—my silence would imply that I had forgotten the kindness of friends but it was only a fear of intruding with my correspondence that kept me silent—I have to thank you very kindly for some little books° which I read with satisfaction & those which put together the 'ayes' & 'noes' of Mr Cobbett may be very useful to plain dealing people as to party they will not see

I look upon Cobbett as one of the most powerful prose writers of the age—with no principles to make those powers commendable to honest praise—the Letters to farmers contain some very sensible arguments & some things that appeared to be too much of party colouring—there is no medium in party matters where there is excess it is always on one side—& that is the worst of it—I am no politician but I think a reform is wanted—not the reform of mobs where the bettering of the many is only an apology for injuring the few—nor the reform of partys where the benefits of one is the destruction of the other but a reform that would do good & hurt none—I am sorry to see that the wild notions of public spouters always keep this reform out of sight—& as extreams must be met by extreams—the good is always lost like a plentiful harvest in bad weather—mobs never were remembered for a good action but I am sorry to see it now &

then verging into the middle classes of society whose knowledge ought to teach them commonsense & humanity for if they have it they never let it get into their speeches

To John Taylor

[early January 1832]

My dear Taylor

I have again been very ill & all unable to write or think or do any thing but thank God I am now better & I mean to keep so if I can—I should have written to you three weeks back but a matter fell in my way that occupied my attentions which were not then fixed but they now are & I hope I have luck in the wind—for Im going to leave Helpstone at spring to occupy a cottage with about 5 acres of land—& the best is that when I get fixed in it; it will be as certain a home as if it was my own—for I shall have a good landlord as Lord Milton owns it & altho I have had some difficulties to leave the woods & heaths & favourite spots that have known me so long for the very molehills on the heath & the old trees in the hedges seem bidding me farewell—other associations of friendships I have few or none to regret—for my father & mother will be often with me—& tho my flitting is not above three miles off—there is neither wood nor heath furzebush molehill or oak tree about it & a Nightingale never reaches so far in her summer excursions—would you believe it but the fact is it is so—but we must put aside such fancys for a season to live in the world by taking it as we find it—& my wishes have grown into resolves to better my self & I feel that I am commencing with a good oppertunity that keeps up my spirits & do you know I feel as happy at this moment as ever I did in my life—for I am looking at a sunny prospect—(there may be clouds & where is the sky without them) & I think that I shall yet live to see myself independant of all but old friends & good health & as the best way to end well is to begin well my desire is to start upon a new leaf—to get out of debt before I leave here & to keep out when I commence a cottage farmer—the place I hear keeps two cows & therefore I shall want a good deal to set me up & start me—I dont much like to meddle with my fund money that is to break it but I cannot get on without it

& so I must do it yet if I could draw a sum upon it I would do so because I fancy I shall be able to replace it as I think of saving somthing yearly by my labour as its poor doing in working for nothing—therefore I want your advice° & that directly for my mind is made up & all that remains is to make a beginning

I have never heard from you since you sent me the old poets neither have I written but that vacancy is under such a heavy cloud that I cannot even turn back to view the prospect—I hope the future will find me a good stock of health for without it all else is nothing—all pleasure to a man in sickness is as gold in a famine of no value & utterly useless—when we look for health by comparisons it is like seeing the sun on a morning after waking from a dream of perpetual darkness—I have found it so & felt it & health is the only current coin for happiness

I wish you had put a few leaves of writing paper here & there in the vol of old poets—for there is no margin in the book for remarks—I have just looked it over—& was dissapointed at the selection I expected to have seen all Withers & also Suckling & Herrick & Crawshaw utterly neglected in spite of that beautiful illustration of the miracle—a miracle of the beautifull itself where he describes the water as blushing into wine & Robert Southwell the author of that fine couplet

> Men trample grass & prize the flowers in may
> But grass is green when flowers do fade away

& many other of the neglected poets who illustrate the gardens of parnassus like the unnoticed blossoms on a summer landscape—were I a popular publisher or a popular author I would publish a cheap vol of these neglected poets as the best specimen of the beautiful in song Mr Southey has the power I have nothing but the will—& I wish he had added to his short accounts of the authors his opinions of their beaut[ies] &c this would have created a taste in the public & been the means perhaps of clearing the way a little further into the wilderness that surrounds these beautiful blossoms which when seen would be taken to adorn the garden as well as the field

A poet that strikes me in this collection as very orignial & true to nature that is very english is William Brown There is a freshness & truth about him that supprised me—there are many consciets in him & when gentlemen & ladys describe rural scenery there is sure to be fanciful imagerys but the fancys of poets are poetry for if their homes be not in the green fields & pleasant places their hearts is—Brown is a sort of Isaac Walton in verse—& many of the popular poets that followed him seem to have made his poems a sort of commonplace book for their descriptions & if they were not fountains of Castalie to inspire them they were certainly good charts to guide them for his pictures are close copys of pastoral scenery

To John Taylor

[after 13 January 1832]

I had been very troubled in mind when your letter reached me for I really thought that the difficulutys the 'red sea' that now lies between me & the 'land of promise' would become impassable for do you know enemies have sprung up where I did not expect them—& a neighbour of mine had told me this morning that mine Landlord a low spirited fellow had been talking it about the town of my backrent—the fact is I owe him now for two years but I thought that my honest intentions would have given him feelings of more delicacy towards me then throwing tokens of my poverty into the mouths of my neighbours for no other purpose then that of insulting me because he is offended at my going to leave the house to better myself—this hurt me in such a manner that I felt the truth of Solomons advice as just 'My son it is better to die then to be poor'—now to get out of these difficultys about twenty pounds would release me for the present can you send me that sum to be settled hereafter & it would be now as a godsend—& then there is the great desert to be crossed & I shall want to start in April & if the money cannot be sold out surely we may get a less sum on its security—I have hopes & they are strong ones that I shall see the expected Caanan but I am so cut down by times that I dont know that I shall weather the storm

To Elizabeth Wilson

Jany 22 [1832]

Dear Madam

I recieved your first letter° & for the neglect in not answering it I beg your pardon—your last letter came to hand last night & to it I reply craving at the same time craving your indulgence to read & think—as I state facts—& as Mr W[ilson] seems to have a share of the inconveniences of life as well as my self I have no doubt he has a portion of common kindness for others in the same situation—I am on the point of leaving Helpstone & am drawing every matter in the way of settlement towards a conclusion as fast as I can & expected every day a final answer of settling my affairs in London for this I waited three months & I have recieved for answer that it cannot be done till May as one of the party° is in Italy—but if any thing turns out in the mean time

To [John Taylor]

[late January 1832]

I did not write sooner because you would know I recieved the dividend by other means & though I have not been over busy to plead any excuse for me I have been burthened with matters that might make apologys for longer absence but I will not trouble my letter with them—I hope you have had some intellagence from Mr Woodhouse as all my anxiety dwells upon that independance of mind that I hope to arive at by using the means which are my own & freeing myself of obligations that burthen & oppress me—I therefore eagerly hope my little money in the funds may be got at because it was not my wish or intention that it should be placed out of my power when I wanted to put it to better uses—therefore now the time is arived that it can be so applied all I wish is that you would act for me as you would act for yourself in such a matter—advice that costs nothing to the giver I have in plenty—& as it is only theory it is worth nothing to my present nessesity—some tell me that cows are excellent profits & some tell me that pigs are excellent profits

& others that ploughed land would be far better then either—& others who have land under the plough say that I am far better off with greensward—& nothing disheartened I hear this confliction of opinions & strife of tongues with the determination to trye & if God gives me health I have a strong hope in the wind that I shall succeed—my whole ambition is to arive at that climax when I can say I owe no man a shilling & feel that I can pay my way—to me this is independance & nothing else—of money I know no other values then of its paying its way & further then that to me it is a worthless matter—show of wealth & pomp of luxury are shadows that never came under the dominion of my wishes—& I often wonder that reasoning man can can keep alive that unreasonable Ape called Pride to exult in riches & think it greatness—As soon as the house is built I leave Helpstone & I wish to leave it out of debt—which I shall not be able to do if I cannot get the money untill May so I hope better tidings & shall be very anxious to hear from you—I enter upon the cottage as a tennant—you speak as if you felt it otherwise—but I cannot look at any right of my having any claims of extra kindness on those who have been kind to me already all my delight is that I have an oppertunity of having such men as the Fitzwilliams & the Miltons for Landlords—for when a man rents anything under them it is as certain as his own & it is as difficult to catch any cottage belonging to them or Lord Exeter as it was formerly of catching a prize in the lottery for in spite of political differences their fame as 'excellent Landlords' are uniform & universal—I wrote to a friend of whom I know nothing further then correspondence alows me to ask his advice as to publishing a Vol of ryhmes but I have heard nothing from him yet & as it is the first presumption I ever took of the kind it is the last—& yet in spite of every difficulty ryhme will come to the end of my pen—when I am in trouble I go on & it gives me pleasure by resting my feelings of every burthen & when I am pleased it gives me extra gratification & so in spite of myself I ryhme on—I have got [*unfinished*]

To [Thomas Pringle]

[after 8 February 1832]

I am the more anxious to write to you to prevent wrong impressions that my silence might lead you very reasonably to fancy—I am not so far a bargain hunter [?] or so bold a fellow to imagine that my ryhming trifles were worth any such remuneration that has been given for them by the publishers of these annuels—only they voluntarily offered it & I accepted it but I am not dissapointed with the reverse of fortune—(for I cannot think these things pay them) & I do assure you you are heartily welcome not only to what you have but to any trifle you may feel inclined to request of me—

—I became a scribbler for downright pleasure in giving vent to my feelings & long & pleasing painful was my struggles to acquire a sufficient knowledge of the written language of england before I could put down my ideas on paper even so far as to understand them myself—but I mastered it in time sufficiently to be understood by others & then became an author by accident & felt astonished that the critics should notice me at all

& that one should imagine I had read the old Poets & that others should imagine I had coined words which were as common around me as the grass under my feet—I shrank from myself with extacy & have never been myself since—as to profit the greatest profits most congenial to my feelings were the friends it brought me & the names that it rendered familiar to my fireside—scraps of whose melodys I had heard & read in my corner—but had I only imagined for a moment that I should hold communion with such hereafter that would have then been to me 'as music in morning'—but I wrote because it pleased me—in sorrow & when happy it makes me happier & so I got one

& when they please others whose taste is better then mine the pinnacle of my ambition is attained—& I am so astonished that I can hardly believe I am myself for no body believed I could do any thing here & I never believed that I could myself—I persued pleasure in many paths & never found her so happily as when I sung imaginery songs to the woodland solitudes & winds of autumn

I should have been very glad to have seen your friend but I have never heard of his being at Deeping lectures on Slavery have been given in the neighbourhood but I thought it was by Mr Buckingham the Traveller°—I have very little interest in the slavedealing arguments but I have a feeling on the broad principle of common humanity that slavery is not only unfeeling but disgraceful to a country professing religion—but then I have an idea that war is as excessive a wrong where mens attributes are founded on the basis of religious right—'do unto others as we would be done unto'—& surely slavery & war must be two very great & very black contradictions to such principles—& yet people argue that blacks were made for bondage & that war was nessesary to keep peace—& so ones qualms are forced to be satisfied—Messrs Smith & Elder sent me a large book for what reason I know not on west Indian slavery°—& I fancied to be sure it was against it but I found that it was in commendation of slavery—written by an ungenerous man & capable of better things

give my hearty good wishes to James Hogg° I am ill but I would travel ten miles to shake him by the hand & wish him success—I saw a ballad of his° in a paper sometime back on the Herding at eve from the pasture which delighted me—tell him to go on with such old fashioned pastorals & time will pay him for all dissapointments—honest Allan wrote some sweet beginnings in the Nithsdale Songs that endeard his memory to my feelings but I fear he has forgot himself since then among Chantrys marble beautys° beautiful indeed but flesh & blood is wanting & this Allan has written of sculptors & painters the [*unfinished*]

To Charles Mossop

[At the end of Apr. 1832 Clare had moved with his family to a cottage in Northborough, three miles from Helpstone. In the *Athenaeum*, 25 Aug. 1832, there appeared this comment: 'Lord Milton has, we understand, bestowed on John Clare, the Northamptonshire poet, a handsome house, with a garden and large orchard, amounting in all to six or seven acres, and when this is considered, in addition to a small annuity—some thirty pounds per year or so—we are bound, not only to praise Lord Milton, but put his name down among the public benefactors to the muse . . .' The *Stamford Bee* and the *Alfred* repeated this story. On 30 Sept. the *Alfred* attempted a correction, followed by the *Bee*, and then the *Athenaeum* in Oct.]

[after 25 August 1832]

My dear Sir

I wish to ask your advice respecting a paragraph copied from the Atheneum into most of the local papers pretending to know of a matter of which I know nothing viz that Lord Milton has given me the Cottage to live in &c &c

Not that I should take any notice of the folly of such gossip further then it troubles me & injures my feelings of a propriety of independance for I came into the cottage with no such feelings or expectations & it is too bad for any one to surmise & publish their surmises for truth—I should hope his Lordship will not be offended at such stories for I cannot help it—nor did I know any thing of it untill two or three days ago when the Editor of the Bee with a friend from London came to see me & they were supprised at my ignorance of the matter saying it was first printed in the Atheneum & copied into most of the others—but I positively told them my expectations were never so high & that I expected to pay rent the same as my nieghbours—& that was all I knew of it—what is to be done should it be contradicted or should it be taken no notice of—I am very unwell & it troubles me in fact a trifle upsets me & my spirits are either elevated to extacy or depressed to nothings—but my intentions as to publishing are earnest & I expect the prospectus will be finished to night—give my best respects to Miss Mossop | yours resp[ectful]ly & [?]

J Clare

To John Taylor

Northborough [6] Septr 1832

My dear Taylor

I had hopes that I should have heard from you about the arival of Mr Woodhouse & that I should have had the happiness of making use of my own money but 'while the grass grows the steed starves' & I am so tethered in difficultys that I can wear against them no longer nor can I put up with the coldness & insults of those to whom I am indebted any longer—for those to whom I owe a few shillings even take advantage of my innabillity to pay & look on me as if I owed them pounds & others to whom I am indebted a few pounds seem to crow over it as if I owed them thousands & all because they know I am poor—therefore with the ad[vice] of a few friends (& that of a young Lady here whose par[ticular] success is so great that she talks of it as accomplished [ ]) I have started to collect subscribers sufficent to enable me to offer the Vol: to advantage to any publisher who chuses & if you like to publish it for me it is at your service if not you will procure me some subscribers which will do me a favour & perhaps reccomend me to a publisher

I feel the situation in which difficulty places me dreadfully but as my staff of independence is broken by that accident that nobody foresees viz a large family an accident that is as dear to me as happiness now—I must do as I can & I should think it is no shame to state the truth of my difficultys as the cause of wishing to make an attempt to get out of them & when I was ill last year my father & mother often said 'John I should like to see another volume printed before we die' & feel at times that I could not rest if they were absent had I not attempted to gratify their wishes as well as my own nessesitys—

If Mr Woodhouse is returned do your earliest oppertunity to serve me for I am as helpless as a child & every thing is going wrong with me

yours sincerely
John Clare

I have nothing as yet on the ground neither cow nor pigs nor any thing else & am in fact worse off then before I entered on the place & to add to the Depressions that distress me there is a paragraph going the round of the papers which is not true not even in shadow & therefore no body could know that which I know not myself & it obliged me to write to the Steward to show that I was no party in giving such a statement publicity for I thought such a feeling might be entertaind by some who did not know me—I heard of it by a person from London of the name of Clarke° who called to see me but I thought it a mistake of his own until I read it myself in the 'Observer' & it hurt me dreadfully—O for the unfriendly friends & the unobtrusive quiet that I enjoyed twenty years ago when I was happy without knowing it & independant without a friend

To Henry Francis Cary

[after 20 October 1832]

My dear Sir

Your kind letter was to me an happiness your philosophy of quietness was better then medicine to my mind for I was enduring ill health & impatience when I recieved it as it was accompanied by a very disagreeable fiction inserted by someone in the Atheneum & for what purpose I cannot tell for if he had any knowledge of my affairs he must know he was writing a falshood & if he had not he ought to have had some charity for the feelings of another when he seems to have such high minded qualitys of his own diction & self pretentions as to become a self authorised counsellor in my affairs & a dictator in the affairs of others—it hurt my ambition for I was seeking independance & not asking charity & had published a prospectus of my intentions to publish a small vol for my own benefit—as I could not get any money from Mr Taylor of my own which he placed in the funds & as he said I had nothing more in profits to recieve then from my publications having recieved not a farthing by the first Vol—it was my only remedy to try my own means to accomplish what I wanted to cover my nessesitys & to set up as a cottage farmer—I felt some vanity that I had a claim to the title of a poet & it was the praise & commendation of men of genius that fostered that ambition & your commendation given early & continued long gave me a pride that the ephemeral opinions of unknown interferences cannot take away—I thought the offering a Vol by subscription could neither hurt my independence or lessen the claim I had to public notice—I wished to be judged of by the book itself without any appeals to want of education lowness of origin or any other foil that officousness chuses to encumber my path with but it seems I must be encumbered never mind I must also write on for ambition to be happy in sadness as verses make me urges me onwards & if I have merit summer insects may anoy but cannot destroy me & if I have not these buzzing authorities are nothings—they neither mar me nor make me—& yet I am sadly teazed & annoyed by their misrepresentations as the[y] must come from enemies in disguise for thank God I am nothing in the sad situation they describe & though some people thinking my promises were put offs never to pay applied at first the rash epithet of law threats to frighten me out of their debt it was but for trifles—& having been frightened for a season & having written to Taylor in this terror several letters & finding his impossibility could give me no remedy I took heart faced my pursuers & told them candidly that if they wished to put their threats in force they had a good oppertunity for I could not prevent it & this avowal which I expected would be the commencement of hostilitys against me brought me peace & turned threats into kindness—so in this truce I wrote this prospectus got it printed & sent it among well known friends about the neighbourhood & candidly asked them for their assistance in making my intentions known to their friends & the hearty readiness in which they all enlisted in my cause set me in good earnest to compleat the scheme as the very best independance I had to get out of difficulty & I sent a printed sheet to Mr Taylor wishing him to aid me with a few subscribers & telling him he should publish the book if he chose but I have not heard a syllable from him of either disapproval or commendment I here send you a prospectus of my little cockleshell—your kindness in my affairs makes me add this trouble to your judgment which my diffidence would not have done had I not recieved your letter yet I wished to ask your advice in the matter & now I shall ask your advice as to a publisher for I think

I have as many subscribers as will carry me into the ocean of public opinion where merit will have its due & that is all I ask for & when I hope success if you laugh at my ambitions I am ready to laugh with you at my own vanity for I sit sometimes & wonder over the little noise I have made in the world until I think I have written nothing as yet to deserve any praise at all so the spirit of fame of living a little after life like a name on a conspic[u]ous place urges my blood upward into unconscious melodys & striding down my orchard & homestead I hum & sing inwardly those little madrigals & then go in & pen them down thinking them much better things then they are untill I look over them again & then the charm vanishes into the vanity that I shall do somthing better ere I die & so in spite of myself I ryhme on & write nothing but little things at last—& these trifles I would willingly trouble your judgment with if you would do me the favour to waste a few hours over them—I thought my old friends had all gone away with the world but I find I have one almost 'the last of the flock' living still in my ways so never mind—our affections increase as our fellowships diminish & I may be happily dissapointed by the many & once more see the 'old familiar faces' as earnest in their affections as ever & then I shall shake hands with old time & be more happy then when old time was new to me

God bless you my dear Sir | I am yours affectionately

John Clare

To Allan Cunningham

Northborough Novr 10 1832

My dear Allan

I was heartily pleased & pleasingly dissapointed to meet with yourself in the shape of a letter for I hardly ever expected to have seen you more so it was a double pleasure which is much better then a single dissapointment & as to my scrawl excuse it for wether to lay it to the pen or to myself I cannot tell but the fact is I can write no better for if I pause my hand trembles then out of all shape & I must go on at a gallop to be understood if so that you can read it at all—

I thank you heartily for your encouragement° in the offer of assisting me in my endeavours to get up to the hill top for one volunteer as the old saying has it is worth fifty pressed men & as the greater part of my ambition is profit & not fame I have little diffidencc in telling you my wishes which is to get as many subscribers as I can get—for the money that was gathered for me by Lord Radstock on which I depended by drawing a portion to start me is so placed in the funds that I am told I cannot get a portion from it & though I do not doubt that it was done with the best intentions yet it put my best intentions in jepordy—for the first Vol brought me nothing & the others when I got some accounts which I cannot understand seem to leave me in debt so I thought there was neither sin nor shame in trying to escape my difficultys in the best way I could & nothing but the publishing a vol: by subscription seemd to make me certain of profit—so I wrote out a prospectus & sent it to the printer before I had any inclination to waver & sent one to Taylor telling him my intentions & giving him the offer to print it if he chose but he has not replied I wish to hurt nobody but I have those around me that make me turn to the practical matters of pounds shillings & pence & though Mr Taylor may have got nothing by the others to induce him to buy I must turn so far a man of business myself as to make the best bargain I can for of the first Vol I never got any thing by a mere trick of the person who introduced it to Mr Taylor stating he had bought it of me & giving me nothing but charging my little accounts with him to Taylor so that in fact I have lost & that if I interperet rightly not less then £40 but as I cannot make out the accounts I must wait the settlement & then I shall see

I have a strong opinion of Taylor & shall always respect him & I think if the matter had been entirely left to business & I had sold them out & out even for a trifle I should have been better off & much better satisfied the charges are so much in these accounts & the items so many that I could but fear & tremble for profit ere I tired my eye to the bottom to look for it—& I cannot but say God protect all hopes in difficulty from the patronage of trade when the cow grows too old in profits in milk she is fatted & sold to the butchers & when the horse has grown too [old to] work he is turned to the dogs—but an author [is] neither composed of the materials nessesary for the profit of butchers meat or dogs meat—he is turned up & forgotten—but I anticipate success for I think I shall succeed very shortly to definite asumptions of being ready for print—& I wait anxiously to hear from Mr Burlowe which I have not yet done & I send him to day a letter with a few verses on the death of the Sun° I mean Scotlands for I saw his end in the papers & felt it—he was kind to me in a notice in my early days of giving me the Lady of the Lake & a gift to the care of a friend Captain Sherwill which I wished to be converted into books viz Burns Works Chattertons Poems & Southeys Nelson & I still possess them among the best valuables in my bookcase—

I have said so much of self that I have left little room for what I most wished to say—I saw some account of your new poem° in the papers & several extracts from your Lives of the painters° which I thought excellent & just what they should be full of anecdote & common sense—& that makes me wish you to go on with your intentions of writing a biography of the Poets—the old ones are the most wanting the notice & when I saw Mr Southey had engaged in the matter I was anticipating a treat but when I saw the vol: it was a dissapointment—all my old favourites which had been made so by Ellises Specimens where here either cut up into living skeletons or ommited as nonentitys unworthy of a shadow of a name—a Biographer may give his opinion on what he likes or dislikes but I like to see an Editor give up their gardens to the readers leisure to chuse what flowers he pleases & not leave us to morsels & lock us out from the whole—

give my best respects to Mrs. C. & I remain dear Allan | yours sincerly

J Clare

To Samuel Simpson

Northborough Novr 10 1832

Dear Sir

I have recieved your subscription° for my little Vol: & thank you & complied with your request of sending you the sonnets you wished for as I think these are what you mean—I am sorry I could not get a frank for I have changed my residence since I last wrote to you—& I wish you had given me directions how the vol: can reach you but I expect it [will] be sent by the publisher to you free of expence at least I shall try to send it so if I can you ask me if my subscription list fills up well I have got somewhere about two hundred just now & expect in the end to be able to publish a thousand copies or at least to dispose of them when published if not subscribed for—I publish the Vol: for myself & so I am sure of the profit

yours respectfully
John Clare

To Eliza Louisa Emmerson

Northborough Novr 13 1832

My dear Eliza

I was delighted to see your handwriting for I have been in such an excess of melancholly that I was obliged to day to send over to deeping for some medicine which I have commenced taking for last night my very brains seemed to boil up almost into madness & my arms & legs burnt as it were with a listless feebleness that almost rendered them useless & I got so fearful of myself that I determined to day to seek a remedy which I am now taking & which will I doubt not relieve me for the doctor is well aware what medicine my constitution needs but it is a sad thing to feel such a debility that will neither bear rest or fatigue long together & I am truly sorry for yourself but you must cheer up & keep on & live to write my epitaph for the great stone which I once mentioned—I am truly sorry that these things should have got into the papers about Mr Taylor & it hurt me much more then if my name only had been mentioned because such things can neither mar me or make me & all I wish now is to stand upon my own bottom as a poet without any apology as to want of education or any thing else & I say it not in the feeling of either ambition or vanity but in the spirit of common sense—last saturday I recieved a parcel of books from Mr How° as a present whose residence I gave wrong in my last to you it is No *13* & in them the numbers of the 'Alfred' & the 'Atheneum' in which those paragraphs were inserted Mr How writes as though he caused the one to be inserted in the 'Alfred' & Allan

Cunningham has written to say he inserted the other in the 'Atheneum' & if I did not believe that the best intentions of serving me placed them there I should have certainly fancied them as no compliments & I wrote to Mr How to tell him that I did not wish to have my poverty printed twice over & also that I felt a stubborn belief that Taylor was a sincere friend & I also corrected the misrepresentation by telling him it was the persons misrepresentations who introduced my poems to Taylor that deprived me of all profits in the first vol: in fact I have brunted the loss of £40 by it if so that the matter is to pass uncorrected—for he never gave me sixpence further than what he charged for to Mr Taylor & when Mr Taylors accounts came down I was astonished to see an item of £20 for copy right & another item of £20 for which I had had nothing—& I wrote to him wishing him to correct the mistakes but as regared the copyright he was silent & as to the other it was he said for 'money & goods' & there was the burthen still on my back & no remedy to remove it—when I thought him a friend he was always whishing me to appear as if he had purchased the vol as he said Taylor & Hessey would deprive him of the profit so I was easy & consented it should be so but I never expected he intended to cheat me into a charge for what I never had—it was to have been *deducted* from the accounts & he *added* it to them & though I never sold the vol I am made the looser & have been duped as it were to purchase my own which is a most damnable herresy—& seeing these things before my eyes I felt determined to do as other folk did sell for the sake of a bargain—when Drury got to Lincoln he wrote two letters to me threatening that if I did not pay him my accounts he should proceed in another way I then wrote to Taylor in fear wishing to turn over all my little property into his & Hesseys hands as I expected the Shark called Law would swallow the whole they then sent down for Drurys bill which he had contrived to make out into nearly as much more as it ought to have been & on my objecting to it he took a great portion off & then I knew it was too much but I had no means of correcting it for I kept no accounts against him so it passed on till I after repeated wishes got Mr Taylors accounts down & to my astonishment I found Drury had sent in in a secret way the above £20 accounts to Taylor a fabrication to a fraction which I expect he paid & so you see who is the cheater—I am always mad at the meaness when I think of it but I am very sorry that Taylor should be brought into the matter for I am sure he is utterly above such things & like myself a man of business only by nessesity—all I wish is that he would clear up a settlement so far that I might be enabled to know how my matters stand in his hands it is an happy thing to be free & if the ballance should turn out against me he shall not loose by me if I can get profit enough by this for I will pay every one to the last farthing & then I shall be happy my creditors if I may so call them to whom I owe trifling sums of money have till lately acted as friends that is depended upon my promises & let me alone but a few of them have got rather impatient from dissapointment & threatened me with law but I turned round like the Stag at bay & took the resolution to state how matters stood with me & that if they chose to put their threats into execution I could not prevent it & although I expected this confession would commence hostilitys it produced a feeling in my favour & one wrote to me in the warmest terms of friendship & gave a proof that he would never hurt me which pleased me much & I shall never forget the kindness—

—two or three days ago I wrote a few stanzas on the memory of Sir Walter Scott & thinking them at first much better then I think them now I wished to have sent them to you but as I had heard nothing I thought 3 letters would bother you so Harry who had been wishing me to send him somthing for a paper or Magazine got into the trouble of them & I have heard nothing as yet from him

—I will send you next a copy of the accounts of my bill—so that you may see what it is for I cannot understand it at all though I have puzzled over it with the very excess of my wisdom in pounds shillings & pence

yours &c &c &c &c | untill I get into sufficient room° to subscribe myself yours very sincerely

John Clare

P.S. remember me very kindly to Mr E.

I must tell you this letter is only half finished & for the want of room I will write you another before the weeks out & fill it up with other trifles

To Joseph Henderson

Northborough April 22. 1833

Dear Henderson

I should be very much obliged to you for a little spinnage seed Lettuce seed Carrot seed & Turnip seed—I have been unwell or I should have sent for them sooner or made a journey for them myself—excuse a short note for I have little inclination to scribble at present

yours &c &c
John Clare

To Henry Edmund Carrington

Northborough Decr 26 1833

My dear Sir

I recieved a kind letter° from you many months back desiring to become a subscriber to my new Vol: & handsomely offering a kindness in the shape of a £5 note & as I answered your letter I felt doubtful many times that yours in reply was lost for nothing has ever reached me here—I was very indisposed at the time & scarcely able to write & though I am in no mood for scribbling even now yet I have taken the resolution to write to you to let you know that if a letter was sent I never recieved it—I think your Father was the author of Dartmoor° a review of which I read sometime back when it jumped into my head that you should be the son of the poet & though perhaps from my inability to read it I am not over tickled with blank verse yet I think the descriptions I met there are good for I never saw the work itself & that they are the productions of a Poet that the next age will know better then this for works of merit lie out of the notice of these days—I have for the last few years suffered severely from indisposition & have been at times incapable of either writing or reading yet I hope I am better & shall wear out of it—as you are connected with a newspaper if any trifle from me would please you to fill up a corner in it they are at your service at any time when I am able to amuse myself with writing them out—a friend of mine° would have called on you this month but he does not reach Bath while° the next & so I thought I would write myself in the mean time I am dear Sir | yours

very sincerly
John Clare

To [John Taylor]

[before 15 February 1834]

I wish to trouble you in fact my wife wishes me to do so or I should not have put it to practice & that is to get a few school books for my childern at the cheapest rate & send down as soon as you can & to stop payment for them next half year—for do you know I wish to make all my childern scholars & the expences for school books make the charges so high that I am troubled often in what way to pay them—& I assure you that if farthings had fractions in the ballance of my bills I should find it useful to find it on my side—I wanted four blank summing books to set down their sums in such as may be charged for 3/6 here & a Question book they use Walkinghams° here but one backed by your own opinion would strike me as the best all is the questions must not be worked in it & I should like it to go through all the rules of Arithmetic in a plain common way—what else I want is a couple of books of extracts or selections in prose & verse which I must leave to your own judgment only I could wish not to have any on Murrays plan which are far from entertaining or good—they learn young people set tasks that are not entertaining to themselves or any body else what I prefer is books that please them to read & please them to remember & I think there are such books to be met with—what I mean is books of good extracts that please every body

To George Darling

[1834–5]

My dear Dr Darling

I write to tell you I am very unwell & though I cannot describe my feelings well I will tell you as well as I can—sound affects me very much & things evil as well [as] good thoughts are continually rising in my mind I cannot sleep for I am asleep as it were with my eyes open & I feel chills come over me & a sort of nightmare awake & I got no rest last night I feel a great desire to come up but perhaps I shall not be able & I hope you will write down directly for I feel you can do me good & if I was in town I should soon be well so I fancy for I do assure you I am very unwell & I cannot keep my mind right as it were for I wish to read and cannot—there is a sort of numbing through my private parts which I cannot describe & when I was so indisposed last winter I felt as if I had circulation in the blood & at times as if it went round me & at other times such a sinking as if I was going to sink through the bed—& though not so bad now I am realy very uneasy in fact I have never been right as it were since then here is all I can say just now but I hope you can send somthing to benefit me give my respects to Taylor & I remain | yours sincerly

John Clare

I fear I shall get worse & worse ere you write to me for I have been out for a walk & can scarcely bear up against my fancys or feelings—

yours &c

J.C.

To Henry Behnes Burlowe

Northborough Novr 12 1834

My dear Harry

I wish to hear how you are & I hope you will write directly to tell me I am ill able to write & as little able to bear dissapointment so write to me directly & it will give me great pleasure to hear from you how are your brothers & all your friends & what are you doing I thank God my Wife & family are all well but as for myself I am scarcely able to do anything yet I feel if I could get to London I should soon be right & I hope I shall be able to get there before long my eldest boy wishes to be remembered to you & is very anxious to get some instructions in drawing he has often wished me to write to you to get him a drawing book & I have not been able to do so before now he has got a box of paints & only waits for some instructions which I hope you will put in your letter & write as soon as you can will you call on Mrs Emmerson as I wish to write to her but cannot tell wether she is at home send me all the news you can & write as soon as you can excuse a short letter & believe me yours very sincerely

John Clare

To Joseph Henderson

Northborough Novr 15 1834

My dear Henderson

Will you give me a few flowers I have been very ill & am scarcely able now to do anything I have just got a proof of the new poems to correct but I can do nothing with it

To George Reid

Northborough Novr 16 1834

My dear Sir

I thank you very kindly for the offer of your kind assistance° though the Poems are not publishing by subscription & the reason was that I could not succeed but I am much better pleased with my success & they are now in the press I dare say I could have got more in the way of profit but I did not like to thrust myself into notice feeling & fearing that the Subscribers might be dissapointed & as they are now published I am independant of all such feelings for I feel assured that if I deserve it the public will do me justice & I am anxious to hope that my friends will not be dissapointed I am sorry to say that I have suffered so much lately from severe indisposition that I am careless almost of either censure or praise untill the kind feelings of my friends revives me but I hope yet to be able to do somthing more & also to be able to write you a longer letter I thank you heartily for your intended present & any thing directed for me at Northborough to be left at the Bull Inn Market Deeping is sure to find me excuse me for the present my dear Sir & believe me | yours sincerely

John Clare

To the Royal Literary Fund

To the Committee for managing the Literary Fund

[late December 1834]

Gentlemen

Owing to the little benefit I have met with from the sale of my Poems & the bad state of my health I find my income quite insufficient for the support of myself & family the sum being somewhere about £37 the truth of which may be known by applying to Mr Taylor & Mr How—which urges me to ask for some assistance to relieve me from the anxiety of seeing a growing family around me without the means of sufficiently providing for it I dare not feel emboldened to ask for any particular sum but I feel that £50 would entirely relieve me from my nessesitys

I am Gentlemen your Obedient Servant

John Clare

To [?Joseph Henderson]

[1834–5]

would you oblige me with a few Shrubs & flowers I am not particuler as to what but I should like a few creepers & have you got a drooping willow & a double blossomed furze & a plant or two of the wild cherry excuse the trouble I give you could you do me a sketch of the old drooping willow in the Island pond I am very fond of the tree so if you can do so

To Joseph Henderson

Northborough Jany 13 1836

My dear Henderson

Will you have the kindness to give me a few shrubs & flowers a few woodbines & somthing my wife likes she calls everlasting° have you got a drooping willow & double blossomed furze my wife also wants a red japonica I am hardly able to say more

God bless you | yours ever

John Clare

To Patty Clare

[In June 1837 Clare was taken to the asylum at High Beech, Epping Forest, to be looked after by Dr Matthew Allen. He was to stay here until his escape in July 1841.]

November 23 1837

My dear Wife

I write to tell you I am getting better I cant write a long letter but wish to know how you all are the place here is beautiful & I meet with great kindness the country is the finest I have seen write & tell me how you all are I cant write a long letter but I shall do better God bless you all kiss them all for me | yours ever my dear wife

John Clare

To Patty Clare

Leppits Hill March 17th 1841

My Dear Wife Patty

It Make's Me More Than Happy To Hear That You & My Dear Family Are All Well—And You Will All Be As Well Pleased To Hear That I Have Been So Long In Good Health & Spirits As To Have Forgotten That I Ever Was Any Otherways—My Situation Here Has Been Even From The Beginning More Then Irksome But I Shake Hands With Misfortune & Wear Through The Storm—The Spring Smile's & So Shall I—But Not While I Am Here—I Am Very Happy To Hear My Dear Boy Mention His 'Brother's & Sister's' So Kindly As I Feel Assured That They Love One Another As They Ever Have Done—It Was My Lot To Seem As Living Without Friends Untill I Met With You & Though We Are Now Parted My Affection Is Unaltered—& We Shall Meet Again I Would Sooner Wear The Trouble's Of Life Away Single Handed Then Share Them With Others—As Soon As I Get Relieved On Duty Here I Shall Be In Northamptonshire—Though Essex Is A Very Pleasant County—Yet To Me 'There Is No Place Like Home'—As My Childern Are All Well—To Keep Them So

Besure & Keep Them In Good Company & Then They Will Not Only Be Well But Happy—For What Reason They Keep Me Here I Cannot Tell For I Have Been No Otherways Than Well A Couple of Year's At The Least & Never Was Very Ill Only Harrassed By Perpetual Bother—& It Would Seem By Keeping Me Here One Year After Another That I Was Destined For the Same Fate Agen & I Would Sooner Be Packed In A Slave Ship For Affrica Then Belong To The Destiny Of Mock Friends & Real Enemies—Honest Men & Modest Women Are My Friends

Give My Best Love To My Dear Childern & Kiss The Little One's For Me Good Bye & God Be With You All Forever

I Had Three Seperate Dream's About Three Of My Boys° Or Your Boys—Frederick John & William—Not Any Ways Remarkable Only I Was In A Wreck With The Latter—Such Things Never Trouble Me Now In Fact Nothing Troubles Me & Thank God It Is So—I Hope The Time Is Not Long Ere I Shall See You All By Your Own Fireside Though Every Day In Abscence Seem's To Me Longer Then Year's

I Am My Dear Wife Your Affectionate Husband
John Clare

P.S. Give My Love To The Dear Boy Who Wrote To Me & To Her Who Is Never Forgotten | God Bless You All
J. Clare

To Mary Joyce

[Clare had by this time come to believe that his childhood love Mary Joyce was in fact his wife; this letter is written in the notebook in which he was writing his two 'Byronic' poems *Child Harold* and *Don Juan*.]

[May? 1841]

My dear Wife Mary

I might have said my first wife & first love & first every thing—but I shall never forget my second wife & second love for I loved her once as dearly as yourself—& almost do so now so I determined to keep you both forever—& when I write to you I am writing to her at the same time & in the same letter God bless you both & forever & both your familys also—I still keep writing though you do not write to me for if a man has a wife & I have two—but I tell it in a couplet with variations as my poetry has been the worlds Horn book for many years—so here it is

'For if a husband will not let us know
'That he's alive—he's dead—or may be so'

No one knows how sick I am of this confinement possessing two wives that ought to be my own & cannot see either one or the other if I was in prison for felony I could not be served worse then I am—wives used to be alowed to see their husbands anywhere—religion forbids their being parted but I have not even religion on my side & more's the pity I have been rather poorly I might say ill for 8 or 9 days before haymakeing & to get my self better I went a few evenings on Fern hill & wrote a new Canto of 'Child Harold' & now I am better I sat under the Elm trees in old Mathews Homestead Leppits hill where I now am—2 or 3 evenings & wrote a new canto of Don Juan—merely to pass the time away but nothing seems to shorten it in the least & I fear I shall not be able to wear it away—nature to me seems dead & her very pulse seems frozen to an iceicle in the summer sun—what is the use of shutting me up from women in a petty paltry place as this merely because I am a married man & I dare say though I have two wives if I got away I should soon have a third & I think I should serve you both right in the bargain by doing so for I dont care a damn about comeing home now—so you need not flatter yourselves with many expec[ta]tions of seeing [me] nor do I expect you want to see me or you would have contrived to have done it before now

—My dear Mary take all the good wishes from me as your heart can feel for your own husband & kiss all your dear family for their abscent father & Pattys childern also & tell Patty that her husband is the same man as he was when she married him 20 years ago in heart & good intentions—God bless you both & your familys also I wish you both to keep in good health & be happy as I shall soon be when I have the good luck to be with you all at home once again—the love I have for you my dear Mary was never altered by time but always increased by abscence

I am my dear Mary your affectionate husband
John Clare

To Eliza Phillips°

[May? 1841]

My dear Eliza Phillips

Having been cooped up in this Hell of a Madhouse till I seem to be disowned by my friends & even forgot by my enemies for there is none to accept my challanges° which I have from time to time given to the public I am almost mad in waiting for a better place & better company & all to no purpose It is well known that I am a prize fighter by profession & a man that never feared any body in my life either in the ring or out of it—I do not much like to write love letters but this which I am now writing to you is a true one—you know that we have met before & the first oppertunity that offers we will meet again—I am now writing a New Canto of Don Juan which I have taken the liberty to dedicate to you in remembrance of Days gone bye & when I have finished it I would send you the vol if I knew how in which is a new Canto of Child Harold also—I am my dear Elize | yours sincerely

John Clare

To Mary Joyce

[Clare escaped from High Beech on 20 July 1841; when he arrived at Northborough three days later, he wrote a prose account of his 'Journey out of Essex' (*AW*, pp. 153–60). This was followed by something close to a 'fair copy' of *Child Harold* in the same notebook; this letter preceded the poem. Clare refused to accept the fact that Mary Joyce had died on 16 July 1838.]

To Mary Clare—Glinton

Northborough July 27 1841

My dear wife

I have written an account of my journey or rather escape from Essex for your amusement & hope it may divert your leisure hours—I would have told you before now that I got here to Northborough last friday night but not being able to see you or to hear where you was I soon began to feel homeless at home° & shall bye & bye feel nearly hopeless but not so lonely as I did in

Essex—for here I can see Glinton church & feeling that Mary is safe if not happy & I am gratified though my home is no home to me my hopes are not entirely hopeless while even the memory of Mary lives so near me God bless you My dear Mary Give my love to your dear & beautifull family & to your Mother—& believe me as I ever have been & shall be My dearest Mary

your affectionate Husband

John Clare

To Matthew Allen

[after 27 August 1841]

My dear Sir

Having left the Forest in a hurry [I h]ad not time to take my leave of you & your family but I intended to write & that before now but dullness & dissapointment prevented me for I found your words true on my return here having neither friends or home left but as it is called the 'Poet's cottage' I claimed a lodging in it where I now am—one of my fancys I found here with her family & all well—they meet me on this side Werrington with a horse & cart & found me all but knocked up for I had travelled from Essex to Northamptonshire without ever eating or drinking all the way save one pennyworth of beer which was given me by a farm servant near an odd house called the plough one day I eat grass to humour my hunger—but on the last day I chewed Tobacco & never felt hungry afterwards—where my poetical fancy is I cannot say for the people in the neighbourhood tells me that the one called 'Mary' has been dead these 8 years° but I can be miserably happy in any situation & any place & could have staid in yours on the forest if any of my friends had noticed me or come to see me—but the greatest annoyance in such places as yours are those servants styled keepers who often assumed as much authority over me as if I had been their prisoner & not likeing to quarrel I put up with it till I was weary of the place altogether so I heard the voice of freedom & started & could have travelled to York with a penny loaf & a pint of beer for I should not have been fagged in body only one of my old shoes had nearly lost the sole before I started & let in the water & silt the first day & made me crippled & lame to the end of my journey

I had Eleven Books sent me from How & Parsons Booksellers some lent & some given me—out of the Eleven I only brought 5 vols here & as I dont want any part of Essex in Northamptonshire agen I wish you would have the kindness to send a servant to get them for me I should be very thankfull not that I care about the books altogether only it may be an excuse to see me & get me into company that I do not want to be acquainted with—one of your labourers Pratts Wife borrowed—'Child Harold'—& Mrs Fishs Daughter has two or three or perhaps more all Lord Byrons Poems & Mrs King late of the Owl Public house Leppits Hill & now of Endfield Highway has two or three all Lord Byrons & one is The 'Hours of Idleness'

you told me somthing before haytime about the Queen alowing me a yearly sallary of £100° & that the first quarter had then commenced or else I dreamed so—if I have the mistake is not of much consequence to anyone save myself & if true I wish you would get the Quarter for me if due* as I want to be independant & pay for board & lodging while I remain here—I look upon myself as a widow or bachellor I dont know which—I care nothing about the women now for they are faithless & decietfull & the first woman when there was no man but her husband found out means to cuckold him by the aid & assistance of the devil but women being more righteous now & men more plentiful they have found out a more godly way to do it without the divils assistance & a man who possesses a woman possesses losses without gain—the worst is the road to ruin & the best is nothing like a good Cow—man I never did like much & woman has long sickened me I should [like] to be to myself a few years & lead the life of a hermit—but even there I should wish from one whom I am always thinking of & almost every Song I write has some sighs & wishes in Ink about Mary—If I have not made your head weary by reading thus far I have tired my own by writing it so I will bid you good bye | & am My dear docter

yours very sincerely
John Clare

give my best respects to Mrs Allen & Miss Allen & to Dr Stedman also to Campbell & Hayward & Howard at Leopards Hill or in fact to any of the others who may think it worth while to enquire about me

* York & Co Peterborough or Eaton & Co Stamford [*Clare's note*]

To George Reid

Novr 17 1841

Dear Sir

When your Letter reached Northborough I was there also—having left Essex or rather made my escape from it on the 23rd of July since which time I have never seen any company or made any visits anywhere Solitude being my chief society & nature my best companion your enquirey to Patty after my health leaves me to say that I am very well that is as well as middling for my mind is as it always has been from a boy—a disappointment I have never had the perusal of a Newspaper for some years & if you have any entertaining incidents in your Scotch Papers I should thank you for the loan of one now & then could you give me any literary News I myself left many Byron Poems behind me but I did not stay to know or hear what became of them & I have written some since I returned with an account of my escape from Essex—I was 3 Nights & 4 days on the road without food & lodging but being used to rough voyages all my life it did not affect my health much only made me very lame in one foot from having a bad shoe on—the sole was nearly off when I started & its keeping on till I got here was little less then a miracle—I am now more comfortable & remain Dear Sir | yours sincerely

John Clare

I think of Thee—A Song°

I think of thee at early day
& wonder where my love can be
& when the evening shadows grey
O how I think of thee

Along the meadow banks I rove
& down the flaggy fen
& hope my first & early love
To meet thee once agen

I think of thee at dewy morn
& at the sunny noon

& walks with thee—now left forlorn
Beneath the silent moon

I think of thee I think of all
How blest we both have been—
The sun looks pale upon the wall
& autumn shuts the scene

I cant expect to meet the[e] now
The winters floods begin
The [win]d sighs through the naked bough
[Sad as] my heart within

I think of thee the seasons through
In spring when flowers I see
In winter's lorn & naked view
I think of only thee

While life breaths on this earthly ball
What e'er my lot may be
Wether in freedom or in thrall
Mary I think of thee

To Charles Clare

Northampton Asylum June 15 1847

My dear Boy

I am very happy to have a letter from you in your own hand writing & to see you write so well I am also glad that your Brothers & Sisters are all in good health & your Mother also besure to give my love to her but I am very sorry to hear the News about your Grandfather° but we must all die—& I must [say] that Frederic & John° had better not come unless they wish to do so for its a *bad Place* & I have fears that they may get trapped as prisoners as I hear some have been & I may not see them nor even hear they have been here I only tell them & leave them to do as they like best—its called the Bastile by some & not with[out] reasons—how does the Flowers get on I often wish to see them—& are the young Childern at home I understand there are some I have not yet seen kiss them & give my love to them & to your Mother & Brothers & Sisters &

my respects To John Bellars° & to your Neighbours on each side of you Mr & Mrs Sefton° & Mr & Mrs Bellars & others who enquire after me I have never been ill since I have been here save a cold now & then of which I take no notice

Believe me my dear Boy | that I remain your Affectionate
Father
John Clare

To Charles Clare

Northampton Asylum [26] Feby 1848

My dear Son

I was very happy to recieve your Letter to hear you was all in good health—your Mother & Brothers & Sisters & as satisfactory tell you I am as well myself thank God for it

When I first came here I saw some of your little Brothers & Sisters little Boys & Girls with Red heads & others also dirty & healthy which satisfied me very well some of them were with your own Sisters which left home before you was born—my dear Boy it does not signifye to a good boy or Girl how they are drest or of what colour the hair is when you are men you will know so—the warmth of our cloathing & not the show is all thats required—Pride is an unnessesary evil—I readily excuse your Brothers John & William for not coming here & in fact beg them not to trouble them selves at all about it unless it would give them pleasure to do so—I tell you all Brothers & Sisters to Love truth be Honest & fear Nobody—Amuse yourselves in reading & writeing—you all have the Bible & other suitable books—I would advise you to study Mathematics Astronomy Languages & Botany as the best amusements for instruction—Angling is a Recreation I was fond of myself & there is no harm in it if your taste is the same—for in those things I have often broke the Sabbath when a boy & perhaps it was better then keeping it in the village hearing Scandal & learning tipplers frothy conversation—'The fields his study nature was his book' I seldom succeeded in Angling but I wrote or rather thought Poems made botanical arrangements when a little Boy which men read & admired I loved nature & painted her both in words & colours better then many Poets & Painters & by Preseverance &

attention you may all do the same—in my boyhood Solitude was the most talkative vision I met with   Birds bees trees flowers all talked to me incessantly louder then the busy hum of men & who so wise as nature out of doors on the green grass by woods & streams under the beautifull sunny sky—daily communings with God & not a word spoken—the best books on Angling are by Piscator° & Henry Phillips° & Sir Humphry Davies° though we must not over look the Father of Anglers Isaac Waltons 'Art of Angling or the Contemplative Mans Recreation' a choice book with all Fishermen & there is many others every way as good—I had hopes I should have seen the Garden & Flowers [before] now—but we cannot reckon on any thing before hand—the future is with providence & unknown till it comes to pass—Like old Muck Rake in the Pilgrims Progress I know nothing in other peoples business & less in whats to come or happen—'There is nothing like home'   give my love to Mr & Mrs Bellars & Mrs Sefton & remember me to all your neighbours who enquire after me particularly old John Green whose words came true & who was the only Person who persuaded me not to come here—you never mentioned your Grandfather   give my love to him & believe my love to you all

while I remain my dear Childern | your affectionate Father

John Clare

To Patty Clare

Northampton Asylum July 19th 1848

My dear wife,

I have not written to you a long while but here I am in the Land of sodom where all the peoples brains are turned the wrong way   I was glad to see John yesterday & should like to have gone back with him for I am very weary of being here—You might come & fetch me away for I think I have been here long enough   I write this in a green meadow by the side of the river agen Stokes Mill & I see three of your daughters & a Son now & then   the confusion & roar of Mill dams & locks is sounding very pleasant while I write it & its a very beautiful Evening   the meadows are greener than usual after the shower & the Rivers are brimful   I think it is about two years since I was first sent up in this hell & not allowed to go out of the gates there never was a more disgraceful deception than this place.

It is the purgatoriall hell & French Bastile of English liberty Keep yourselves happy & comfortable & love one another by & bye I shall be with you perhaps before you expect me There has been a great storm here with thunder & hail that did much damage to the glass in the neighbourhood hailstones the size of Hens Eggs fell in some places Did your brother John come to Northborough or go to Barnoak his Uncle John Riddle came the next morning but did not stay. I thought I was coming home but I got cheated I see many of your little Brothers & Sisters at Northampton weary & dirty with hard work some of them with red hands but all in ruddy good health some of them are along with your Sister—Ruth Dakker who went from Helpstone a little girl Give my love to your Mother Grandfather Brothers & Sisters & believe me my dear Childern | hers & yours very affectionately

John Clare

To Charles Clare

Northampton Asylum Octr 17. 1848

My dear Son

I am glad to hear from you & write agen directly to say I am quite well & never was better in my Life thank God for it. I am very glad to hear that your Mother & brothers & Sisters are quite well also your Aunt Sophy Uncle & Aunt Riddle & make them all the same return from me

We have had a very Large Flood here the largest that has been known for many Years & it seems not to have gone down yet—I think I shall not be long now before I see you & as I have so particularly enquired after each & all of you so lately in my last I shall only say God bless you all now & forever—live happy & comfortable together in your old house at home for go where we will & be as we may *always* remember 'There is no place like Home' be good childern & be kind to your Mother & always obey her wishes & you will never do wrong I always found it so myself & never got into error when I did it

Your Brother John promised Mr Knight° to send him with

your Brothers & Sisters consent to lend him the lone of a Volume of M.S. Poems in Your Possesion—you have my free consent to do so as soon as you like

I am my Dear Charles your Affectionate Father
John Clare

To [Mary Howitt]

[This is a bizarre letter, in that although it appears to be addressed to Mary Howitt (1799–1888), whose husband William had been responsible for *The Book of the Seasons* (1831), the final paragraph (picking up Clare's asterisk in the margin of the second) addresses the dead poet Jeremiah Wiffen (1792–1836). The Howitts seem to have visited Clare twice, once in July 1844, and again in Dec. 1846. A copy of *The Book of the Seasons* (6th edn. 1840) is inscribed 'John Clare | From his friend | Mary Howitt'.]

[1848–9?]

My dear Madam

I have heard you sent me one of your Vols 'The Book of the Seasons' by the Revd Mr Jones° which I went for as soon as I hear'd it & he had lent it to a young Lady a Friend of mine so I could not think it long in coming—but Mr Wiffen who had sent me a like present of his 'Apsley Wood'° having told me that you would expect a Letter from me to say I recieved it safe I write in the mean time to say that when it comes in my possesion I will write agen to tell you how I like it

I was unlucky enough to leave Mr Wiffens Poem behind me somewhere in Northampton or where I am which I told him & though I had intended to have written him a Letter perhaps *my thanks to him thro' your hands may do as well for do you know in these sort of places I own nothing but the cloaths on my back & hardly them—& when I want to write to a friend I have neither Pen ink nor paper which I do not like to explain frequently not knowing the cause—I can assure you my home is never In such places as these—my fancy wont even have a bed in

* Some passeges of the Poem 'Apsley wood' put me strongly in mind of 'Child Harrold' as well worthy of Byr[o]n himself & one of the short poems 'the last but one' as very like the strength & style of the same writer—I should have written much sooner but I have no communication with pen & Ink & can only write with a pencil—I thank you kindly in giving me the hint that Mary Howitt expected a letter to thank her for her kindness in sending me her book of The Seasons

them she fancys on & lyes elsewhere—have you read Whartons 'Ode to fancy' I used to like it—I have poetical sweathearts too which my fancy dwells on as it did when I was single so in writing of these as my fancy dictates they grow imperceptably into a Vol & then I call it Child Harold of which I wrote much both in Essex & here which I did & do meerely to kill time & whose more proper Title might be 'Prison Amusements'

I am my dear Madam yours very affectionately
John Clare

To Charles Clare

Northampton Asylum April 28th 1849

My dear Son Charles

I am happy to hear from you at any time but more particularly now as I am quite lost in reveries & false hums I am now in the ninth year of my Captivity among the Babylonians & any news from Home is a Godsend or blessing I am glad to hear your Mother & brothers & Sisters are all well as this Letter leaves me at this present thank God for it & also my Grand Childern God bless them kiss all the little ones for me & tell them it was sent from their Father—for I have no money to send them sweet meats or Playthings or Books—The Sherwood Forresters name is Mr S. C. Hall° & not Knight as you write he has been here & said he would Call & see you he Left me the same little book 'The Upland Hamlet & other Poems'

I know of no 'three or four Volumes of M.S. Poems that have not been Published' as we searched them all over & compleated every fragment for the Press but if you think otherwise you may send them when you like & where you like—for I know nothing but of one Vol which I partly filled the last five months I was at Home & I think I reccolect somthing of the others which I brought home with me send them by all means—I know of none which he prefers but cant you send the 'Three or Four Volumes' of MSS as they are & let him see what he wanted himself—do just as you please & you will do right enough—you tell me you will write to me again before long Do so as soon as you can & let it be about home & those who live there tell me how the Flowers go on & read books of Knowledge dont forget you[r] Latin & Greek & Hebrew nor your Mathematics & Astronomy for in them you have Truth when I was a day Labourer at Bridge Casterton & courted your Mother I knew Nine Languages & could talk of them to Parsons & Gentlemen & Foreigners but never opened my Mouth about them to the Vulgar—for I always lived to myself—dont forget you have Bibles & Prayer Books—& never act Hypocrisy for Deception is the most odious Knavery in the World—Stick to Truth & 'shame the Devil'—Learning is your only wealth Mathematics Astronomy & Mechanics should be your 'Common Place Book' God Bless you all Together & believe me my dear Childern | your Affectionate Father

John Clare

To Charles Clare

June 1st 1849.

My dear Boy

I was very happy to have so long a Letter from you & to hear that you was all well & to hear that the Garden is prosperous & that you & your neighbours are all well & happy—Spring & Summer came in beautifull & the crops of Grass & corn are plentifull & give promise of Haytime & Harvest & Plenty

You told me to enquire of you about my old Neighbours & Labouring Companions of my single Days—There is William & John Close do they live at Helpstone yet & how are they—how is John Cobbler of Helpstone I worked with him when a single Man & Tom Clare we used to sit in the Fields over a Bottle of Beer & they used to Sing capital Songs & we were all merry together how is John & Mary Brown & their Daughter Lucy & John Woodward & his Wife & Daughter William Bradford & his Wife & A. & E. Nottingham & old John Nottingham & his Wife Sally Frisby & James Bain & old Otter the Fiddler & Charles Otter & John & Jim Crowson—most of us Boys & Girls together—there is also John & James Billings & Will Bloodworth & Tom & Sam Ward & John Fell & his Wife & John King & Mr & Miss Large & Mr & Miss Bellars on the Hill & Mr

Bull & all enquiring Friends & Mrs Crowson many are dead & some forgotten & John & Mrs Bullimore the Village Schoolmistress & Robin Oliver & his wife & Will Dolby & his Wife & Henry Snow & his Wife & Frank Jackson & his Wife Richard Royce & his Wife & Daughter & Jonothan Burbidge & his Wife & Daughter & all I have forgotten remember me kindly to—for I have been along while in Hell—how is Ben Price & Will Dolby for I liked Helpstone well—& all that lived in it & about it for it was my Native Place—how is Thomas Porter of Ashton he used to be my Companion in my single Days when we loved Books & Flowers together & how is Charles Welsh of Bainton—my fondness for Flowers made me acquainted with him which has wore many Years & his Wife too & Daughters for they are all old Friends—Give my Love to your Brothers & Sis[ters] & Grand father & Neighbours & ever [believe] me | your Affectionate Father

John Clare

To Charles Clare

Novr 7th [1849] Asylum Northampton

My dear Charles

I ought to have answered your Letter before now but I have to go down below for Ink & Paper & forgot all about it till this Morning—You never tell me my dear Boy when I am to come Home I have been here Nine Years or Nearly & want to come Home very much—You need not mind about Writing often only in your next say when Johnny is coming to fetch me away from this Bastile—Have you four Boys got each an hebrew Bible & a Harry Phillips on Angling—how do you get on with the Flowers—how are your Sisters & your Mother & Grandfather your Three Brothers & your Neighbours Give my Love to them all & Helpstone People Likewise—Take care of my books & M.S.S. till I come—to your Neighbours on each side of you give my best respects—& to Mary Buzley & old Mr Buzley if alive—& believe me my dear Son | Your Affectionate Father

John Clare

To John Clare

[1849–50]

My Dear John

I have not heard from you so long—how do you get on—I wrote to your brother Fred a few Days after Christmass & supposed that he was with You keeping the Holiday—'Love one another'—& be a happy Family & I will be as usual when I get oppertunity—for there is no oppertunity for it here there is neither room nor time for pleasure or commonsense we are always wrong ways—& may we all be wrong ways for ever

Amen

To Mary Collingwood

Mary Collingwood

[1849–50]

My dear Mary Collingwood

I long to see you & have Loved from the first Night of my capture here

Betsey Averey

Mary Ann Averey

My Dear Mary

but there is no faith here so I hold my tongue—& wait the end out withou[t] attention or intention—'I am that I am'—& done nothing Yet

yours &c

J Clare°

To Eliza Dadford

[1849–50]

My dear Eliza

How I long to see you & kiss that pretty Face—I mean 'Eliza Dadford' how I should like to walk with you in the snow where I helped to shake your carpets & take the oppertunity we neglected then to kiss on the green grass & Love you even better then before

> Some promises are broke as soon as made
> & silent Love is sweet thats never spoken
> The churchyard grass looks pleasant where the maid
> Looked Love in smiles in Memorys pleasing Token

I am My Dear Eliza Dadford yours forever
J. Clare

To Patty Clare

[1849–50]

My dear Wife

I have wrote some few times to enquire about yourself & the Family & thought about yourself & them a thousand othe[r] things that I use to think of the childern—Freddy when I led him by the hand in his childhood—I see him now in his little pink frock—sealskin cap—& gold band—with his little face as round as a apple & as red as a rose—& now a stout Man both strangers to each other the father a prisoner under a bad government so bad in fact that its no government at all but prison disapline where every body is forced to act contrary to their own wishes 'the mother against the daughter in law & the daughter against the mother in law' 'the father against the son & the son against the Father'—in fact I am in Prison because I wont leave my family & tell a falshood—this is the English Bastile a government Prison where harmless people are trapped & tortured till they die—English priestcraft & english bondage more severe then the slavery of Egypt & Affrica while the son is tyed up in his manhood from all the best thoughts of his childhood bye lying & falshood—not dareing to show love or remembrance for Home or home affections living in the world as a prison estranged from all his friends still Truth is the best companion for it levels all distinctions in pretentions Truth wether it enters the Ring or the Hall of Justice shows a plain Man that is not to be scared at shadows or big words full of fury & meaning nothing when done & said with them truth is truth & the rights of man—age of reason & common sense are sentences full of meaning & the best comment of its truth is themselves—an honest man makes priestcraft an odious lyar & coward & a filthy disgrace to Christianity—that coward I hate & detest—the Revelations has a placard in capitals about 'The Whore of Babylon & the mother of Harlots' does it mean Priestcraft I think it must—this rubbish of cant must soon die—like all others—I began a letter & ended a Sermon—& the paper too

I am dear Wife yours ever
John Clare

To Dean Dudley

[Dean Dudley, the American genealogist and writer, visited Clare in Mar. 1850. He recorded the visit in *Pictures of Life in England and America: Prose and Poetry* (Boston, 1851), in which he included a smartened-up version of Clare's letter and poem.]

April 3rd 1850

Dear Sir

I am glad to hear of you & am sorry you are going to leave us & our Country so soon without having the oppertunity of seeing you agen

But I believe your Country America is more pleasant then ours is here & that you will be happier in it—Love of country is very strong in most people—& 'Home sweet Home' is a Melody for many other Eears then mine

Where Flowers are God is & I am free—°

I remember giving Mr Baker° a Copy of Verses on May day but have forgot what they where but I think they where somthing about the Ma[y] & he said when I gave him them he would alow none to copy them

On your return to New England give my very best respects to Mr Dana° & Mr Whittier° for the pleasure their respective Works have afforded me—I here send you a Song written today just before I got your Letter—'Dinah a Ballad'

I am yours sincerely
John Clare

Song

I' the sunshine o' the Season i' the springtime o' the year
When small birds find their songs agen & wilding flowers appear
When sunshine i' the blue sky was shineing all abroad
I met a lovely fair maid a going down the road
The Shepherds purse & groundsell too were breaking into bloom
& bumble Bees about the flowers beginning where to hum
I met my lovely Dinah a coming down the Glen
The envy o' the lasses & the favourite o' men

I met my lovely Dinah in her handsome gown o' Green
When her cheeks burnt like the rose bush as handsome as a queen
& all about the footpath the d[a]iseys silver stars
& pileworts golden studs whose burnish nothing mars
Where littered bye the pathside & all about the grass
& there I went with Dinah a beautifull young Lass
Accross the old inclosure where the birds began to sing
I courted lovely Dinah at the starting o' the Spring

I courted lovely Dinah & thus to her did say
My beautifull young creature sweeter then rose o' May
If you'll be mine love I'll be yours We'll tenderly agree
While the grass upon the ground is green & bloom bursts on the tree
To fondle in each others arms from rising sun till night
& mix untill we loose ourselves in ravishing delight
Where whitethorn shows its tender green & chaffinch builds its nest
O how I love to lean awhile on Dinahs happy breast

To Charles Clare

April 24th 1850 Northampton Asylum

My dear Son Charles

I shall just write to tell you that I am quite well & never was better—I imagine you have been to the Post Office every Day since you wrote—I thought you had forgotten me altogether—

till I heard from you—I have got nothing to write about at all for I see nobody & hear nothing—give my best Love to your Mother Brothers & Sisters—Neighbours & [ ] get on for I am still fond of Flowers

I rather fancy I shall see you shortly & in the mean time believe me my Dear Charles your Affectionate Father

John Clare

'He that is down need fear no fall
'He that is low no pride
'He that is humble ever shall
'Have God to be his Guide'
John Bunyan

To Mary Collingwood

[This letter in code, and the following two letters, are in an almanack for 1850. The code is a simple one, involving the removal of all vowels and the letter 'y'; it none the less poses some problems, and not all the decodings can be regarded with absolute trust. Clare rather perversely finds himself resorting often, but not regularly, to a coded form of 'and' rather than the ampersand; and there are times when he cannot sustain his renunciation of vowels.]

To Mary Collingwood

[1850]

M Drst Mr Cllngwd

M nrl wrn t & wnt t hr frm Nbd wll wn M r hv m t n prc & wht hv dn D knw wht r n m Dbt—kss's fr tn yrs & lngr stll & lngr thn tht whn ppl mk sch mstks s t cll m Gds bstrd & whrs p m b shttng m p frm Gds ppl t f th w f cmmn snse & thn tk m hd ff bcs th cnt fnd m t t hrds hrd

Drst Mr r fthfll r d thnk f m knw wht w sd tgthr—dd vst m n hll sm tm bck bt dnt cm hr gn fr t s ntrs bd plc wrs nd wrs nd w r ll trnd Frnchmn flsh ppl tll m hv gt n hm n ths wrld nd s dnt believe n th thr nrt t mk mslf hvn wth m drst Mr nd sbscrb mslf rs

fr vr & vr

Jhn Clr

My Dearest Mary Collingwood

I am nearly worn out & want to hear from you Nobody will own me or have me at any price & what have I done Do you know what you are in my Debt—kisses for ten years & longer still & longer than that when people make such mistakes as to call me Gods bastard & whores pay me by shutting me up from Gods people out of the way of common sense & then take my head off because they cant find me it out herods herod

Dearest Mary are you faithfull or do you think of me you know what we said together—you did visit me in hell some time back but dont come here again for it is a notorious bad place worse and worse and we are all turned Frenchmen foolish people tell me I have got no home in this world and as I dont believe in the other [? any rate] to make myself heaven with my dearest Mary and subscribe myself yours for ever & ever

John Clare

To Mary Ludgate

[1850]

My dear Mary Ludgate

This cms wth m kind Lv t hpng t wll fnd n gd hlth s t lvs m t prsnt thnk Gd fr t whn thnk f n m pllw 'Ngls whspr' bnn Dr m Ngl dr Dv Hrt f hrts 'Dmnd f m——'—& thsnd thr lv whsprs f th n th scrlt & grn Gwn whl l lstng & grtfd t hr thm sngng th prs's

Hw s Hlln Mr Grdnr ftn lk twrds hr cttg & snd kss's n Dvs wngs bt sh nvr cms t t rcv thm—f r wll I m hpp f r ll cnt tll Gd blss & kp m dr dghtr frvr & vr | dr Dghtr

Jhn Clr

T Mr Ldgt Wht Hrt Nn | vr Brg Nrthmptn

My dear Mary Ludgate

This comes with my kind love to you hoping it will find you in good health as it leaves me at present thank God for it when I think of you on my pillow 'Angels Whisper' bonny Dear my Angel dear Dove Heart of hearts 'Diamond of May'—& a thousand other love whispers of thee in thy scarlet & green Gown while I lie listening & gratified to hear them singing thy praises

How is Hellen Maria Gardiner° I often look towards her cottage & send kisses on Doves wings but she never comes out to receive them—if you are well I am happy if you are ill I cant tell God bless & keep my dear daughter for ever & ever | dear Daughter

John Clare

To Mary Ludgate White Hart Inn | Over Brig Northampton

To Hellen Maria Gardiner

[May 1850]

M Dr Hlln Grdnr

Hp t wll n hppnss nd hlth—nd tht r prtt fc kps th rs blm s t ws whn mt—b th frdls—xxxxx xxx xxx xxx kss's hw s Crln r Sstr—M drst Hlln Mr hw lng t pt m rm rnd r btfl nck nd r chk nd lps—'Thn drst Hlln ll lv n mr'—M dr hlln hw shld lk t wlk wth n th bnks f th rvr & gthr wld flwrs nd hnt brds Nsts—bt hv bn tn rs n prsn—nd cnnt s n thng f plsr r pstm—Lv nd nj yr slf m dr Hlln Mr nd b rslf fr hr w r hmd [? tll] m scrl m wn nm—stll m mslf snsbl s ver ws

m drst Hlln Mr | m rs sncrl

Jhn Clr

My Dear Hellen Gardiner

I hope you are well in happiness and health—and that your pretty face keeps the rosey bloom as it was when I met you by the firdales—xxxxx xxx xxx xxx kisses how is Caroline your Sister My dearest Hellen Maria how I long to put my arm round your beautiful neck and your cheek and lips—'Then dearest Hellen I'll love you een more'—My dear hellen how I should like to walk with you on the banks of the river & gather wild flowers and hunt birds Nests—but I have been ten years in prison—and cannot see anything of pleasure or pastime—Live and enjoy yourself my dear Hellen Maria and be yourself for here we are homed [? till I am scarcely] my own name—still I am myself sensible as ever I was

my dearest Hellen Maria | I am yours sincerely

John Clare°

To William Knight

Asylum Northampton July 8th [18]50

Dear Knight

I write to you agen with scarcely one thought in my Head how do you get on at Birghmingham°—remember me to the Literary Lady you mention in your Letter though I do not know her I know some of her friends Miss Landon Miss Cook° Mrs Hemans & Mary Howitt & Remember them still perfectly—I am still wanting like Sternes Prisoners Starling° to 'get out' but cant find the Way I had a Letter a fortnight ago from my youngest Son Charles who sends his best respects to you with the rest of the Family—He tells me that Mr Henderson has left Milton for Wentworth or I thought of spending a pleasant day with him on my return home—I have had up to this 2 or 3 half ozs of Pigtail from Osborns the last about a fortnight or three weeks ago—Write to me when you can for I am very lonely by times—I am without Books or Amusements of any kind & have got nothing to kill time or turn out 'Prison Amusements' what few books I have had I lost somehow or other—all I have left is 'Fishers Young Mans Best Companion'° which I bought my self

I am Dear Knight faithfully yours

John Clare

To Charles Clare

July 25th 1851

My dear Son

I got your Letter safe & was pleased to hear from U as I thought it a long while since I heard from any of U—How are your Brothers & Sisters & your Grandfather & Neighbours—& 'Country Cousins'

How is your Mother & Uncle & Aunt at Barnack I hope U send the young ones to School—besure not to forget that—how is your Grandfather—tell John I shall be glad to see him—Give my Love to all your Brothers & Sisters & believe Me my Dear

Charles your Sincere Father

John Clare

P.S. I wrote so far the day before Yesterday & then left off thinking to finish it in Ink—but I can ask a few more Questions with my Pencil how is Mary Buzley & is Miss Parkinson at Northborough still—How is John Woodward his Wife & Daughter How is Peach Large Mary Large & her 4 or 5 Sisters how is Mary Burbadge & her Mother & Father & does your Brother Jhon ever see Jane Sisson & her Brother William or her Father or Mother tell Jhon to remember me to Dame Porter & Ann & Thomas & also to Betsey Newbon & her Brother & Father & Mother & believe me My Dear Boy | your

Affectionate Father

John Clare

To Patty Clare

March 7th 1860

My Dear Wife

This comes with my kind Love to you & the Childern & my Father & Mother hoping it will find you all well I would have written sooner but had no oppertunity is Mr Sefton & Mrs Sefton living & the two Sons well how is William & his wife & also the neighbours give my love to Wm & Sophy Kettle also to their two Sons & the Daughter—how is Champion John Junr & Frederick & also William Parker Clare & Frederick & Anna Maria Eliza Louisa Sophia & Julia give my love to Mrs Kettle Fanny Temp & to all enquiring friends

your loving husband till Death

John Clare

To James Hipkins

[James Hipkins, of 2 Smith Square, Westminster, had written to Dr Edwin Wing about Clare. Wing replied: 'In reply to yours of the 6th inst respecting John Clare I beg to inform you he is still living and in good bodily health though very feeble in mind and still the subject of many mental delusions. I endeavoured to induce him to write a few lines to you and to make an effort at poetical composition but I could get nothing from him but the few words I enclose.' This is Clare's last extant letter.]

March 8th 1860

Dear Sir

I am in a Madhouse & quite forget your Name or who you are you must excuse me for I have nothing to commu[n]icate or tell of & why I am shut up I dont know I have nothing to say so I conclude | yours respectfully

John Clare

APPENDIX I

Much of the correspondence between Drury and Taylor in 1819 and 1820 was concerned with Clare's finances, and the desirability or otherwise of a written agreement between the respective parties. This was a matter taken up again by Lord Radstock at the end of 1820. The following is a series of notes made by Taylor and Hessey early in 1820; the final three points are on a separate sheet.

Text: MS Northampton 47 (in Taylor's hand)

1. We are told by Drury that a MS. copy of the 'Setting Sun' was the first Piece of Clare's Compositions which he had ever seen or heard of, and that he knew nothing of the printed Prospectus when he called on Clare—
2. Clare paid Henson [£] 1/5/0 for the Prospectuses, & was even compelled to discharge the Reckoning at the Public House which Henson had incurred by coming over to Helpstone for the Money.
3. Clare had only *seven* subscribers, after his Prospectus were distributed.
4. Henson refused to give Clare credit for the Expense of printing the Book, unless he could obtain 100 Subscribers or pay him 10£ in advance.—This was in Decr 1818.
5. At this Time Drury called on Clare, & in April 1819 he purchased the MSS. from Clare for 10£. with a promise of more if the Work was Successful—
6. In April 1819 Drury sent T & H the MSS. for their Opinion, which being favourable was followed by an arrangement between T & H. & D. to this Effect—That T & H shod. superintend the Publication of the Poems requiting the Author according to their Ideas of his Deserts, & that D. shod. partake of whatever Profits they might realize, in an equal Degree with them.
7. T & H. proposed these Terms to D. refusing to engage in the Work unless they had the Privilege of doing what they might think Justice to the Author.
8. They desired D. to increase the Allowance to Clare, making the Sum advanced 20£.
9. They selected, corrected, & published the Poems which form the present Vol. advising with the Author small Alterations &c.
10. They wrote the Introduction,—without making any Charge for editing &c.
11. They proposed receiving Clare in their own House & giving him Education & Support till he should be qualified to take the Office of Teacher in the National School.—
12. They pledged themselves to O[ctavius] G[ilchrist] & other Friends of Clare to give 100£ to Clare whether the Work succeeded or not,—so far back as Nov 12 1819—
13. They offered to give their Advice to Clare without Emolument or Advantage, on all future Occasions, let who would be his Publishers, in a letter dated Nov 30th.

14. On Jany 16 the Book was published, when they sent Clare 20 Copies (1st & 2nd Edit) for his Friends.
15. They have given away the profit of more than 100 Copies to the Subscribers & Patrons who have made Presents to Clare—
16. After the Earl Fitzwilliam & Lord Milton had given Clare 20£ they wrote to Earl F. acquainting him with their Desire to raise an Annuity for Clare to which they subscribed 100£. & this brought 100£ more from his Lordship—
17. Hearing that Clare had articled himself to a Bookseller to allow him 3/4ths of all his future Works, they broke through the Agreement, & caused it to be burnt, by offering to give that Bookseller equal Profits with themselves in all they might hereafter publish for Clare—
18. They have expressed their Intention to Clare & all his Friends to give him at least *half* of all the Profits that may arise from the present or future Works, taking all Responsibility of publishing upon themselves alone—

1. The Agreement entered into by John Clare with E. Drury shall be destroyed by Taylor & Hessey on the Day they receive it from ED.—
2. The published & unpublished Works of John Clare shall be under the Management of T & H. who agree to give to ED an equal Share with themselves in all Profits arising from the Publication of such Works, after the Deduction of Expenses, & of Sums given to the Author.
3. As Managers of the Publication of these Works, T & H. shall have the Power of giving to John Clare any Sums they think proper, either out of, or in Anticipation of, the Profits of the said Works, provided that ED be not called on by T & H to make good any Advances of theirs which the Profits when realized are inadequate to cover.—

APPENDIX II

In August 1829 Clare was sent a copy of the accounts for his three published volumes, which prompted a complex correspondence between Clare and Taylor, and Clare and Drury. With the accounts was an explanatory letter from Taylor.

(i) Taylor to Clare Tuesday, 4 August 1829

Text: MS Northampton 44 (*copy*)

My Dear Clare

This *Volume* of Accounts will be I fear a difficult work for you to understand without I write a few Notes upon it by way of Illustration—

The principal Account is that which is called the Cash Account and which is marked A page 1 & 2—By this it appears that you have received Cash from me, (or I have paid Cash *for* you) to the Amount of [£]141.8.8 more than is due to you. N.B. In this Account you will notice that your Half yearly Dividend was reduced from [£]9.7.6. to [£]7.17.6 in the year 1823, by a charge which Government made in the Value of the 5 p Cent public Funds, in which Stock or Funds your Subscription Money was Invested.

B. is a Statement of that Subscription Account, shewing who contributed to it, & how much, & what was done with the Money.—The Balance of [£]2.17.6 is carried to your credit in the Cash Acct A.

C. is a Statement of the Profit & Cost of the 4 Editions of your 'Poems'.—The first returned 20£ for the Copyright which was paid you by Drury—the 2nd and 3rd Editions repaid the 100£ paid to your Subscription by T & H. & E.D. The 4th Edition is now on sale, and it wants [£]5.1—to return the Expenses which I have incurred upon it. There is a loss therefore at present upon the Edition, but to cover it there is a Stock which *when sold* will amount to [£]66.2.3 of which one half will be yours, deducting Commission.

D. is the Statement of the Village Minstrel.—Here is a Profit realized of [£]28.2.0 carried to your Credit in the Cash Account A. with Stock which when sold will amount to 276£ of which sum, deducting Commission, one Half will be yours.

E. is the Account of the Shepherd's Calendar—& it shews that I am out of pocket at present [£]63.4.0 on that Book.—when all the copies are sold, there will be a *profit* of about 40£ of which one half will be yours.

F. is the Book Account, as it stands in T & H's Ledger and in mine.—I have charged you the same price, for the copies you have had of your works, that I myself, in these Accounts, have paid for them.—The Amount is carried to your Debit in the Cash Account A.

From all these Accounts it will appear—

First, that you have received a Profit of [£]148.2.0 in all, on the Books which have been sold—

Second, that you will be entitled to the Half of 377£ (or about 188£) more, when all the present Copies are disposed of, if they are sold at the regular prices.—

Third, that of this latter sum I have paid you 141£. on Account, which leaves you 47£ only dependent on the future sale of the present copies.—

This sum of 141£ with the 63£ remaining outlay on the Shepherds Calendar makes my advance in the whole about £204.

If you see anything that looks like an Error in these Statements let me know, & I will explain or rectify it.—

I am, My dear Clare, Very sincerely yours,

J.T.

(ii) The Accounts A–F are in MS Peterborough F3 (A, B, D, E, F) and MS Bodleian Don c.64 (C).

On Account A Clare has added in pencil:

In this cash account there is nothing alowed me for my three years writing for London Magazine I was to have £12 a year & this with £7 given to them for me by a Duchess & never sent me makes viz

3 years writing for Mag	£36
Duchess Subscription	7
	£43 never yet accounted for

On Account C Clare has written in pencil:

How can this be—I never sold the Poems for any price—what money I had of Drury was given me on account of profits to be recieved—but here it seems I have got nothing & am brought in minus twenty pounds of which I never recieved a sixpence—so it seems that by the sale of these four thousand copies I have lost that much—& Drury told me that 5000 Copies had been printed tho 4000 only was accounted for

On Account F Clare has written in pencil (of notebooks and paper sent to him):

Stuck in the parcel & sent but not ordered this paper mentioned must be what they copied the poems on & as the poems were kept I shall pay for no copying—they kept all the MSS & sent down copies I otherwise had no paper of them at all it was all given me by a friend

NOTES

1 *'Sonnet' in the prospectus.* 'The Setting Sun' was printed by Henson in Clare's 'Proposals for publishing by subscription a Collection of Original Trifles' in 1818.

2 *Taylor & Hessey London.* An apparently unique proof copy of *PD* exists in the Houghton Library at Harvard University; the title-page reads: *Poems, Songs and Sonnets by John Clare*, with the imprint Taylor and Hessey, London, 1819. There is a similar mock title-page in Peterborough MS A42.

Casterton. Clare worked as a limeburner at Casterton in 1817, and then as a gardener; he left for Pickworth, but returned in spring 1819, before leaving in Nov. because of a disagreement over wages.

alow its Insertion. In his reply, Holland said he could not refuse the dedication of 'The Woodman', which duly appeared in *VM*.

your company. Holland reported, 'Agreeable to Your wish I called on Mr Drury. As far as I can judge he is Your friend.'

3 *Lord Viscount Milton.* Lord Milton, of Milton Hall, was Charles Fitzwilliam, son of Charles William Wentworth Fitzwilliam, 3rd Earl Fitzwilliam. Clare usually distinguishes between father (Fitzwilliam) and son (Milton).

shape most Suitable. Taylor decided against a dedication for *PD*, partly because Lord Milton was abroad at the time and never replied to Clare's request.

'Memoir'. Drury had sent Taylor a brief account of Clare's life, for use in the Introduction to *PD*.

Lame Man at helpstone. Parker Clare suffered from severe rheumatism; Taylor wrote in the Introduction to *PD*, 'He is now a helpless cripple, and a pauper, receiving an allowance of five shillings a week from the parish.'

National School. Nothing came of the plan to train Clare as a teacher (see Appendix I).

4 *the present it enclosed.* Drury told Taylor (5 Feb. 1820) that Strong had sent Clare £1.

5 *'Reccolections after a Ramble' &c.* 'The Peasant Boy' became 'The Village Minstrel'; all three poems were published in *VM*.

'The Lodge House' & 'Robs Terrors of Night'. These tales were not published in Clare's lifetime; but see *AW*, pp. 87–96.

'Kirk White'. Henry Kirke White (1785–1806), the son of a butcher in Nottingham, produced his first volume of poems in 1803. Holland and Drury both encouraged Clare's interest in his work. Sherwill presented Clare with *The Remains* on 12 Feb. 1820.

6 *'Crazy Nell'.* In *AW*, p. 103, Clare writes, ' "Crazy Nell" was taken from a

narative in the Stamford Mercury nearly in the same manner it was related I was very pleasd with it and thought it one of the best I had written and I think so still'.

Milton Hall. Clare visited Milton on 6 Feb., and Burghley House, seat of the Marquis of Exeter, on 21 Feb. (see *AW*, pp. 116–17).

public. Lord Radstock had written, in the *Morning Post*, of Clare's visits to the nobility.

London. Clare's first visit to London, with Octavius Gilchrist, took place in Mar. 1820.

'Patty of the Vale'. Clare married Martha Turner (1799–1871), the 'Patty' of his poem (printed in *PD*), on 16 Mar. 1820 at Casterton Magna. The reference here is to the calling of the banns.

a friendly Gent. The drawing, by Frank Simpson, nephew of the Gilchrists, was never used, despite Clare's repeated promptings.

7 *as you proposd.* Hessey reassured Clare (14 Mar. 1820) that the violin he had promised Clare was on its way; a similar reassurance came a few days later from Taylor about a copy of Lord Radstock's portrait.

Woodhouse. Richard Woodhouse (1788–1834), barrister and friend of Keats.

Percival. The Revd John Percival (1788–?), a writer and friend of Keats and Taylor.

drury. Drury's chief quarrel was with Taylor, who appeared to have ousted him from Clare's concerns. Clare had been persuaded to sign an agreement, according to which Drury would publish all Clare's writings, and Clare would receive a quarter of the profits. By 24 Apr. 1820 Drury had surrendered the 'Agreement' (see Appendix I).

stuntly. i.e. rudely, abruptly.

8 *& Keats too.* Keats's criticism, according to Taylor, was 'that the Description too much prevailed over the Sentiment'.

a Subscription. Radstock had begun a subscription list, and by mid-April about £300 had been collected.

9 *a Banker.* A. Hoare, a member of the famous banking family, had written to Clare, enquiring about his circumstances.

'Curries Burns'. The Works of Robert Burns, ed. James Currie, first appeared in 1800.

'Blair'. Hugh Blair's *Sermons* (1819), inscribed by Lord Radstock, were sent on by Taylor on 12 Feb. 1820.

11 *Scott.* Sir Walter Scott was to give money for some books; also a copy of *The Lady of the Lake*, which he declined to sign.

'AB'. This was Dawson Turner (1775–1858), botanist, antiquary, and patron of John Sell Cotman.

12 *Lord Nelson.* Joshua White, *Memoirs of the Professional Life of the Right Honourable Horatio Lord Viscount Nelson* (1806).

12 *2nd Edit.* Taylor replied (27 Apr.), 'There are 270 Copies left of the 2nd Edit but I think they will all be gone in another Week.'

13 *gentleman from Cambridge.* The Revd Chauncey Hare Townsend visited Clare in Apr., leaving a sonnet to Clare, dated 18 Apr. 1820, later published (defectively) in the *Morning Post* (see *AW*, pp. 123–4).

not in Q. i.e. not in the mood.

Quarterly. An unsigned review, by Gilchrist, appeared in the *Quarterly*, 23 (May 1820), 166–74.

14 *my complaint.* Sherwill attributed Clare's ill health to the general excitement of writing and publication; he urged calmness and regularity.

his Lordships misfortune. Radstock had fallen down a stone staircase.

the cottage. There were rumours that Lord Milton was going to build a cottage for Clare.

Plumptre. The Revd James Plumptre (1770–1832), vicar of Great Gransden, Huntingdonshire, sent his *Original Dramas* (1818), *Four Discourses on Subjects relating to the Amusement of the Stage* (1809), and a *Collection of Songs* (3 vols., 1806–8).

15 *prize for poetry.* Townsend's 'Jerusalem', which had won the Chancellor's English medal at Cambridge in 1817, was published in *Cambridge Prize Poems* (1820).

16 *any such thing.* Clare's paraphrase of the 148th Psalm held a prominent position in *VM* (he had in fact tried to get it published in the *Stamford Mercury* in 1819).

17 *Keats.* Keats's final volume appeared in June 1820.

your Essay. Taylor was planning, partly as a result of the reception given to Keats, 'An Essay on English Poesy'.

18 *'Ways of a Village'.* Sometimes referred to as 'Week in a Village', this became 'The Village Minstrel'.

'Midnight'. This was not published in *VM*.

19 *plasters.* Townsend sent some 'rheumatick applications' for Clare's father, together with a copy of James Beattie's poem *The Minstrel* (1771–4).

writing songs. Drury had persuaded Clare to write songs to be published by, among others, James Power of the Strand. Mrs Emmerson, Taylor, and Hessey were all uneasy about the venture.

20 *'my good old chuckey'.* This became Clare's common term of endearment for Taylor.

Lord Radstocks letter. Taylor had expressed anxiety upon hearing that Clare had written '*an independent* letter' to Lord Milton about Radstock.

21 *some other paper.* Townsend's 'Sonnet' appeared, corrected, in the *New Times*, 24 May.

Hiltons sket[c]h. Hilton's portrait of Clare, sent on 17 May, was engraved by Edward Scriven as the frontispiece for *VM*.

22 *the verse on your worthy self.* Clare's poem 'To Captain Sherwill Jun:' (Peterborough MS B2, 136) contained stanzas addressed to Sherwill and Radstock, and concluded with a postscript addressed to Taylor.

'book sellers'. The review, by Gilchrist, commented that booksellers 'are . . . rarely deficient in shrewdness'.

the fancy. Taylor had sent *The Fancy* ('The Poetical Remains of the late Peter Corcoran'); Clare, in his postscript, rightly guessed the author to be Reynolds.

23 *Hayden Corri.* 'The Meeting', included in Taylor's Introduction to *PD*, was set to music by Haydn Corri (1785–1860), in a setting performed by Madame Vestris in Drury Lane and, most probably, Covent Garden (see *AW*, p. 130).

24 *Campbell & Rogers.* Thomas Campbell (1777–1844) and Samuel Rogers (1763–1855) were two of the most popular poets of the day.

25 *false delicasy.* 'The Country Girl' had been omitted from the 2nd edn., 'Dolly's Mistake' and 'My Mary' from the 3rd. Further 'diplomatic' excisions proposed by Lord Radstock would be effected in the 4th edn. Hessey replied, 'Whether it be false or true delicacy which raises the objection to these pieces it is perhaps hardly worth while to inquire.'

primpt up. i.e. dressed up primly, prudishly.

26 *muscles.* i.e. muzzles.

'Scriven'. Edward Scriven (1775–1841) engraved Hilton's portrait of Clare, for the frontispiece to *VM*.

Hyp. 'Hyperion, a Fragment' was the final poem in Keats's 1820 volume.

27 *'Powers'.* James Power (1766–1836), best known as publisher of Moore's *Irish Melodies*, set to music by John Stevenson (1808–34).

Revd Mr Hopkinsons. The Revd Samuel Edmund Hopkinson (1754–1841) was vicar of Morton with Hacconby, Lincs., 1795–1841; he was also rector of Etton, Northants., 1786–1828, and, for about 30 years, JP for Kesteven and the Liberty of Peterborough. For Clare's amusing account of his visit see *AW*, pp. 121–3.

Grimsthorp castle. Grimsthorpe Castle (built by Vanbrugh), not many miles from Morton, was the seat of the Duke of Ancaster.

my friend. Frank Simpson.

28 *'Tothill fields'.* J. H. Reynolds, whose 'The Fields of Tothill' had appeared in the anonymous *The Fancy* (1820).

mean to be in London. Clare's next trip to London did not materialize until May 1822.

the 2 lines. Argument still raged over what Radstock called 'radical slang' in 'Helpstone' and 'The Dawnings of Genius', and Taylor was inclined to give way.

29 *the cirscumstance.* Taylor wanted to know if Drury had seen an MS or printed copy of 'The Setting Sun', the poem in the prospectus for *PD*; he

thought Gilchrist's article in the *Quarterly* was inaccurate. Taylor apologized on 12 Dec. 1820 for having been mistaken, and for having relied on Drury's written word ('Deceit of this kind I cannot overlook'); see *AW*, pp. 21–2.

29 *dechyher*. i.e. decipher.

Hiltons news. Hilton became an RA in 1819.

his advice. Taylor wrote (29 Sept. 1820), 'I think he [Keats] wishes to say to you that your Images from Nature are too much introduced without being called for by a particular Sentiment . . . his Remark is only applicable now & then when he feels as if the Description overlaid & stifled that which ought to be the prevailing Idea.' There was no correspondence between Keats and Clare.

old Peggy. i.e. Pegasus.

the 'nob' of 'sir John'. Taylor wrote, 'Your Nob, Sir John, will grace the 3rd [edn.] and that will be out—when? why, in 12 months more I hope.'

30 *my friends poems*. C. H. Townsend, presumably.

proof sheet poet. S. Messing, of Rutland, whose *Poems on Various Subjects* appeared in 1821; Clare saw some of these in proof.

J[ames] D[rury]. Edward Drury's brother, and publisher of songs. It is conceivable that Clare has momentarily confused the two.

'Close of Eve'. Published in *VM* as 'Rural Evening'.

To the Ivy. Published in *VM*.

32 *G[ilchrist]'s verses*. Presumably 'The Invitation', Clare's poem printed by Gilchrist in his 'Account of John Clare . . . ', *LM* 1 (Jan. 1820), 7–11.

33 *my last blunder*. Clare had expostulated at an advertisement for the new volume in the *New Times*, and had also complained about his not seeing the proofs.

Bishop of Bristol. The Revd John Kaye (1783–1853), elected Master of Christ's College, Cambridge, in 1814; under the Enclosure Act of 1809 certain mutual benefits were established between Helpstone and Christ's College.

wild flowers. 'The Wildflower Nosegay', published in *VM*.

'St Caroline' or 'George 4th'. The 'bill of pains and penalties' against Queen Caroline, which had been pending since July 1820, was voluntarily abandoned, after much agonized debate in Parliament, in Nov. There was a general rallying to her cause, against George IV. The scandal became a test case for political allegiances.

34 *poets & fiddlers'*. Cf. Southey, *Life of Nelson* (1814), ch. VI.

'martinmass Eve'. This was not published in Clare's lifetime.

'the Cress gatherer'. This was published in *VM*.

'Reccolections' &c. 'Recollections after a Ramble' appeared in *VM*, but without these lines.

35 *Sonnet to Autumn.* Printed in *VM.*

36 *reeve.* i.e. pull, twist.

Lord Liverpool. Robert Banks Jenkinson, 2nd Earl of Liverpool (1770–1828), Prime Minister from 1812 to 1827.

37 *Woodhouse.* Richard Woodhouse became a joint trustee with Taylor for the fund money, in Sept. 1820.

39 *swore at Highgate.* A reference to the custom of 'swearing on the horns' at the Gate House, Highgate.

40 *letter I shoud have had.* A letter from Taylor, intercepted by Drury in Dec. 1819.

put in despotic. Lord Radstock wanted changes to some lines in 'Helpstone'; he had also pencilled in the margins of 'The Peasant Boy', 'This is radical slang'.

41 *'Gastrels Institutes'.* Francis Gastrell, *The Christian Institutes: or, The Sincere Word of God* (1707), presented by Radstock in an edn. of 1812.

all is vanity'. Cf. Matt. 11: 7 and Eccles. 1: 2; otherwise, Clare seems to be aspiring to a vaguely 'biblical' prose.

42 *the hunting song.* 'Milton Hunt' was not included in *VM.*

43 *one of the Songs.* i.e. 'Dropt here and there upon the flowers'.

44 *these Songs.* The composer was Frederick Crouch (1783–1844); Taylor commented, 'The Music of the Songs by Crouch is very silly & common-place . . . I cannot notice it in the Introduction without disapprobation, so it must pass in silence.'

Poor Scotts death. John Scott (1783–1821), the first editor of the *LM*, had died in Feb. 1821 in a duel with Jonathan Christie (friend of John Gibson Lockhart).

Elm trees. Taylor said he would try to save them; he quoted part of this letter in the Introduction to *VM.*

45 *'Sketches of my Life'.* These were sent on 3 Apr. 1821.

46 *To Time.* Published in *VM.*

47 *Keats Epitaph.* 'Here lies one whose Name was writ on Water'. Taylor had written, 'If I had seen this Inscription on a Stone in a Country churchyard I should have felt that it recorded the Death of a Poet,—or at least of an uncommon Man.' Keats had died on 23 Feb. 1821.

sketches of my life. See *AW*, pp. 1–26.

'Lolham Brigs'. Lolham Bridges constituted a local landmark, but were not Roman. Taylor recorded his own visit to the spot, and the origin of Clare's poem 'Langley Bush', in *LM* 4 (Nov. 1821), 540–8.

48 *To the Memory of Keats.* Published in *VM.*

50 *Song.* Published in *VM.*

Dr Noehden. Georg Heinrich Noehden (1770–1826), who worked in various capacities at the British Museum, was author of a German grammar and a book on numismatics.

52 *hipt.* i.e. vexed.

your approbation. Taylor wanted Clare to 'try his hand' at an article for the *LM*, which he had taken over after Scott's death.

lines on Lord R[adstock]. i.e. 'To Lord Radstock', published in *VM*, but not in the Introduction.

53 *all the charm is fled*'. 'Eve of St Agnes', st. xxvi.

Barry Cornwalls Endless amusments. Bryan Waller Procter ('Barry Cornwall') (1787–1874) was renowned for his songs and poetic dramas.

54 *Humphrey Nixons letter.* See the 'Letter from Mr Humphrey Nixon, De omnibus rebus et quibusdam aliis', *LM* 3 (June 1821), 628–32 (most probably by J. H. Reynolds).

mortgagously. One of Clare's 'rustic' coinages.

'*Walter Selbey*'. There had been a number of articles in the *LM* on 'Traditional Literature', with particular reference to ballads about Eleanor and Walter Selby.

57 *the injurd quean.* Queen Caroline died 7 Aug. 1821; for his earlier comments on her, see the letter to Hessey, 1 Dec. 1820.

last twin childern. A reference to the two volumes of *VM*.

Mathews. Charles Mathews (1776–1835), famous for his one-man entertainments (or 'At Homes'), particularly the *Travels in Air, on Earth, and on Water*, which was published in 1821 and reached its 20th edn. within the year. See the following letter.

Mr Bunney. Joseph Bunney, of Whittlebury, had written to Clare with an invitation on 11 Aug. 1821.

the late Wests. Either the painter Benjamin West (1738–1820) or the local poet of the same name, author of *Poems, Translations and Imitations* (Northampton, 1780).

Sonnet. Not published in Clare's lifetime.

58 '*Air Earth & Water*'. See preceding letter to Taylor. Clare mentions various characters in Mathews's drama: the 'Polly Packet' is a boat that dominates the action in Act III; the 'silly fellow' is Mr Theophilus Tulip, 'an overgrown idiot' who keeps asking his parents for medicaments.

'*Village Sketches*'. Nothing along these lines was published in the *LM*.

59 *parcel.* Taylor sent the proofs of the Introduction to *VM* on 29 Aug.

thats settled. Taylor had got word of Clare's impatience at the delay: his response was to suggest that Clare find another publisher.

mistakes in the proofs. These corrections were incorporated into the Introduction, except that Richard Turnill was not mentioned by name.

60 *do as you please.* Taylor had written, 'Clare has created more of these never-dying forms, in the personification of things inanimate and abstract,—he

has scattered them more profusely about our paths, than perhaps any poet of the age, except one.' Taylor agreed that 'everyone can stick in their own favorite'. As there was no proper 2nd edn. the change back did not occur.

that lowly dwell'. Cf. Judg. 6: 37–40.

Albermarle Bookseller. John Murray, Byron's publisher.

61 *'Wanderings in June'*. Published in *SC*.

A Reflection in Summer. Published in *LM* 4 (Oct. 1821), 400.

62 *noveltys*. Taylor sent, on 2 Nov. 1821, both the *LM* and the *Monthly Magazine*.

P[hillips]. Sir Richard Phillips (1767–1840) established the *Monthly Magazine* in 1796; always a figure of controversy, he disputed the theory of gravity. There was a review of *VM* in the *Monthly Magazine*, 52 (Nov. 1821), 321–5.

Mr Carys opinion. Taylor reported H. F. Cary's favourable verdict: 'He speaks I assure you in such very high Terms of the Work that you need not care for the slip slop Criticism of Sir R. Phillips.'

Incognita. Eliza Emmerson had sent a sonnet, addressed to Clare and signed 'Incognita', to the *Morning Post*; Taylor had declined it for the *LM*.

companions. Taylor threatened to bring some of the 'Londoners' up to visit Clare, including Allan Cunningham and 'Peter Corcoran' (i.e. J. H. Reynolds).

63 *the Author of the visit*. The reference is to Taylor's account of his 'Visit to John Clare', *LM* 4 (Nov. 1821), 540–8.

Mermaid of Galloway. Taylor and Hessey had just published Allan Cunningham's poems in one volume.

Opium. Thomas De Quincey.

Cooks oracle. J. H. Reynolds.

New Monthly. There was a tepid, unsigned review of *VM* in the *New Monthly Magazine*, 3 (Nov. 1821), 579.

'Patchwork skreen for the Ladies'. Hessey told Clare that a poem had been reprinted in the *Guardian* on 8 Oct., from *La Belle Assemblée*; in fact the *Guardian* (7 Oct.) reprinted 'On Leaving London' from *Ackermann's Repository*.

'Summer'. Clare's sonnet 'A Reflection on Summer' was printed in *LM* 4 (Oct. 1821), 400.

64 *the dream*. 'Superstition's Dream: A Poem' (unsigned), *LM* 5 (Feb. 1822), 163–5; as Taylor was to promise, it would appear in Clare's next volume, 'with your name'.

'the Deserter'. There seems to be no extant poem with this title.

while. i.e. until.

'Jockey & Jenney'. Published in *SC*, as 'Jockey and Jenny: or, The Progress of Love'.

65 *'Bachelors Hall'*. This was occupied by John and James Billings, 'a sort of meeting house for the young fellows of the town' (*AW*, p. 41).

'Life death & Eternity'. This last poem appeared in *LM* 5 (June 1822), 531, and in *SC*; the other two poems remained unwritten.

66 *a 'nov[el]'*. Drafts for this survive in Peterborough MS A46.

'The Misterey'. There are versions in Peterborough MS A57, 62; B6, 22.

'Bradgate Park'. 'Bradgate Park, the Residence of Lady Jane Grey', signed E[dward] H[erbert] (i.e. J. H. Reynolds), *LM* 5 (Feb. 1822), 166–74.

67 *hipt*. i.e. annoyed.

ill sucess. Taylor wrote on 5 Dec. 1821: 'about 800 Copies I believe have been sold of the *Minstrel* . . . we printed 2000'. He offered consolation on 18 Feb.: 'It is certain that the last work does not [sell] like the first, but you must remember that the first was a surprise to everybody, that it excited the strongest Sympathy & that numbers bought it from a regard for the Author's Circumstances . . .'

'to Spring'. This could be, among other possibilities, 'The Approach of Spring' or 'The Pleasures of Spring'.

68 *London*. Clare spent the last ten days of May and most of June in London.

my promise. See the following letter. For Clare's comments on the problems of shopping in London see *AW*, pp. 139–40.

69 *Sophy*. Clare's sister.

Bristol. E. V. Rippingille, the painter, was in London during Clare's visit, but back in Bristol on 20 June, hoping for a visit from Clare.

my coming home next week. In fact, Patty gave birth on 13 June to a daughter, Eliza Louisa. Mrs Emmerson, on 17 June, regretted that a 'necessity' had forced Clare to leave London early.

'reeling ripe'. Cf. *The Tempest*, v. i. 279, 'And Trinculo is reeling ripe'.

70 *Bloomfield*. Robert Bloomfield lived at Shefford, Bedfordshire, from 1814 until his death in 1823.

Lambs last paper. Elia, 'A Complaint of the Decay of Beggars in the Metropolis', *LM* 5 (June 1822), 532–6.

Beggars Opera. The Beggars Bush was a public house in Holborn: see *AW*, p. 132.

a mysterious hint. Cary reassured Clare that there must have been some misunderstanding; but there were other suggestions that Clare might have caused offence e.g. 'by saying you wished the churches were all in ashes and the parsons sent to beg their bread'.

71 *hospitality*. For Clare's description of his visit to the Cary household see *AW*, pp. 136–7.

'Lives of the poets'. Cary was contributing to *LM* a series of unsigned articles, a 'continuation' of Johnson's *Lives*.

Lyddal Cross. 'The Twelve Tales of Lyddal Cross' appeared in *LM*, Jan. 1822.

14 lines. This sonnet was published in *LM* 6 (Oct. 1822), 335.

'Summer Walks'. Cary encouraged Clare in this venture, which was to form part of *The Shepherd's Calendar*.

72 *Percey Green*. Clare wrote several poems under this pseudonym, and a few appeared in *LM*. Peterborough MS A24 is a quarto MS book with a mock title-page: 'Edmund & Helen or the Suecide | A Story of Love | with other Poems | By Percey Green | "Kissing & cutting of throats" | Sir W. Scott'. This particular poem was not published in Clare's lifetime.

73 *'The Parish'*. Clare told Hessey on 4 Jan. 1823 that he had finished his satire; but it was never published in his lifetime. See *The Parish*, ed. Eric Robinson and David Powell (1985).

the 2nd Edit:. The 1st edn. of *VM* (1821) consisted of two volumes. The 1st had as frontispiece Scriven's engraving of Hilton's portrait; the 2nd was to have had a picture of Clare's cottage, but De Wint's drawing was not thought suitable. He was intending to produce another version, but never did, and another artist, William Cowen, was employed.

74 *To the Deity*. Not published in Clare's lifetime.

Cowie. See the preceding letter. William Cowen (1797–1861), born in Rotherham, earned the patronage of Earl Fitzwilliam, and was known for his Irish landscapes. His drawing of Clare's cottage was engraved for the so-called 2nd edn., which appeared in May 1823 and was no more than the remaining 1,000 copies left over unbound from the 1st edn.

75 *Lamb*. Charles Lamb sent Clare his own *Works* (1818) and Thomas Browne's *Tracts*, in an edn. of 1822.

Tomas. Thomas Bennion, Taylor's clerk.

heavey wet. Beer, ale, or porter.

present. Lamb had sent a signed copy of *Elia: Essays which have Appeared under that Signature in the London Magazine* (1823).

Elia dead & Weathercock dead. The Jan. volume of *LM* contained [Charles Lamb], 'A Character of the Late Elia', By a Friend, and [T. G. Wainewright], 'James Weatherbound: or, The Weathercock Steadfast for Lack of Oil. A Grave Epistle'.

76 *'Francis Turner Esqr'*. Hessey asked Clare to sign a copy of his poems and return it to him for presentation to Francis Turner (1785–1864), the barrister who had helped Richard Woodhouse draw up the deed of settlement of Clare's fund money and would not accept a fee. Sharon Turner (1768–1847) was a lawyer and historian, Dawson Turner (1775–1858) the botanist and antiquary who had once written to Clare signing himself simply 'A.B.'.

'good angel on the devils horn'. *Measure for Measure*, II. iv. 16.

tankard. Weatherbound's 'Grave Epistle' (see above) addressed Clare: 'Never shall his [Elia's] companionable draught cause thee an afterlook of anxiety into the tankard!'

78 *a Critique or Essay. Four Letters from the Rev. W. Allen, to the Right Hon. Admiral Lord Radstock, on the Poems of John Clare, the Northamptonshire Peasant* (1823). Taylor refused to publish this in *LM*, and Mrs Emmerson and Lord Radstock agreed to finance the printing, by Murray, of 500 copies.

79 *the last poem.* 'To an Early Friend', sent to Hessey, 17 May 1823, and published in the *Scientific Receptacle*, 1 (July 1825), 223–5, and subsequently in *RM*. Mrs Emmerson assured herself that she was the dedicatee.

80 *Gilchrist is done.* Gilchrist died 30 June 1823.

82 *my nessesitys.* Hessey had sent £15 on 26 Dec., Taylor £10 on 31 Dec. 1823.

'Harvest home'. In a letter of 13 Oct. 1823 Hessey had suggested a month-by-month plan for *The Shepherd's Calendar* which included 'September—Harvest Home—A Capital Subject— describe a real Scene'.

one hundred sonnets. Northampton MS 17 (1824) is entitled *A Collection | Of Sonnets | Descriptive of | Appearences in the Seasons | And other Pictures in | Nature*; there is a sequence of 25 sonnets. *The Midsummer Cushion* (Peterborough MS A54) was to overflow with sonnets.

84 *offr.* i.e. over.

Popes difenition. A crude paraphrase of Pope's 'Discourse on Pastoral Poetry' (1704).

'Love & Flattery'. Not published in Clare's lifetime.

86 *Young.* Edward Young, *Night Thoughts*, iv. 842. Mrs Emmerson presented Clare with a copy of Young on 24 Feb. 1820.

what shall I do. By 15 May 1824 Clare had decided to come up to London.

87 *Brooks.* The Revd Joshua William Brooks (1790–1882), curate of East Retford, 1821–7, sent Clare a long letter on 27 Apr. 1824, referring to his tract, 'The Word of God Concerning All who are in Trouble or Affliction'.

Blackley. William Blackley, a Wesleyan Methodist on the Stamford circuit.

88 *a farmers son.* Nicholas Stratton, *Poems on Various Subjects, Written Chiefly during the Season of Youth* . . . (1824).

89 *a friend of mine.* Most probably Joseph Henderson: Hessey (5 Oct. 1824) sent the *LM* and a letter from Cary via Henderson.

school book. Anna Laetitia Barbauld, *Lessons for Children from Two to Three Years Old* (1779).

getting well. Clare had returned from London 8 Aug. 1824; his illness had not been cured by the visit, nor by the pills sent on by Hessey from Dr Darling.

Life of Chatterton. This had appeared in *LM*, June 1820. Clare noted in his Journal that he was reading Chatterton between 12 and 15 Sept. 1824.

90 *'period of a mile'.* Pope, 'Fourth Satire of Dr John Donne, . . . Versifyed', ll.72–3.

91 *Noyes.* Robert Noyes (1730–98), *Distress: A Pathetic Poem* (1783).

Crow. William Crowe (1745–1829), 'Lewesdon Hill'.

Brerewood. Thomas Brerewood (d.1748), 'The Four Seasons'.

Vernon. W. Vernon's 'The Parish Clerk' appears in *The Lady's Poetical Magazine: or, Beauties of Poetry* (1791), presented to Clare on 25 Mar. 1820 by Mrs Emmerson.

Fawkes. Francis Fawkes (1720–77) was famous for this song.

Woty. William Woty (1731–81), author of 'The Inscription' and compiler, with Fawkes, of *The Poetical Calendar* (1763).

'Walks in a Forest'. This poem (1794) was by Thomas Gisborne.

Greaves. i.e. Richard Graves (1715–1804).

L[andon]. Laetitia Elizabeth Landon (1802–38), famous for the *Improvisatrice* (1820), killed herself with prussic acid.

Watts. Alaric Alexander Watts, poet and editor of various journals, presented Clare with his *Poetical Sketches* (1824).

92 *enclosed letter.* To Mrs Wright, according to Clare's Journal, 'requesting her to give me a bulb of the "Tyger lily" & a sucker of The "White Province Rose"'.

Hessey. Clare recorded in his Journal that '[Artis] told me that he went three times & sent oftener for the M.S.S. which they did not send at last'.

the poem. Clare sent his 'The Vanitys of Life', as an old poem he had found, for publication in the *Sheffield Iris.*

93 *'brother bard'.* Weston, editor of Robert Bloomfield's *Remains* (1824), had written to ask if Clare had any letters from Bloomfield.

94 *Three Sonnets on Bloomfield.* These appeared in the *Scientific Receptacle*, 1 (July 1825), 306–7. The second was included in *RM.*

97 *Young Lady.* Elizabeth Kent, the botanist.

the alterations. Hessey wrote (30 June 1825): 'in future he [Taylor] is to publish & I to sell books'.

98 *my friend Emmerson.* Mr and Mrs Emmerson had visited Clare, partly to recuperate from the death in August of Lord Radstock.

101 *'European Magazine'.* 'The Gipsy's Song' and the 'Essay on Popularity' (both unsigned) were published in the *European Magazine*, 1 (Nov. 1825), 280–2 and 300–3 respectively.

improvements. Alaric Watts made several alterations to Clare's 'Song' that appeared in the *Literary Souvenir* (1826), 410.

102 *my intentions.* Mrs Emmerson told Clare (11 Dec. 1825) that Mr Emmerson had been to see Taylor: half of *SC* was already set up in type and Taylor 'proposed to publish one Vol with the Months & *close* the book with a few *Tales*—leaving the rest of the "Tales" for a 2nd Vol.'.

104 *Miss Kent.* Elizabeth Kent had written, about her projected book on birds, on 19 Jan. 1826; nothing came of this project.

104 *Bristol.* Rippingille, chiding Clare for not writing, invited him to Bristol.

105 *slumber in a storm*'. Goldsmith, *The Traveller*, l. 312.

106 *looked for every day.* The Clares' fourth child, John, was born on 16 June 1826.

for sale. The 'Life' was never in a state to be offered for sale.

Silks & Maoganys. Rippingille (22 Mar. 1826) had scoffed at the painters of his day: 'There is Mr. Fag's silk or Mahogany so like those substances that it is quite wonderful. These are things that people can see & feel with their fingers ends without scratching their heads . . .' The probable reference is to the amateur portrait painter Rogert Fagan (d. 1816).

107 *Elton.* Sir Charles Abraham Elton (1778–1853), scholar, translator, writer, and patron (at Clevedon Court, near Bristol) of the arts. Clare had written to him, and hoped to visit him in Bristol.

108 *his Bill.* Drury had written on 27 June 1826, saying he had received a statement from Taylor and Hessey, claiming more than £100. He wanted to know about his own claims, for cash advances to Clare, to cover the costs of *VM*, medical advice for Clare's mother, the binding of books. Taylor was anxious to 'get the old account settled, & when that is done I shall be glad to have no further dealings with him'.

109 *Franks.* Frank Simpson.

VanDyk. Harry Stoe Van Dyk (1798–1828), a minor versifier, was brought in to help with the editing of *SC*, but he pleased nobody. His financial concerns in the West Indies increasingly took his mind off Clare's poems.

110 *Octaves Drawing.* Octavius Simpson, brother of Frank, was a landscape artist.

conduct of the Marquis. Taylor wrote, 'I am surprised to hear that the Marquis has not thought of paying you either for the Books or Dedication.—Of course he will not consider the former a Gift, even if he does not consider the latter an Honour.'

111 *the bad sale of the new Poems.* Taylor wrote, 'The Season has been a very bad one for new Books, & I am afraid the Time has passed away in which Poetry will answer.'

Colbourns Novels. Henry Colburn (d. 1855) was famous for the widely disseminated cheap novels he published.

Darleys Play. George Darley's *Sylvia: or, The May Queen*, was to be published before Christmas.

112 *Liverpool.* i.e. Hilton's triptych *The Crucifixion*; Hilton, married to De Wint's sister, was made keeper of the Royal Academy in 1827.

113 *British Museum.* In 1826 Cary was appointed assistant keeper of books at the British Museum.

114 *a series of the living ones.* i.e. *The Poetical Album* (1828–9).

Booksellers. Hunt and Robinson were one of many firms that went bankrupt in 1826.

Darwins poetry. Erasmus Darwin (1731–1802): Clare possessed edns. of *The Botanic Garden* (1825) and *The Temple of Nature* (1824).

116 *the crush.* Behnes had sent a bottle of eau-de-Cologne for Patty, and some toys for the children.

3 Songs. These were by Mrs Emmerson.

a brother Poet in the Table book. Hone's *Table Book* (8 Aug. 1827) contained an account of Robert Millhouse (1788–1839), a weaver and soldier, best known for his poem *Vicissitude* (1820).

118 *Baxter & Royce.* Neighbours in Helpstone.

a Friend of mine. Mrs Emmerson.

119 *'J. Billings'.* This poem has not survived.

121 *'Roman Coins'.* As a result of archaeological excavations at Castor, several people were offering old coins for sale; Taylor had expressed an interest.

two fellows of Peterbro. See *AW*, pp. 49–51.

'Spirit of the Age'. Samuel Carter Hall (1800–89) edited the *Spirit and Manners of the Age*, in which some of Clare's poems appeared.

122 *overrun the constable.* i.e. run into debt.

123 *the Epitaph.* This seems to have been for a Mr J. Fryer, of Hambleton, whose death was reported on 21 Mar. 1828.

Wilsons. Samuel Wilson, bookseller at Stamford, partner of John Drakard.

Princess Vittoria. William Behnes (1794–1864), sculptor and draughtsman, brother of Henry, wanted Clare to write a poem for the engraving of his bust of Princess Victoria, to be published in the *Juvenile-forget-me-not* (1829); Clare did so.

Mrs Halls Evergreen. Anna Maria Hall (1800–81) edited many journals, but not one called 'The Evergreen'; but see previous note.

To my kind friend E[liza] L[ouisa] E[mmerson]. 'May Morning: Addressed to E.L.E. by the Northamptonshire Peasant' appeared in the *Amulet* (1834), 298.

125 *tell me if such will do as Imitations.* Taylor was not encouraging, and the poem was not published in Clare's lifetime.

126 *Steward.* The Revd John Steward, of Market Deeping, wrote on 22 Apr., inviting Clare to dinner; he did not expect Clare to walk in this weather, and a friend would be sending his horse.

129 *bookselling business.* Clare had tried to sell his own books.

copper medal. Hundreds like this were struck to commemorate Vice-Admiral Vernon's capture of Porto Bello in 1739: Commodore Brown was with him in the ship, the *Hampton Court.* Vernon was the opponent of Sir Robert Walpole, who advocated a less bellicose policy.

129 *poor Van Dyk.* Harry Stoe Van Dyk had recently died.

130 *Boston.* Henry Brooke, of the *Boston Gazette*, persuaded Clare to visit Boston in Sept.

Memoirs of Byron. Leigh Hunt, *Lord Byron and Some of His Contemporaries* (1828), caused an uproar when published.

131 *the Translations.* Volumes in Taylor's 'Interlinear Series', or 'Locke's System of Classical Instruction'.

later Mathematical publications. Taylor announced on 21 Oct. the publication of Darley's *Geometrical Companion.*

132 *russia backs & corners.* i.e. smart leather binding.

134 *your very kind Presents.* Behnes sent on 22 Dec. two bottles of wine for Patty and a bottle of brandy for Clare.

135 *taste for the Fancy.* Clare's interest in prize-fighting is a theme that runs through his life and work; for Jones the Sailor Boy see *AW*, p. 144.

Stratford. i.e. Mrs Emmerson's house at Stratford Place.

your Bust. This is the bust of Clare now in Northampton Public Library; Behnes was also supposed to be painting Mrs Emmerson, 'our good Friend of Avon'.

136 *Mr Ackerman.* Ackermann's *Forget-me-not* for 1829, edited by Frederick Shoberl, contained Clare's song 'O the voice of woman's love' and 'On a Child Killed by Lightning' (pp. 68 and 272 respectively).

137 *repe[ti]tion.* Taylor had warned against repetition; Darley was not much more enthusiastic.

the best Annual. Allan Cunningham's *Anniversary* appeared only once, in 1829; it contained Clare's 'Ode to Autumn', several pieces by Cunningham, 'The Temptation' by Proctor (Barry Cornwall), and two poems by Darley.

his play. Darley's *Sylvia* (1827).

New Work on Religion. Hessey's *Library of Religious Knowledge* was to begin publication on 31 Jan. 1829.

Trigonometry. Clare's copy of Darley's *System of Popular Trigonometry* is dated 1835.

138 *Burke of 'Modern Athens'.* William Burke (1792–1829) was tried in Edinburgh for a series of gruesome murders, and convicted on the evidence of his accomplice William Hare.

Hunt & Thurtells. John Thurtell (1794–1824), a notorious gambler, was hanged for murder, 9 Jan. 1824, after a dramatic trial; Joseph Hunt was found guilty as an accessory before the murder, but his death sentence was commuted to transportation for life.

the 'Statute'. 'Helpstone Statute: or, The Recruiting Party', not published in Clares' lifetime.

the other. Either 'To E.L.E. on May Morning' or 'To E.L.E.'.

139 *to the 'Glowworm'*. 'The Glowworm', by A. Ferguson, Esq., appeared in the *Anniversary* (1829), 65.

Spirit of the Age. Hall announced on 4 Mar. 1829 that he was now in charge of the *Spirit and Manners of the Age*, and would pay 8 guineas a sheet. See Clare to Hall, 13 May 1828.

140 *a letter from friend Cunningham*. Cunningham wrote on 6 Apr. 1829, 'Your verses to Miss Landon are the very best you ever composed.' But on 30 July he wrote to say that the *Anniversary* had ceased publication.

Miss Frickers. Mrs Emmerson reported (14 July 1828), 'I am told by my friends the Miss F.s, that Allan C., is *much pleased* with *our* contributions—pardon my vanity!!' Clare recalls (*AW*, p. 137) meeting the Misses Fricker at Mrs Emmerson's: he was not greatly impressed.

141 *Mr Pringle*. Thomas Pringle (1789–1834), poet and editor of *Friendship's Offering*.

142 *somthing in prose*. Cunningham's advice (on 6 Apr. 1829) had been 'to turn your hand to prose your poetic spirit will embellish all you do and there is always a market for it.'

this half sided epistle. The left-hand side of the inner sheet is blank.

143 *poor Humphry*. [William Hone], *Poor Humphrey's Calendar* (1829).

144 *their accounts*. Henderson sent Taylor's account on 15 Aug. 1829, suggesting Clare write to Watts for clarification.

148 *'Guesses at truth'*. [Augustus William and Julius Charles Hare], *Guesses at Truth*, by two Brothers (1827), published by Taylor, but not in Clare's library.

poor Mrs Wright. Mrs William Wright, of Clapham, who used to send Clare flowers and cuttings, had died.

152 *your flattering request*. John Drakard wrote (21 Dec. 1829) asking Clare for help with a new paper he was going to publish on 5 Jan. 1830: this was the radical *Stamford Champion*.

153 *publishing in the country*. Mrs Emmerson wrote (21 Dec. 1829): 'I cannot advise you on the subject of publishing your "little vol. of trifles", unless I could *know more* of the *merits* of the case—certainly, I do not think you ought to publish a Volume in your *own part* of the World.' William Sharp had passed on some proposals from Samuel Carter Hall.

154 *where is Charles Lamb*. Cary replied that he had not seen Wainewright or Lamb since last summer: Wainewright was living at Turnham Green, Lamb at Enfield, with his sister, 7 miles from London.

'sales & bankrupts'. In spite of country-wide depression, Parliament resisted attempts to institute an investigative select committee.

royal fashions too. The reference is to the scandal surrounding the reconstruction of Buckingham House to form Buckingham Palace: the wings of the forecourt became such a laughing-stock they had to be demolished.

154 *Lawrence.* Sir Thomas Lawrence, President of the Royal Academy, died 7 Jan. 1830.

155 *Ettys.* William Etty (1797–1840), RA 1828, friend of Hilton; see *AW*, pp. 145–6.

beautiful verses. In a letter of 20 Jan. Robertson told Clare that his wife had made a pleasing addition to her verses upon him. Apparently the family name was almost interchangeable with Robinson.

156 *Balmerinos.* Arthur Elphinstone, 6th Earl Balmerino (1688–1746), who fought at Culloden, was captured and executed.

Mr Nell. R. Nell, a Stamford bookseller.

158 *intended kindness.* De Wint was sending on a drawing requested by Clare.

where are you. Darley's last surviving letter to Clare is dated 14 Mar. 1829, and there seems to be no reply to this letter. Darley left England for France in late summer, 1830.

159 *the candle at both ends'.* Tobias Smollett, *The Expedition of Humphry Clinker.* Clare had an edn. of 1827.

160 *Allen.* i.e. Allan Cunningham.

Shee. Martin Archer Shee (1769–1850), the successor to Sir Thomas Lawrence as President of the Royal Academy.

Wilkie. David Wilkie (1785–1841), appointed, on Lawrence's death, painter-in-ordinary to the Crown.

gossip you desired. Mrs Emmerson wrote (10 Mar. 1830), 'So you are studying the rules of "Grammar" . . . let me have the pleasure of a gossiping letter from you.'

161 *Paul Pry.* i.e. a very inquisitive person.

162 *flats.* i.e. clowns.

163 *no difference.* George IV died 26 June 1830.

how the devil they get there'. Cf. Pope, 'Epistle to Dr Arbuthnot', ll. 171–2.

Mr Dales. The Iris: A Literary and Religious Offering (1830), ed. Thomas Dale and L. T. Ventouillac.

165 *a Girl.* Sophia, born 24 July 1830.

your success. Taylor had told Clare (6 Jan. 1830), 'Hessey is very well, & likely to get forward as a Book & Print & Picture Auctioneer.'

166 *the honour of her husband'.* Cf. Prov. 12: 4.

167 *school.* The plans to get Frederick into Christ's Hospital came to nothing.

Miss Lamb. Mary Lamb, tended by her brother Charles after she had killed their mother, appeared to regain some of her sanity early in 1830, but her health soon deteriorated; she died in 1847.

Hazlitts death. Hazlitt died on 18 Sept. 1830.

168 *Lord Althorp.* John Charles Spencer, Viscount Althorp (1782–1845), was Leader of the House of Commons for 1830, and an active supporter of the Reform Bill.

quiet in our neighbourhood. In answer to Taylor's question, 'Are the People tolerably quiet in your Neighbourhood? Certainly the Times are awful . . .'

169 *not in parliment).* Henderson told Clare on 1 Feb. 1831 that as Lord Milton was no longer an MP there was no franking for the servants.

lesks. i.e. the groin.

170 *Jones. Attempts in Verse, by John Jones, an Old Servant, with Some Account of the Writer by Himself, and an Introductory Essay on the Lives and Works of our Uneducated Poets* (1830). Southey's Introduction made no reference to Clare. J. G. Lockhart reviewed the volume, *QR* 44 (Jan. 1831), 52–82.

a line or two in Italics. Part of Jones's poem 'On the death of Miss Sadlier Bruere' was quoted in Lockhart's review.

Poesy a Maying. Published in the *Bee* (24 June 1831), and commended by Mrs Emmerson as 'a sweet garland of thought'. Taylor sent Clare's letter, with the sonnets, to a friend who would show them to the publishers Smith, Elder and Co.

171 *intend their death'.* Clare is quoting from *2 Henry VI*, IV. iv. 31–2, 35–6.

172 *Horn on the Psalms.* George Horne, *Commentary on the Psalms* (1771).

the Vols you sent me. Taylor sent an anthology edited by Southey, *Selected Works of the British Poets, from Chaucer to Jonson* . . . (1831); he suggested Clare make notes in the margin (they might even be published).

one shilling per copy. Taylor was not selling more than twelve copies a year of Clare's poems. He hoped someone might buy them at a shilling a copy in sheets.

William Brown. William Browne, *Britannia's Pastorals* (1613, 1616); Clare quotes the second song of Book II.

173 *Surry.* Clare quotes from one of eight sonnets in the volume by Henry Howard, Earl of Surrey (1517?–43).

Wither. George Wither (1588–1667) was represented by 'The Shepherds Hunting'.

174 *cottage farming.* Henderson and Mrs Emmerson were both talking about a vacant cottage at Northborough, which had land with it large enough for two cows.

175 *'Album Verses'.* Lamb's *Album Verses* (1830) were published by, and dedicated to, Edward Moxon, with financial support from Samuel Rogers.

Sir J. Sir John Trollope lived at Casewick House, Stamford, but owned Ashton, a hamlet of Ufford. There were the remains of a manor house at Torpel, SE of a large wood known as The Lawn.

176 *some little books.* Mrs Marsh sent Clare '3 Numbers of Cobbetts penny tracts which Mr Clare may keep'.

178 *your advice.* Taylor wrote, 'I cannot comply with your Request to sell out of the Funds till Mr Richard Woodhouse returns from Italy, for he is joint

Trustee with me . . . If the Money can be sold out for your own Use, it shall be done.'

180 *your first letter.* Elizabeth Wilson and her father Samuel wrote several times from 1828 onwards, reminding Clare of his debts.

one of the party. Richard Woodhouse, a Trustee.

183 *Mr Buckingham the Traveller.* James Silk Buckingham (1786–1855) was an author and traveller who established the *Athenaeum* in 1828. Pringle had told Clare that an agent of the Anti-slavery Society had been talking at Market Deeping.

west Indian slavery. Alexander Barclay, *A Practical View of the Present State of Slavery in the West Indies* (1826), which was a conservative retort to James Stephen, *The Slavery of the British West India Colonies delineated* . . . (1824–30).

Hogg. James Hogg (1770–1835) was on his first visit to London.

a ballad of his. 'When the Kye comes home', printed in the *Stamford Champion* (1 Feb. 1831).

Chantrys marble beautys. Sir Francis Chantrey (1781–1842) was the sculptor for whom Allan Cunningham acted as an assistant.

186 *Clarke.* James F. Clarke (1812–75), a doctor who visited Northborough with his uncle Thomas Clarke (editor of the *Bee*), and sent some medicines for Clare.

189 *your encouragement.* Allan Cunningham admitted sending a piece about Clare to the *Athenaeum*, and offered to do all he could for Clare.

190 *death of the Sun.* 'Genius', prompted by Walter Scott's death on 21 Sept. 1832, was published in *RM*.

your new poem. The Maid of Elvar.

Lives of the painters. Cunningham was working on vol. vi of *Lives of the British Artists*, and was planning one on the poets.

your subscription. Samuel Simpson, of Lancaster, wrote on 1 Nov. 1832, reminding Clare that he had asked, some time ago, for some of Clare's sonnets in his own hand; he sent 10s. for a subscription.

191 *Mr How.* Jeremiah How, a relative of the Peterborough printer Charles Jacob, announced on 30 Oct. 1832 that he was coming in as a partner in the publication of *RM*; he took responsibility for notices in the *Athenaeum* and the *Alfred.* His address was 13 Ave Maria Lane, London, i.e. the same as that of the publisher George Byrom Whittaker.

193 *sufficient room.* Clare has to cram his final lines into the small space at the head of the letter.

194 *a kind letter.* Carrington, of the *Bath Chronicle*, had written on 23 Aug. 1833 to say he would like to be a subscriber to the new volume.

Dartmoor. Noel Thomas Carrington (1777?–1830), *Dartmoor* (1826).

a friend of mine. Thomas Emmerson.

195 *while.* i.e. until.

Walkinghams. Francis Walkingame, *The Tutor's Assistant: Being a Compendium of Arithmetic, and a Complete Question-book* (1751).

197 *kind assistance.* George Reid, an accountant, wrote from Glasgow on 6 Nov. 1834, offering to get some subscribers for Clare's next volume; he was also anxious to send Clare some books.

198 *she calls everlasting.* Henderson's reply reads, in part, 'I have sent you a few evergreen shrubs to decorate your cottage ground with and also a few flower roots including some chrysanthemums the plants I beleive Mrs Clare calls everlasting.—I have sent a man to help you to plant the shrubs, so you will probably be able to get them in to day.'

200 *Three Of My Boys.* Frederick, John, and William were born respectively on 6 Jan. 1824, 16 June 1826, and 29 Apr. 1828; Charles Clare was born on 4 Jan. 1833.

202 *Eliza Phillips.* This letter comes in Northampton MS 8 at the end of *Don Juan.* Although she was most probably a real person, Eliza Phillips has not been identified.

my challanges. Clare laboured under the delusion that he was a prize-fighter. Northampton MS 8 contains a pathetic 'Challenge To All The World' by 'Jack Randall'.

homeless at home. The 'Journey out of Essex' included these words: 'so here I am homeless at home and half gratified to feel that I can be happy any where . . .'

203 *8 years.* '3' would be correct, but Clare has written '8'.

204 *sallary of £100.* The Queen Dowager had contributed 20 guineas towards a subscription fund which was opened in 1840: the target figure of £500 was never reached.

205 *A Song.* From *Child Harold.*

206 *your Grandfather.* Parker Clare died in 1846, at the age of 82.

Frederic & John. Frederick had died in 1843; John was to visit in 1848.

207 *John Bellars.* The Bellairs family lived at Woodcroft Castle: see *AW*, pp. 54–5.

Mr & Mrs Sefton. Samuel Sefton married Clare's first daughter Anna; after her death in 1844 he married her sister Eliza Louisa.

208 *Piscator. The Practical Angler* (1842).

Henry Phillips. The True Enjoyment of Angling (1843).

Sir Humphry Davies. Davy, *Salmonia: or, Days of Fly Fishing* (1827).

209 *Mr Knight.* William F. Knight, the steward at the asylum, 1845–50, responsible for transcribing most of Clare's asylum verse, was contemplating the publication of some of Clare's poetry.

210 *Mr Jones.* Quite probably William Arthur Jones (1818–73), the Unitarian

minister, an intimate friend of George Baker, the antiquary, and resident in Northampton 1842–9.

210 *'Apsley Wood'*. 'Apsley Wood', in Spenserian stanzas, was the principal poem in Wiffen's *Aonian Hours* (1819).

211 *Mr S. C. Hall.* It was, in fact, Spencer Timothy Hall (1812–85), author of *The Upland Hamlet* (1847), which he presented to Clare.

214 *J Clare.* At the end of this letter, Clare has written: 'Sally Mason'; a fainter pencil continues the list: 'Betsey Ashby | Mary Bolland | Maxey', after which comes the line, 'gently John gently John'.

216 *& I am free*—. Clare's poem 'Poets love nature' concludes with a variation of this line.

Mr Baker. George Baker (1781–1851), topographer and historian, and brother of Anne Elizabeth Baker (1786–1861), compiler of a *Glossary of Northamptonshire Words and Phrases* (1854).

Mr Dana. Either Richard Henry Dana, jun. (1815–82), author of *Two Years Before the Mast* (1840), or his father, the poet (1787–1879).

Mr Whittier. John Greenleaf Whittier (1807–92), the poet.

220 *Hellen Maria Gardiner.* See the following letter; an undated letter is from a Caroline Gardiner (possibly her sister), niece of Octavius Gilchrist.

John Clare. After this letter is the note: '1850 May 12th Plumbs Pears & Apple Trees are in bloom & the Orchards are all blossoms'.

221 *Birghmingham.* Knight was appointed clerk and steward of the Borough Asylum at Birmingham on 30 Jan. 1850; he resigned in 1892.

Miss Cook. Eliza Cook (1812–89) edited *Eliza Cook's Journal*, 1849–54.

Starling. See 'The Starling: Road to Versailles', in Sterne's *A Sentimental Journey* (1758).

Best Companion'. George Fisher, *The Instructor: or, Young Man's Best Companion* (1727).

INDEX